RESEARCH IN HUMAN CAPITAL AND DEVELOPMENT

Volume 6 • 1990

FEMALE LABOR FORCE PARTICIPATION AND DEVELOPMENT

Editorial correspondence pertaining to articles to be published should be sent to:

Professor Ismail Sirageldin, Series Editor
Department of Population Dynamics
The Johns Hopkins University
School of Hygiene and Public Health
615 N. Wolfe Street
Baltimore, Maryland 21205

All other correspondence should be sent to:

JAI PRESS INC.
55 Old Post Road No. 2
Greenwich, Connecticut 06830

RESEARCH IN HUMAN CAPITAL AND DEVELOPMENT

A Research Annual

FEMALE LABOR FORCE PARTICIPATION AND DEVELOPMENT

Editor: ISMAIL SIRAGELDIN
Department of Population Dynamics
The Johns Hopkins University

Co-editors: ALAN SORKIN
Department of Economics
University of Maryland

RICHARD FRANK
School of Hygiene and Public Health
The Johns Hopkins University

VOLUME 6 • 1990

JAI PRESS INC.

Greenwich, Connecticut *London, England*

55 Old Post Road No. 2
Greenwich, Connecticut 06830

JAI Press Ltd.
118 Pentonville Road
London N1 9JN
England

ISBN: 1-55938-032-2

Manufactured in the United States of America

CONTENTS

LIST OF CONTRIBUTORS

Sulayman Al-Qudsi — Office of National Health Plan
Ministry of Public Health
Safat, Kuwait

Richard Anker — Employment, Planning, and Population Branch
International Labor Organization
Geneva, Switzerland

Isak Aytac — Department of Sociology
University of Maryland, College Park

Susan Elster — Department of Social Science
Carnegie–Mellon University

Richard Frank — Department of Health Policy and Management
The Johns Hopkins University
School of Hygiene and Public Health

Eltigani E. Eltigani — Population Studies Center
Faculty of Economics and Rural Development
University of Gezira
Wad Medani, Sudan

Mark Kamlet — Department of Social Science
Carnegie-Mellon University

Ruth Levine — Department of Population Dynamics
The Johns Hopkins University
School of Hygiene and Public Health

John Mullahy Yale University

David Salkever Department of Health Policy and Management
The Johns Hopkins University
School of Hygiene and Public Health

Nasra Shah Office of National Health Plan
Ministry of Public Health
Safat, Kuwait

Jody Sindelar Yale University

C. Matthew Snipp Department of Rural Sociology
University of Wisconsin
Madison

Alan Sorkin Department of Economics
University of Maryland

Catalina H. Wainerman Centro de Estudios de Poblacion—CENEP
Buenos Aires, Argentina

Rebeca Wong Department of Population Dynamics
The Johns Hopkins University
School of Hygiene and Public Health

INTRODUCTION

During the past twenty years, there has been a rapid and sustained increase in the labor force participation of women (particularly married women) throughout the world. Much of this labor force growth has been concomitant with the rapid economic and social changes that have occurred in both developed and developing countries. The growth in female labor force participation is also associated with significant changes in reproductive behavior, women's socioeconomic roles and status, and the structure and stability of families and households. These issues have significant conceptual and policy implications; however, they are not fully understood. There is, for example, a large degree of diversity in female labor force participation rates among and within developed and developing countries. Attempts to understand these diversities have gone in three directions: measurement, specification, and empirical. In this volume, an attempt is made to elucidate some of these issues.

The first portion of this volume considers conceptual and methodological problems associated with measuring labor force growth among women. The Frank and Wong study analyzes the literature on labor supply and fertility in developed countries. They focus on econometric issues and discuss the advantages and disadvantages of recursive, simultaneous and reduced form models. A summary of empirical studies of the effect of fertility on labor force participation is presented for each of three models indicated above.

The Levine paper considers occupational segregation by gender and its relevance for female labor supply. Three different explanations of gender segregation are examined: (1) the neoclassical; (2) the segmented labor market theory; and (3) the "Marxist-feminist." The paper concludes with a discussion of gender based occupational status and its effect on fertility behavior.

The study of Anker considers the degree to which official labor force participation statistics for women in developing countries understate the actual labor contribution of women. Focusing on a 1983 survey of approximately 1,000 rural households in Egypt, he develops four distinct definitions of labor force behavior. Rates vary from 12 to 81 percent, depending on the measure of labor force participation used. Gender of interviewer and sex of respondent were also discussed in terms of their impact on female labor force participation.

Wainerman's study also considers the accuracy of the census measurement of the female labor force in developing countries. The paper focuses on data collected in Paraguay. Surveys were carried out in Asuncion, the country's capital city, and in the rural area of the Piribebuy district. According to the author, the "official" definition of female labor force behavior would exclude as much as five-sixths of rural female workers. The paper concludes with a discussion of importance of developing more comprehensive measurements of labor force participation of women in rural areas of developing countries.

The second part of the volume presents three empirical studies of female labor force participation in the United States. The Elster and Kamlet study begins with a thorough review of the recent economic and sociological literature concerning women's labor force behavior in the United States. Subsequently, they focus their research on the effect of income aspirations and social class on women's labor force decisions. Data are taken from the 1970 and 1980 Census for the Pittsburgh area. This study takes a dynamic view of the formation of income aspirations and recommends a number of interesting topics for further research.

The work by Mullahy and Sindelar is one of the very few economic studies of the effects of mental illness on labor market decisions. This is an important issue because the six months prevalence rate for mental illness in the United States is 19 percent. Aside from consideration of the impact of mental distress on the labor force participation of women, the paper also considers the effect of inclusion of health status variables on labor supply models.

The Salkever paper focuses on the labor force participation of single women with children. A comparison is made between those mothers with and without disabled children. The advantage of this study, compared to earlier work, is that the former uses a much larger data set that concomitantly includes a greater number of disabled children. As the number of single women with children is steadily increasing, the results of this paper are of growing policy importance.

The final section of this volume presents three studies of female labor force participation in developing societies. Each of the societies under consideration is experiencing rapid social change.

The Snipp-Aytac study is a detailed analysis of the American Indian female labor force. Using data from the 1980 Census, they consider the labor force behavior of women living both on reservations and in urban areas. This is the first major study of the American Indian female labor force ever undertaken. The effects of both demand and supply characteristics on labor force behavior are presented.

The Shah and Al-Qudsi paper analyzes female labor force participation in Kuwait. Kuwait has had very rapid economic growth associated with the growth in oil exports. Because over half of the female work force in Kuwait is comprised of expatriates, the study provides a separate analysis for Kuwaiti and non-Kuwaiti women. The paper also measures the degree of earnings discrimination against women working in Kuwait by their ethnic origin. Some discussion of future economic prospects for women in Kuwait is also presented.

The Eltigani paper focuses on female labor force behavior in rural Sudan. To be specific, the study concerns those women who live in close proximity to the Gezira scheme, a large scale irrigation project begun in 1925. The major crop that is grown is long-staple cotton. One interesting phenomena, which is analyzed in the paper, is the increasing use of hired workers instead of the female labor of the farm household. Another issue that is discussed is the substitution of machinery for female workers in cotton harvesting. This is leaving much of the female work force in a vulnerable economic position.

Much effort has gone into the production of this volume. Aside from the contributors, the anonymous referees, and numerous colleagues who provided suggestions to improve the contents of this volume, we would like to thank Ruth Levine, who performed the dual role of being a contributor as well as careful editor. As usual, Ruth Skarda performed the excellent job of retyping the entire manuscript and preparing the authors' index. Finally, our acknowledgement to the careful editors of JAI Press in the preparation of the final manuscript.

Ismail Sirageldin
Alan Sorkin
Richard Frank
Editors

PART I

CONCEPTUAL AND METHODOLOGICAL ISSUES IN FEMALE LABOR PARTICIPATION

EMPIRICAL CONSIDERATIONS FOR MODELS OF FEMALE LABOR SUPPLY AND FERTILITY IN DEVELOPED COUNTRIES

Richard Frank and Rebeca Wong

I. INTRODUCTION

During the latter part of the twentieth century it has been repeatedly observed that women who participate in economic activities have fewer children than women who do not (Kasarda, Billy, & West, 1986). In addition, the greatest increases in female labor force participation have been among mothers. Because of these trends, there has been a considerable interest among policymakers as to the extent to which economic and social forces affect both fertility and labor force activities of women.

Specifically, policymakers are concerned with the consequences of various social policies on both the labor market and family structure. For instance, the degree to which the structure of Aid to Family with Dependent Children (AFDC)

Research in Human Capital and Development, Vol. 6, pages 3–16.

ISBN: 1-55938-032-2

discourages women from working and encourages fertility has been a point of extensive debate in recent years (Blau & Robins, 1986). Similarly, new proposals to subsidize child care services are designed to create work incentives for single mothers, yet another consequence of this policy may be to further encourage childbearing. Related issues arise when one addresses public policy regarding abortion, contraception, and the minimum wage. All have potential impacts on both the labor market activities of women and fertility.

The purpose of this paper is to highlight issues of concern to researchers interested in the empirical estimation of female labor supply models and who choose to consider fertility a relevant factor in the labor supply decision.[1] We review issues of estimation in the context of developed countries.

In this review of studies on fertility and labor supply we take as a point of departure the one-period static model of household production put forth by Willis (1973). This model of household decision making specifies an objective function with two arguments: child services (including quality and quantity dimensions) and a composite commodity of other services. These services are produced by the household using time inputs of various members and other inputs that can be purchased in the market (such as food, clothing, and shelter). Thus the pursuit of the objectives is constrained by the available time, the income (earned and unearned) of the household, and input prices (wage rates and prices of market goods). Maximization of the objective function subject to the constraint leads to demand functions for child services and other services.

The focus of this review is on attempts to empirically assess the relationship between fertility (or family composition) and labor supply of women. The empirical models are generally derived from the household production framework and may be viewed as conditional demand functions for leisure (labor supply) and child services. We focus primarily on the structure of empirical models used to study the labor supply-fertility relationship. We pay particular attention to the trade-offs between various practical concerns in the implementation of these empirical models. The paper is organized as follows: the second section discusses estimation strategies for studying the labor supply-fertility relationship. The third section presents results from the literature in the context of the approaches taken to estimation. A set of conclusions is presented in the final section.

II. ESTIMATION ISSUES

One of the questions that much research on fertility and labor supply seeks to address is how family composition affects female work effort. Researchers attempting to answer this question empirically are faced with a dilemma. It involves relying on various strong assumptions to obtain estimates of parameters that are of policy interest, versus using less restrictive models that do not give straightforward insights into the important policy question. In this section we focus on this trade-off and offer an approach to obtain estimates of the impact of family structure on female labor supply.

A simple approach to the specification of an econometric model examining the effect of family structure on labor supply is to enter indicators of family structure directly into the supply function.[2] This is essentially a conditional supply function (or conditional demand for leisure function). The supply model might take the form:

$$H = H(W, X, F, g) \tag{1}$$

where: W is the wage rate;
X is a vector of exogenous regressors;
F is a measure of family structure (e.g., age-specific number of children);
and g represents unmeasured attributes of the individual that determine labor supply (e.g., attitudes or mental health status).

This model requires that g and F be orthogonal in order to obtain consistent estimates of the impact of family structure on labor supply (dH/dF). This is a very strong assumption and is unlikely to be met. For example, if individuals believe they are ill-suited to become parents, then this propensity might be represented as an element of the vector g. This would imply writing an equation for family structure (or fertility) of the following form:

$$F = F(W, Z, g) \tag{2}$$

where: Z is a vector of regressors that may be the same as X in (1) above (this point will be taken up in detail below).

Clearly, the error term in an empirical formulation of Equation (1) would be correlated with the variable F. The consequences of such a situation have been traced by Rosenzweig and Schultz (1983). They show that estimates of the impact of a variable such as family structure on labor supply will be biased. This can be seen by differentiating Equation (1) with respect to F:

$$dH/dF = H_F + H_g\,(g_F) \tag{3}$$

where: H_F, H_g, and g_F are partial derivatives.

Equation (3) states that estimates of dH/dF will be biased by the extent of correlation between g and F. This is similar to a simultaneous equations bias problem. However, it is possible to argue that family structure is predetermined at any point in time when a labor supply decision is made. This does not address the possibility that an unmeasured factor appears in both Equations (1) and (2). We refer to this as a recursive model with correlated errors. Thus, while estimation of Equation (1) will simply allow one to obtain estimates of the policy parameter of interest, it comes at the cost of bias.

The possibility that family structure is endogenous in labor supply models has led to a number of efforts to estimate a structural model of labor supply and fertility (Schultz, 1978, 1980). A major difficulty confronting attempts at joint estimation of fertility and labor supply has been model identification. Each study specifying a structural model of labor supply and fertility imposes identifying restrictions. These have usually been justified on practical grounds rather than on a theoretical basis. For example, Schultz (1978, p.291) remarks:

> If Mincer is correct . . . only a reduced form can be estimated for either fertility or labor supply. This appears to me no longer to be an adequate reason for not estimating the underlying structural parameters. Nonetheless, it should be obvious that the choice of identifying restrictions, in this case, remains somewhat arbitrary.

The specific problem of identification in these models stems from their theoretical basis. Most models of labor supply and fertility have originated from household production models such as those of Willis (1973) and DeTray (1973). These models typically specify a household's objective function as consisting of three arguments: child services, leisure, and a composite commodity. This objective function is maximized subject to a full income constraint reflecting prices of goods, services and time, the available time and wealth. This maximization problem can be solved to obtain demand functions for child services, leisure, and a composite commodity.

A major implication of this theoretical formulation is that the 3-equation demand system described above consists of a common set of exogenous (right-hand side) variables. Thus, the demand for child services, leisure (or supply of labor) and the composite commodity are each determined by the same set of economic, environmental, and technical factors. This is, of course, true of all demand systems (Theil, 1982). Imposition of identifying restrictions on these types of models is therefore inconsistent with their theoretical basis.

There is an alternative to attempting to specify and estimate a structural model of labor supply and fertility. This is to estimate each endogenous variable as a function of exogenous influences derived from the household production model's constraints. (Lehrer & Nerlove 1982, McCabe & Rosenzweig, 1976a; 1976b, 1981; Mincer, 1962). Relevant exogenous variables might include the female's wage rate (actual or imputed), her spouse's wage, household wealth, the female's educational attainment, and the price of child care services. The results obtained from adopting this approach are unbiased estimates of the impact of the exogenous influences in the model on each of the endogenous variables.

The obvious shortcoming of relying on the reduced form models of labor supply and fertility is that one does not obtain direct information on the policy question of interest. Thus, the researcher appears to be confronted with choosing among (1) biased estimates of the parameter of interest when the recursive model is used; (2) difficult to interpret results of the parameter of interest when a structural model is chosen;[3] or (3) consistent estimates of factors that are not of direct policy interest.

A first step that can be taken that may assist in choosing an approach is to test for stochastic regressors within the recursive model. Performance of a specification test such as those proposed by Hausman (1978) or Wu (1973) could be used to determine whether the family structure variable is endogenous. It appears, however, that these specification tests tend to reject the exogeneity hypothesis in nearly all cases. This would result in infrequent use of the recursive approach, leading the researcher back to the reduced form.

Perhaps the most promising approach to resolving the dilemma is to rely primarily on panel data for analyzing fertility and labor supply. The advantage of panel data is that it offers: (a) the ability to test cross-sectional assumptions about the presence of unobserved individual effects (often referred to as heterogeneity), and (b) the possibility to "control" for unmeasured individual effects on outcomes of interest, if they do exist. This would allow one to make use of the conditional demand for leisure specification given in (1) above (the recursive model) without relying on the assumption that F and g are orthogonal. To demonstrate this, let us return to Equation (1) and rewrite it in the following manner:

$$H_{it} = a + X_{it} B_{it} + c_{it} F_{it} + g_i + u_{it} \qquad (1')$$

where: i indexes individuals;
t indexes time; and
u is a random disturbance term.

If one can assume that F is strictly exogenous (in the sense that it does not depend on H_{it}) and that g is time invariant (at least over the observed time period of the panel), then one can test for the presence of individual effects and obtain consistent estimates of the B and c parameters (Chamberlain, 1985).

In order to estimate a model such as (1′), one may make use of the fixed effects estimator. For a simplified version of model (1′), where $H_{it} = B'X_{it} + g_i + u_{it}$ the fixed effects estimator of B is

$$B = [\text{sum } (X_{it} - X_i)(X_{it} - X_i)']^{-1} \text{ sum } (X_{it} - X_i)(H_{it} - H_i) \qquad (4)$$

The estimate of B will converge to the true B if there is sufficient variation in $(X_{it} - X_i)$. Returning to Equation (1′), this means that an estimator such as that in Equation (4) will "control" for the effects of the time invariant individual effects such as g. The implication is that the covariance between F and the error term will be zero. The second term in Equation (3), $H_g(g_F)$ would now be zero because $dg/dF = 0$ with the fixed effects model.

The benefits of this approach are that (a) one can directly estimate the model of policy interest (the conditional demand for leisure model given in Equation (1)); (b) one can test for the assumptions upon which cross-sectional studies are based; and (c) one need not impose either arbitrary restrictions on the structural model or encounter difficulties in interpretation of results. These benefits come largely at the cost of assuming strict exogeneity of F and H.

The conclusions derived from this discussion are rather straightforward. First, one faces a choice among a set of restrictive assumptions that must be imposed in order to empirically assess the relationship between family structure and female labor force participation. Second, our preference is to rely on the exogeneity of H and F and to adopt an empirical strategy that allows for (1) a minimal set of assumptions about unobserved influences on H and F; (2) no arbitrary identifying restrictions for structural models; and (3) a reasonably simple method to obtain estimators of the parameters of interest.

The consequences of these conclusions for data are also quite direct. The entire approach proposed depends on microlevel household data that are collected repeatedly over time (panel data). The intense focus by economists on problems of labor supply during the 1960s and 1970s led to the development of important panel data sets in developed countries. Most notable in the United States are the Panel Study on Income Dynamics and the National Longitudinal Surveys. Both data sets offer detailed information on individuals, including their investments in human capital, family structure, and the characteristics of other household members. Recent developments of longitudinal surveys of households and individuals in Sweden and Australia make cross-national comparisons of fertility and labor supply possible.

One study that has adopted a strategy similar to the one proposed here is that by Heckman and Macurdy (1980). In their analysis, eight years of the panel data from the Panel Study on Income Dynamics are considered. The analysis was designed primarily to examine the extent to which female labor supply responded to "shocks" to household income. In the process of specifying a labor supply model they used several measures of family structure as explanatory variables. They used a fixed effects tobit estimator to obtain parameter estimates. In all cases they found that female labor supply was negatively related to fertility.

III. EMPIRICAL EVIDENCE FROM DEVELOPED COUNTRIES

The significant difference in the fertility levels between women who participate in labor market activities and those who do not is considered virtually universal in developed countries. This generalized finding has been summarized in several literature surveys, for example, by Andorka (1978), Standing (1983), and Kasarda et al. (1986). The finding holds for almost every measure used for female work and fertility.

We focus on the issue of the empirical estimation of the effect of fertility on labor force participation (dH/dF). This issue has been addressed in the literature, using multivariate analyses with a variety of data sets and methodological approaches. In view of the estimation issues discussed in the previous section, we are especially interested in assessing the sensitivity of estimates of this relationship to the estimation strategy adopted.

We classify a group of empirical studies according to the model specification used. This specification relates to the treatment of the family structure (or fertility) and labor supply variables in the empirical model. We consider that the models can be classified as recursive, simultaneous, or reduced form. The Appendix gives a detailed description of each category.

Table 1 summarizes an illustrative group of studies according to the type of

Table 1. Estimated Values for dh/dF According to Type of Model Used

	Type of Model		
Author(s)	*Recursive*	*Simultaneous*	*Reduced Form*
Weller (1977)			
Butz & Ward (1979)	N.A. $dF/dW < 0$		
Fleischer & Rhodes (1979)	0		
Lehrer & Nerlove (1982)	$= 0$ < 0		
Lehrer & Kawasaki (1984)	N.A.		
Stolzenberg & Waite (1984)	$= 0$ < 0 > 0		
Schultz (1985)	N.A. $df/dW < 0$		
Rosenzweig & Schultz (1985)	$= 0$ < 0		
Bloom (1986)	N.A.		
Osawa (1988a)	N.A. $dF/dW < 0$		
Osawa (1988b)	N.A. $dF/dH{\cdot}W < 0$		
Schultz (1978)	< 0	< 0	
Waite & Stolzenberg (1976)		< 0	
McCabe & Rosenzweig (1976)			N.A. $dH/dW > 0$
Heckman & Macurdy (1980)	< 0		

model used. The estimated value for *dH*/*dF* is negative in most cases, with a few studies finding a nonsignificant or positive effect. We cannot conclude from these findings that the relationship between female labor force participation and fertility is unambiguously inverse. There is a wide variation among the studies with respect to other factors—beside the estimation strategy. Some of these factors are: the timing of the decisions modeled; the variables assumed subject to choice; the level of measurement; the operational definition of the main variables; and the data sets and population of interest studied.

Note also in Table 1 that not all studies covered in this summary have estimates for *dH*/*dF*. Several studies have obtained the effect of wages on fertility; these are reported, after noting that *dH*/*dF* was not available (N.A). in the particular study.

Table 2 presents a summary of the same studies considered in Table 1, incorporating a classification by some of the factors of interest mentioned. In a similar summary, for different purposes, Keeley (1981) reviewed empirical research on labor supply and found extreme diversity of wage and income elasticities. This was attributed to the different underlying assumptions made by the researchers. These assumptions referred to functional specification, sample selection, and measurement of dependent and independent variables. For our case we will elaborate on the *dH*/*dF* effect according to the model specification used in the studies, and will highlight the difference in assumptions made by the researchers.

Studies With a Recursive Model

Among the studies using a recursive model, there is variability in the process modeled and the timing of the decisions. For example, Fleischer and Rhodes (1979) model a lifetime labor force decision (measured by work history) as a function of total fertility. Lehrer and Nerlove (1982) use the same approach, but consider a series of period decisions (measured by proportion of time worked in different periods of the life cycle). Heckman and Macurdy (1980) model labor supply decisions in a life cycle context, using U.S. panel data. On the other hand, Stolzenberg and Waite (1984) use a period analysis approach on the decision to participate in the labor force in a given period of time, by studying the effect of cumulative fertility by age of children.

Although all the studies in this group used U.S. data, the population of interest varied. These studies considered all women regardless of their participation in the labor force, but differed in the selection of women according to their marital status (see Table 2). For the studies in this category, the results for *dH*/*dF* are such that they confirm the hypothesis that there is greater time intensity of younger children. For example, the effect of family structure on female labor force was insignificant in Fleisher and Rhodes, where the effect of fertility seems to work through its effect on wages. In Stolzenberg and Waite, the magnitude of the negative *dH*/*dF* effect decreases for older children. When *F* is measured as

Table 2A. Summary of Studies According to Various Factors of Interest

Author(s)	*Timing of Process*	*Choice Variables*	*Variables Definition*
Weller (1977)	Period; static		Several measures of LFP; children ever born
Butz & Ward (1979)	Life cycle; static	Wages; fertility	TFR; ASFR; proportion of employed wives; female hourly earnings
Fleischer & Rhodes (1979)	Life cycle; static	LFP	Work history; total living children
Lehrer & Nerlove (1982)	Life cycle; static	LFP; fertility	Proportion of time worked; live births
Lehrer & Kawasaki (1984)	Sequential; static	Fertility; child care mode	Intended fertility; current c.c. mode
Stolzenberg & Waite (1984)	Period; static	LFP	Participation; children by age
Schultz (1985)	Time series	Fertility	TFR; age specific birth rates
Rosenzweig & Schultz (1985)	Life cycle; panel	Fertility; LFP; others	Proportion of time worked; children born
Bloom (1986)	Life cycle; static	Wages; length birth interval	Hourly wages; age at first birth
Osawa (1988a)	Period; static	Fertility	Children ever born
Osawa (1988b)	Time series	Fertility	Desired family size
Schultz (1978)	Life cycle; static	LFP	Annual hours worked; children by age, and ever born
Waite & Stolzenberg (1976)	Life cycle; static	Plans on LFP; plans on fertility	Intended LFP at age 35; intended total number of children
McCabe & Rosenzweig (1976)	Period; static	LFP; family size; others	Children ever born; number annual hours worked
Heckman & Macurdy (1980)	Life cycle; panel	LFP	Annual hours worked; participation

Note: LFP = labor force participation; TFR = total fertility rate; ASFR = age specific fertility rate.

Table 2B. Summary of Studies According to Various Factors of Interest

Author(s)	*Unit of Observation*	*Data Set*
Weller (1977)	Married women, husband present	U.S. 1/100 1960, 1970 Census
Butz & Ward (1979)	Country	U.S. time series 1948–1975
Fleischer & Rhodes (1979)	Married women, husband present	U.S. NLS
Lehrer & Nerlove (1982)	Unmarried women	U.S. 1973 National Survey of Family Growth
Lehrer & Kawasaki (1984)	Working women, two-earner households	U.S. 1976 National Survey of Family Growth
Stolzenberg & Waite (1984)	Women, and Areas	U.S. 1970 Census 1/100 sample
Schultz (1985)	Counties	Sweden time series 1860–1910
Rosenzweig & Schultz (1985)	Women ever married	U.S. longitudinal NFS, 1970 & 1975
Bloom (1986)	Working women	U.S. 1985 CPS
Osawa (1988a)	Women, 20–59	Japan 1975, close to Tokyo
Osawa (1988b)	Country	Japan time series Census 1960–1980
Schultz (1978)	Married women	U.S. 1967 CPS
Waite & Stolzenberg (1976)	Women, age 14–24	U.S. Longitudinal study of labor market, Waves 1968–1973
McCabe & Rosenzweig (1976)	Households, both spouses present	Puerto Rico 1970 1/100 sample
Heckman & Macurdy (1980)	White women, age 30–65	U.S. PSID Waves 1968–1975

Notes: NLS = National Longitudinal Survey.
NFS = National Fertility Survey.
CPS = Contraceptive Prevalence Survey.
PSID = Panel Study of Income Dynamics.

number of children above the age of 13, the dH/dF effect turns positive. Lehrer and Nerlove find that the dH/dF effect changes over the life cycle of unmarried mothers. The effect is negative but not significant when women have school-age children; it gains significance when women have children of child-rearing age.

Studies With a Simultaneous Equations Model

Two studies included in the summary used a simultaneous equations model. They coincide in that both conceptualized decisions in a life cycle context, and in that they find the same general results. However, Schultz (1978) considers fertility and labor supply behaviors of married women in the United States, while Waite and Stolzenberg (1976) study intentions among young women, ages 14–

24, in the United States. Hence, the operational definition of the variables of interest differs. Schultz used annual hours worked, number of children in the household by age group, and children ever born. Waite and Stolzenberg use intended labor force participation at age 35 (dummy), and intended total number of children.

In order to obtain an estimate of the *dH/dF* effect, both studies use Two-Stage-Least-Squares, and find that the effect is significant and negative. In addition, Schultz finds that the effect is larger if children are in preschool age.

Studies With a Reduced Form Model

Only one of the studies included in the summary estimated a reduced form model. McCabe and Rosenzweig (1976) assumed that female labor force participation and family size are jointly determined by a common set of exogenous variables. They used a period approach, using data from Puerto Rico. The study used number of annual hours worked and a cumulative measure of fertility, with a sample of households with both spouses present. The findings support the hypothesis that children raise the demand for time at home.

In the analysis of the findings from our illustrative group of studies, no clear patterns of results emerge by the strategy used. Although at first glance there are indeed differences in the estimated *dH/dF* effects (see Table 1), the results are not really different in substance. When analyzed in more detail, they seem to confirm the hypothesis that small children raise the demand for the woman's time at home. Hence, it would appear that it was the measure used that determined the significance and sign of the general finding for *dH/dF*. This would help explain the differences in results among the studies in the category of recursive models. Keeley (1981) addresses issues of the correct specification of the independent variables in labor supply functions. Here, we have highlighted the household structure variable, given that our concern was labor supply of women.

One aspect deserves to be highlighted: most of the empirical literature deals with cross-sectional individual data, using individual behavior models. The number of studies in the literature that use a macrolevel of measurement is limited (see, for example, Schultz, 1985; Butz & Ward, 1979; Osawa, 1988). This may be due to the additional complications that arise in the definition of the main variables across time and across countries in studies of female labor supply. The emergence and growth of the informal sector in some countries implies that the definition of what are considered market work activities for women may vary widely.

In conclusion, the empirical evidence seems to imply that the estimated value for *dH/dF* is ambiguous. If the conditions of employment of women in a modern industrial society are such that reduce the conflict between mother and worker roles, that is, if working and caring for small children is facilitated, then the inverse relation between employment and fertility decreases, or disappears. For example, Osawa (1988) for Japan, finds similar fertility among wives not in the labor force and those working as unpaid family workers, whereas those working outside the home have lower fertility rates. This point is also illustrated by Schultz (1978), who finds that the dH/dF effect is larger if children are of preschool age, among married women in the United States.

IV. CONCLUSION

We have presented practical considerations of the empirical approach used to estimate the effect of fertility on female labor supply in developed countries. We have outlined advantages and disadvantages of the various model specifications, according to the use of recursive, simultaneous, or reduced form models. We conclude that the preferred approach of estimation is a recursive form that involves a fixed effects estimator. This requires household level panel data that have been increasingly available for developed country analyses in recent years, and should become even more so in the future.

We reviewed a group of existing empirical findings for developed countries, concluded that the results are sensitive to the measures of fertility used, and found that there is no clear pattern of results according to the type of estimation strategy adopted. However, despite variations across studies, both in estimation strategy and other factors (related to the data sets and model specification), the findings are indicative of significant negative responses of female labor supply to family composition.

APPENDIX

Types of Models

Recursive with correlated errors; *F* endogenous

$$H = H\ (F, \ldots)$$
$$F = F\ (\ldots\ldots)$$

Recursive with no correlated errors; *F* exogenous

$$H = H\ (F, \ldots)$$

Simultnaneous; *F* endogenous

$$H = H\ (F, \ldots)$$
$$F = F\ (H, \ldots)$$

Reduced Form; *F* endogenous

$$H = H\ (\ldots\ldots)$$
$$F = F\ (\ldots\ldots)$$

Note: This definition of recursive or reduced-form does not necessarily correspond to the definition found in the econometric literature. The use of the terms here is to reflect the form of the model as it relates to the fertility and labor force participation variables, and to how they are specified in the empirical model with respect to each other.

NOTES

1. Female labor supply is broadly defined as the participation of a woman in economic activities, beyond the household work. Fertility is broadly defined as the number of children a woman has, and takes various forms in empirical research. It is sometimes replaced by family composition, meaning, the number of family members of different ages, including children.

2. We will not take up issues of selection bias and endogeneity of wages as they have been extensively covered in the literature.

3. One problem of interpretation arises if, for example, fertility (as measured by number of young children) is found to have a negative impact on labor supply. This may be because certain key exogenous variables may have impacts that are of opposite signs on the two endogenous variables.

REFERENCES

Andorka, R. (1978). *Determinants of fertility in advanced societies*. New York: The Free Press.

Blau, D. M., & Robins, P. K. (1986, January). Labor supply response to welfare programs: A dynamic analysis. *Journal of Labor Economics, 4*(1).

Bloom, D. E. (1986, October). *Fertility timing, labor supply disruptions, and the wage profiles of American women*. Harvard University (Discussion Paper 86–8).

Butz, W. P., & Ward, M. P. (1979, June). The emergence of countercyclical U.S. fertility. *American Economic Review, 69*(3).

Chamberlain, G. (1985). Heterogeneity, omitted variable bias and duration of dependence. In J. Heckman & B. Singer (Ed.), *Longitudinal analysis of labor market data*. Cambridge: Cambridge University Press.

Cochrane, S. H. (1979). *Fertility and Education: What do we Really Know?* Baltimore, MD: The Johns Hopkins University Press.

DeTray, D. N. (1973). Child quality and the demand for children *Journal of Political Economy 8*(2), 70–90.

Fleischer, B. M., & Rhodes, G. F., Jr. (1979, March). Fertility, women's wage rages, and labor supply. *American Economic Review, 69*(1).

Hausman, J. A. (1978). Specification tests in econometrics. *Econometrica, 46*(6), 1251–1271.

Heckman, J. J., & Macurdy, T. A. (1980). A life cycle model of female labour supply. *Review of Economic Studies, 47*.

———. (1981). New methods for estimating labor supply functions: A survey. In R. G. Ehrenberg, (Ed.), *Research in Labor Economics* (Vol. 4). Greenwich, CT: JAI Press.

Jones, E. F. (1982). Socioeconomic differentials in achieved fertility. *World Fertility Survey Comparative Studies, ECE Analyses of WFS Surveys in Europe and USA* (No. 21). International Statistical Institute, Voorburgh, Netherlands.

Kasarda, J. D., Billy, J. O. G., & West, K. (1986). Status enhancement and fertility. *Reproductive Responses to Social Mobility and Educational Opportunity*. New York: Academic Press.

Keeley, M. C. (1981). Labor supply and public policy: A critical review, Chapter 4, Academic Press.

Lehrer, E., & Kawasaki, S. (1984). Child care arrangements and fertility: An analysis of two earner households. unpublished mimeograph.

Lehrer, E., & Nerlove, M. (1982). An econometric analysis of the fertility and labor supply of unmarried women. In J. Simon & T. Lindert (Eds.), *Research in Population Economics* (Vol. 4). Greenwich, CT: JAI Press.

McCabe, J. L., & Rosenzweig, M. R. (1976a). Female labor-force participation, occupational choice, and fertility in developing countries. *Journal of Development Economics, 3*.

———. (1976b). Female employment creation and family size. In R. G. Ridker (Ed.), *Population and Development*. Baltimore, MD: The Johns Hopkins University Press.

Mincer, J. (1962). Labor force participation of married women: a study of labor supply. In H. G. Lewis (Ed.), *Aspects of Labor Economics*. Princeton: Princeton University Press.

Osawa, M. (1988, July). Working mothers: Changing patterns of employment and fertility in Japan. *Economic Development and Cultural Change, 36*(4).

Rosenzweig, M. R., & Schultz, T. P. (1985, December). The demand for and supply of births: Fertility and its life cycle consequences. *American Economic Review, 75*(5).

Schultz, T. P. (1978). The influence of fertility on labor supply of married women: Simultaneous equation estimates. In R. G. Ehrenberg (Ed.), *Research in Labor Economics* (Vol. 2). Greenwich, CT. JAI Press.

———. (1980). Estimating labor supply and functions for married women. In *Female labor supply* theory and estimation. Princeton, NJ: Princeton University Press.

———. (1985). Changing world prices, women's wages, and the fertility transition: Sweden, 1860–1910. *Journal of Political Economy, 93*(6).

Standing, G. (1983). Women's work activity and fertility. In R. A. Bulatao, & R. D. Lee (Eds.), *Determinants of Fertility in Developing Countries* (Vol. 1). New York: Academic Press.

Stokes, C. S., & Hsieh, Y. (1983, August). Female employments and reproductive behavior in Taiwan, 1980. *Demography, 20*(3).

Stolzenberg, R. M., & Waite, L. J., (1984, May). Local labor markets, children and labor force participation of wives. *Demography, 21*(2).

Theil, H. (1982). *The system-wide approach to microeconomics*. Chicago: University of Chicago Press.

Tienda, M., & Glass, J. (1985, August). Household structure and labor force participation of black, Hispanic, and white mothers. *Demography, 22*(3).

Van Esterik, P., & Greiner, T. (1981, April). Breastfeeding and women's work: Constraints and opportunities. *Studies in Family Planning, 12*(4).

Waite, L. J., & Stolzenberg, R. M. (1976, April). Intended childbearing and labor force participation of young women: Insights from nonrecursive models. *American Sociological Review, 41*.

Welch, F. (1979). Effects of cohort size on earnings: The baby boom babies' financial bust. *Journal of Political Economy, 87*(5).

Weller, R. H. (1977, February). Wife's employment and cumulative family size in the United States, 1970 and 1960. *Demography, 14*(1).

Willis, R. J. (1973). Economic theory of fertility behavior. *Journal of Political Economy, 81*(2), 14–65.

Wu, D. (1973). Alternative tests of independence between stochastic regressors and disturbances. *Econometrica, 41*, 733–750.

OCCUPATIONAL SEGREGATION BY GENDER:

RELEVANCE TO LABOR SUPPLY AND FERTILITY RELATIONSHIPS

Ruth E. Levine

I. INTRODUCTION

Founded or false, the notion that men and women differ in their productive abilities is continuously reinforced by the division of labor by gender. Casual observations, as well as a host of careful studies, tell us that both the split between domestic and labor market activities, and occupational segregation by gender, form a dominant pattern in industrialized and developing societies, contemporary and historical (Blau & Jusenius, 1976; Mackintosh, 1984; Rogers, 1980). The level of women's labor force participation has been shown to vary by several orders of magnitude over time, and among regions; and definitions of male and female occupational roles have shifted (Benería & Roldán, 1987; Strom, 1987). Despite this, the clarity of the distinction between the work that is

Research in Human Capital and Development, Vol. 6, pages 17–25.

ISBN: 1-55938-032-2

appropriate for women and that which is appropriate for men remains sharp in any given setting.

Childbearing—or the potential for childbearing—is at the heart of the matter. Orthodox economists and dual labor market theorists alike acknowledge that women's biological role in reproduction has been inextricably linked to their roles in domestic production and within the labor market. Typically, a trade-off is envisioned between income-generating activities, or labor force participation, and domestic production, particularly childbearing and child care. This hypothesized trade-off, which is supported by a substantial body of empirical work, predicts that working women will have lower fertility rates than will nonworking women, and that, among workers, women with higher fertility rates will have lower career-orientation and be concentrated in "static," low-paid occupations. In this way, women's fertility behavior is thought to condition their occupational choices.

If reproduction is at the core of gender segregation of work, then we have reason to ask whether occupations and, more particularly, rigid gender assignment of productive roles, affect reproduction. An examination of the causes and consequences of occupational differentials can shed light on the conceptual and empirical questions of the links between a women's work in the labor market and her work in the home, including the bearing and raising of children. Consideration of gender-based occupational patterns demands that we explicitly assess assumptions about the nature of labor market operation, and the interactions between individual decisions and structural constraints.

II. DEFINITIONS AND DIMENSIONS

Simply put, gender-segregation is the allocation of employment opportunities by gender (Hall, 1985). The vague term "employment" can be decomposed into three dimensions to analyze the characteristics and dynamics of segregation. These dimensions allow detailed comparison of the allocation of workers to different types of production, and the division of activities and authority among workers producing the same commodity (Thompson, 1983).

First, "employment" can mean field of activity, such as road construction, domestic service, chemical manufacture, oil refining or retail sales. These fields, corresponding to the content of the work and the location within the economy, often are aggregated into broad productive sectors (i.e., primary, secondary, and tertiary). Second, "employment" can refer to occupational category; for example, professional, technical, bureaucratic, clerical, agricultural, and so on. These occupational categories identify the work process, and the level and type of skill or training required. Third, "employment" can mean position within an occupational category. Workers may be employers, supervisory or nonsupervisory employees, self-employed, cooperative workers, or hold other positions. Position within employment refers to the relative status of the worker, not the characteristics or the production or the product.

In a vast range of settings, gender-segregation of employment is manifested within each of these dimensions, though the mechanisms may vary. Differentials are observed in the proportions of men and women employed in different fields of activity, with women being disproportionately represented, most strikingly, in the service sector and specific parts of the manufacturing sector, such as light assembly and textiles. Gender segregation among occupational categories also is widely found; women cluster in clerical, teaching, parts assembly, and certain technical and retail sales categories. Similarly, women's position within employment systematically differs from men's. Women are represented disproportionately as nonsupervisory employees, not owners, or self-employed (Hall, 1985).

Gender-based differences along each of these dimensions are correlated with differences in remuneration for work and opportunities for advancement. Employees in the traditionally "female" fields of activity, occupational categories, and positions are, in nearly all cases, paid less than are employees in traditionally male employment. Similarly, the typical woman's job is not a rung on a career ladder or a progressive occupation; instead, it is static, a dead end.

III. EXPLANATIONS OF GENDER SEGREGATION

Although the existence and endurance of gender-segregation in the labor market is plain to see and rarely disputed, the explanations for it constitute a substantial and long-standing debate. According to the neoclassical-human capital perspective, occupational gender differentials can be taken as evidence of a labor market that responds appropriately to heterogeneity of workers' productive capabilities and preferences. The common thread among all neoclassical variants is the assumption of a competitive labor market in which differentials in employment and wages stem from current or previous choices made by workers and potential workers (Hall, 1985; Mincer & Polachek, 1974).

> The neoclassical mode assumes perfect competition where, in equilibrium, all jobs are viewed by workers as equivalent and all workers are viewed by employers as a homogenous entity. . . . Under conditions of perfect competition, the labor market is assumed to operate continuously, producing uninterrupted flows of labor services at appropriate prices. (Sirageldin, Sherbiny, & Serageldin, 1984, p.16).

Recognizing that a key to women's work force choices lies in their roles within the family, neoclassical economists have elaborated the New Household Economics. This views a household as a decision-making unit that both produces and consumes satisfaction-yielding services, sending one or more members to the labor market to earn the income necessary to satisfy the household's needs.

Occupational choices are considered endogenous to the dichotomous labor force participation decision, with the focus on supply-side factors, including workers' preferences. Women, thought to be more committed to the home than the work place, choose to prepare themselves (through investments in human capital) for occupations that are relatively compatible with domestic production: jobs requiring little skill or formal training, which are easy to enter and for which the opportunity cost of leaving is relatively low; or occupations that allow women to care for their children while working. From this view, women are paid less than men because they have lower educational attainment, on average, and because they choose to enter and leave the labor market more frequently. Synergistically, "crowding" of women into particular occupations tends to bring down the average wage (Becker, 1981; Blau & Jusenius, 1976; Dex, 1985; Mincer, 1962).

The foundations and implications of the New Household Economics can be challenged if we allow for the possibility that the market mechanism is not a means of achieving allocative efficiency—the perfect match between labor supply and demand. For this, we turn to the segmented labor market theory. While the neoclassical approach has built an explanation that concentrates on supply influences affecting which women work, the segmented labor market perspective shifts the focus to which jobs women do, and the demand for female labor.

The theory of segmented markets has taken widely varying forms in developed and underdeveloped contexts, but a basic core exists: The labor market is seen as inherently noncompetitive. Intentional and systemic barriers restrict workers to particular types of employment, independent of productive potential. There are multiple labor markets, and workers have access to a given market because of their race, gender or other attribute. In segmented markets, "workers face different earnings functions depending on their location in the labor market. . . . [W]orkers in the less-favored group earn less than similarly qualified workers in some other group" (Fields, 1980, p.2).

Discriminatory structures explain the concentration of racial minorities and women in jobs offering low pay, poor working conditions, and few opportunities for advancement (Blau & Jusenius, 1976). Most essential to segmented market theory is the notion that segmentation is *endogenous* to the labor market, not an externally generated imperfection (Sirageldin, Sherbiny & Serageldin, 1984).

Typically, the labor market segments are seen as the primary sector, in which the occupations are characterized by relatively high pay, good working conditions and potential for career advancement; and the secondary sector, which is comprised of low-skill, high turnover, low-pay work, providing few, if any, chances for betterment.[1] Specific categories of workers find employment in one of the sectors, but there is almost no movement between the sectors. Women and racial minorities, it is argued, are generally restricted to the secondary sector (Bowles, 1973; Piore, 1975; Reich, Gordon, & Edwards, 1973).

> [E]conomic mobility between these two sectors [is] sharply limited, and hence workers in the secondary sector are essentially trapped there. . . . [T]he secondary sector is marked by pervasive underemployment because workers who could be trained for skilled jobs at no more than the usual cost are confined to unskilled jobs. (Wachter, 1974, p.639)

The benefits of segmented markets for capital can be summarized: over-concentration of workers in particular occupations artificially generates a relative surplus of labor, which maintains low wages and fosters divisions among the work force (Reich, Gordon, & Edwards, 1973). And, as several case studies have convincingly shown, in developing settings the informal labor force provides products and services that are vital to large-scale capital, at much lower cost than is possible within the formal sector (Arizpe, 1978; Bromley & Gerry, 1979; Nash & Fernandez-Kelly, 1983; Portes & Benton, 1984; Young, 1982).

Starting with the premise that the market is inherently noncompetitive, the interpretation of the economic behavior of women takes a different course. Simply put, the direction of causation is reversed. If women are confined to a secondary labor market, this confinement results in their limited investments in human capital, low levels of labor force participation, and concentration in low-paying, static occupations. Investment in human capital provides little, if any, payoff: For workers confined to the secondary sector, the returns-to-education are lower than for workers in the primary sector. On-the-job experience is also not as beneficial to disadvantaged workers.

> [B]outs of unemployment and/or employment in the secondary sector increase the likelihood of future unemployment and/or low wage employment. Employment in the secondary sector, rather than contributing positive on-the-job training, imparts negative human capital. (Taubman & Wachter, 1986, p. 1196)

A theoretically related, yet distinct, analysis of gender-segregation of employment roughly can be labeled as "Marxist-feminist"; it is an attempt to understand the conjuncture between women's historic and contemporary oppression, and economic forces in developed countries. More recent efforts have been made to extend the work to developing settings (Benería, 1982; Benería and Roldán, 1987). From Marxism comes an understanding of the primacy of the mode of production in establishing social relations; from feminism comes a sensitivity toward the roots and effects of patriarchal power. From this perspective, women lose the economic game not because they have been dealt an unlucky hand or make the wrong choices, nor because the other players cheat. Women lose because the rules of the game ensure that they will lose—and that they will continue to play.

The initial assumption is that socially constructed gender differentials are a mechanism to generate and reinforce material exploitation of women under capitalism. The Marxist-feminist approach argues that opportunity differentials in the labor market benefit capital in several ways. First, such differentials generate surpluses of cheap labor. When women are marginal workers, the labor supply that can be tapped to keep average wages low. Second, the work that women perform in the home is a type of unpaid production that is necessary for the biological and social reproduction of the labor force (Mackintosh, 1984; Thompson, 1983).

In an attempt to avoid economic reductionism, Marxist-feminists have devoted substantial attention to the origins of beliefs and ideology related to the sexual division of labor, though there is hardly consensus about what those origins might be (O'Brien, 1981). At the least, the self-perpetuating nature of division of labor is explored in both theoretical and empirical dimensions, and the question of women's choice is reformulated.

IV. LESSONS FOR THE FERTILITY-LABOR FORCE QUESTION

The discussion has concentrated on the segregation of employment by gender, and its possible explanations. Now I turn to look more closely at the relationship between labor force behavior and fertility. Very generally, the pattern expected and observed is an inverse relationship between fertility and labor force participation, and a correlation between high fertility and employment in low-paying, static occupational locations.

The labor-force fertility connection has generated distinct concentrations, depending on setting: In developed economies, attention has been given to changes in women's labor supply with delays in childbearing and declines in total fertility; conversely, in developing settings, considerable concern has been given to the declines in fertility that might be induced by an increase in female education and economic opportunities.

Traditionally, gender-segregation of employment has attracted little attention in research devoted to household decision making and fertility behavior. Rather, gender-based differences in labor market location have been taken for granted, or implicitly assumed away. Empirically, most research has used the variables of employed/not employed or hours worked, without attention to the absolute or relative occupational location of the worker. Gender is a variable used to adjust estimation of potential wages, but the reason for the need for such adjustment has rarely been examined. When one or more characteristics of a woman's occupation has been taken into consideration, for instance, in studying the question of maternal-worker compatibility, the comparisons made have been between the various types of work that women do, and not between men's and women's work.

I argue that gender-based differentials in occupational location are intimately tied to fertility behavior, under either of the explanations of gender-segregation.

Under the New Household Economics, women's specialization in child care and housework is a necessary starting point for the joint explanation of women's labor force participation, occupational location and fertility. This specialization, reflected in both educational and occupational choice, is described in Becker's (1981) *A Treatise on the Family:*

> Women not only have a heavy biological commitment to the production and feeding of children, but they are also more biologically committed to the care of children in other, more subtle ways. Moreover, women have been willing to spend much time and energy caring for their children because they want their heavy biological investment in production to be worthwhile. . . . [Biological] differences can be distinguished by the assumption that an hour of household or market time of women is not a perfect substitute for an hour of the time of men when they make the same investments in human capital. . . . [W]omen invest mainly in human capital that raises household efficiency, especially in bearing and raising children, because women spend most of their time at these activities. (pp. 21–23)

Several implications emerge. First, a social behavior—women's allocation of time between the labor market and the home—is traced directly to gender-specific biology (pregnancy and childbirth). Second, the social behavior is a function of gender-specific preferences and is the outcome of choice. Third, inherent gender differentials exist in the productive outcomes of investment in human capital, such as education. Fourth, women's decisions about investments in human capital are based on a desire to maximize the efficiency of household production. Within this fundamentally functionalist perspective, the economic position in which women find themselves is a result of women's reproductive roles, and the choices those roles induce within a fully competitive labor market.

Whether we view the labor market as competitive becomes central to the conceptualization of the link between women's work and fertility. Relaxing the assumption of the competitive labor market greatly enriches our understanding of that relationship.

From the segmented labor market view, women "specialize" in home production not out of choice, but out of lack of opportunities to enter the labor market or move from job to job, sector to sector. Opportunities may be restricted based not only on gender, but also on stage in the life cycle. Unmarried women may be given greater employment opportunities than married women; women with young children may be barred from any type of employment. It is not workers' choices but rather their lack of choices that determines labor force behavior.

What are the implications for understanding why nonworking women have fewer children than do working women, and why different patterns of fertility are observed among different types of employment? Barriers to labor market participation and mobility may induce high fertility in several ways. First, women may be restricted to (or choose) lower levels of education, or nontechnical training, if they perceive that job opportunities are limited. Low educational attainment, in turn, is correlated with low levels of labor force participation, participation in noncareer-oriented occupations and high fertility aspirations.

Second, if the available jobs are static—poorly paid, with low costs associated with interruption—women are likely to leave employment when conflicts with domestic responsibilities emerge. It is neither specialization in domestic work nor preferences that result in a concentration of women in low-paying jobs, but rather the restriction into such jobs that pushes women toward the home, and toward childbearing.

Third, if women with young children cannot find work—or cannot find satisfying work—because of employer discrimination (or lack of access to affordable child care), the opportunity costs associated with an additional birth are very low. Young mothers may remain at home, and have more children, because of a lack of alternatives. Once more, barriers effect an inverse relationship between participation and fertility.

Fourth, the types of jobs available to women, which are typically service-oriented and low-status, reinforce women's social roles as wives and mothers. Women with such employment are likely to have relatively little economic autonomy and power within the home, and may be unable to be major actors in determining their own childbearing or domestic responsibilities (Standing, 1983).

We are left with a circle of causation and reinforcement: women are limited to a narrow range of occupational opportunities in part because they have given actual or expected fertility behavior; and their fertility behavior is partially a result of their actual or expected employment opportunities. The research required to deepen understanding of the economic and demographic status of women is not that which makes a linear path out of this system. Rather, it will focus on the ways in which the limitations in economic and domestic realms reinforce one another, and the ways in which the process can be changed.

NOTE

1. In this context, primary and secondary sectors should not be confused with productive sectors (i.e., extractive, manufacturing, service, and so on).

REFERENCES

Arizpe, L. (1978). Mujeres migrantes y economía campesina: Análisis de una cohorte migratoria a la ciudad de México, 1940–1970 [Migrant women and peasant economy: Analysis of a cohort of migrants to Mexico City, 1940–1970]. *América Indigena, 38*(2), 303–326.

Becker, G. (1981). *A treatise on the family*. Cambridge, MA: Harvard University Press.

Benería, L. (1982). Accounting for women's work. In L. Benería (Ed.), *Women and development: The sexual division of labor in rural societies* (pp. 119–147). New York: Praeger/ILO.

Benería, L., & Roldán, M. (1987). *The crossroads of class and gender: Industrial homework, subcontracting, and household dynamics in Mexico City*. Chicago: University of Chicago Press.

Blau, F. D., & Jusenius, C. L. (1976). Economists' approaches to sex segregation in the labor market: An appraisal. In M. Blaxall, & B. Reagan (Eds.), *Women and the workplace: The implications of occupational segregation* (pp. 181–244). Chicago: University of Chicago Press.

Bowles, S. (1973). Understanding unequal economic opportunity. *American Economics Review, 63*(2), 346–356.

Bromley, R., & Gerry, C. (Eds.). (1979). *Casual work and poverty in third world cities*. New York: Wiley.

Dex, S. (1985). *The sexual division of work: Conceptual revolutions in the social sciences*. London: Wheatsheaf.

Fields, G. S. (1980). *How segmented is the Bogata labor market?* (Staff Working Paper 434). Washington, DC: World Bank.

Hall, R. H. (1985). *Dimensions of work*. Beverly Hills, CA: Sage.

Mackintosh, M. (1984). Gender and economics: The sexual division of labour and the subordination of women. In K. Young, C. Wolkowitz, & R. McCullagh (Eds.), *Of marriage and the market: Women's subordination internationally and its lessons* (pp. 3–17). London: Routledge & Kegan Paul.

Mincer, J. (1962). Labor force participation of married women: A study of labor supply. In National Bureau of Economic Research, *Aspects of labor economics* (pp. 63–73). Princeton, NJ: Princeton University Press.

Mincer, J., & Polachek, S. (1974). Family investments in human capital: Earnings of women. *Journal of Political Economy, 82*(2 Part 2), S76–S108.

Nash, J., & Fernandez-Kelly, M. P. (Eds.). (1983). *Women, men and the international division of labor*. Albany, NY: State University of New York Press.

O'Brien, M. (1981). *The politics of reproduction*. Boston, MA: Routledge & Kegan Paul.

Piore, M. J. (1975). Notes for a theory of labor market stratification. In R. C. Edwards, M. Reich, & D. M. Gordon (Eds.), *Labor market segmentation*. Lexington, MA: Heath.

Portes, A., & Benton, L. (1984). Industrial development and labor absorption: A reinterpretation. *Population and Development Review, 10*(4), 589–611.

Reich, M., Gordon, D. M., & Edwards, R. C. (1973). A theory of labor market segmentation. *American Economic Review, 63*(2), 359–365.

Rogers, B. (1980). *The domestication of women: Discrimination in developing societies*. New York: Tavistock.

Sirageldin, I., Sherbiny, N. A., & Serageldin, M. I. (1984). *Saudis in transition: The challenges of a changing labor market*. New York: Oxford University Press.

Standing, G. (1983). Women's work activity and fertility. In R. Bulatao & R. Lee (Eds.), *Determinants of fertility in developing countries* (pp. 517–546). New York: Academic Press.

Strom, S. H. (1987). Machines instead of clerks: Technology and the feminization of bookkeeping, 1910–1950. In H. I. Hartmann (Ed.), *Computer chips and paper clips: Technology and women's employment* (pp. 63–97). Washington, DC: National Academy Press.

Taubman, P., & Wachter, M. L. (1986). Segmented labor markets. In O. C. Ashenfelter, & R. Layard (Eds.), *Handbook of labor economics 1* (pp. 1183–1217). New York: North Holland.

Thompson, P. (1983). *The nature of work: An introduction to debates on the labour process*. London: Macmillan.

Wachter, M. L. (1974). Primary and secondary labor markets: A critique of the dual approach. *Brookings Papers on Economic Activity, 3*, 637–693.

Young, K. (1982). The creation of a relative surplus population: A case study from Mexico. In L. Benería (Ed.), *Women and development: The sexual division of labor in rural societies* (pp. 149–176). New York: Praeger/ILO.

METHODOLOGICAL CONSIDERATIONS IN MEASURING WOMEN'S LABOR FORCE ACTIVITY IN DEVELOPING COUNTRIES:
THE CASE OF EGYPT

Richard Anker

I. INTRODUCTION

The present volume in the annual series on *Research in Human Capital and Development* is concerned with female labor force participation. Two other papers in this section provide theoretical overviews and explanations for this situation. The papers in parts 2 and 3 present empirical analyses to explain either the determinants of women's labor force participation or how women's labor force participation affects other behavior such as fertility, child health and mental health status.

All of these discussions and analyses are based on the size and distribution of women's labor force activity—as measured by statistics. Official macrostatistics,

Research in Human Capital and Development, Vol. 6, pages 27–58.

ISBN: 1-55938-032-2

for example, may indicate that *x* percent of women are in the labor force; that the profile of age specific participation rates are shaped as an inverted-U; that *y* percent of "working" women are in an agricultural occupation; that *z* percent of these women are working as unpaid family workers, and so on. Then, based on these macrolevels and trends, theoretical frameworks are developed. For the empirically-oriented studies on the other hand, microhousehold- and individual-level data are relied upon. Thus, survey data are analyzed using multivariate statistical techniques to explain, for example, why certain women are in the labor force and others are not.

It is almost a non sequitur to say that analyses and reviews such as those contained in this volume are only as good as the data upon which they are based. Unfortunately, such an obvious statement has been in the past all too often ignored or downplayed by scholars engaged in empirical analyses. Such a cavalier attitude toward female labor force data is, however, misplaced, because there is considerable evidence that female labor force data are subject to large measurement errors, and that these errors are not randomly distributed across population subgroups; indeed, there are important examples where the estimated size of the female labor force has doubled, tripled or quadrupled based on results of successive labor force surveys or on results from successive questions in particular surveys.

Reasons for the well-known instability of estimates of the female labor force can be found in how labor force participation is defined, how questionnaires are constructed and how field work techniques are used to collect these data. The bottom line, however, is that available data on the female labor force are sensitive to a number of factors related to its measurement and so should not be taken at face value in a rush toward empiricism or theoretization.

This paper concentrates on difficulties in the measurement of women's labor force participation. The intention is to indicate how and why estimates of female labor force participation vary from survey to survey, from region to region, and from country to country *due to nonbehavioral* factors related to its *measurement* rather than to underlying social-economic-demographic factors that help to explain variations in human activity. It is our feeling that unless analysts and readers fully understand what is being represented by data on female labor force activity, there is a high probability that incorrect conclusions will be drawn and inappropriate policies will be formulated. In this discussion, we rely heavily on results from a methodological labor force survey from rural Egypt (and to a lesser extent to a similar methodological survey from rural India), where information was collected in a controlled experiment on the measurement of labor force activity of over 1,000 (1,600) adult women using different labor force definitions; different types of questionnaires; male and female interviewers; as well as self-respondents and proxy-respondents.

The remainder of this paper is structured as follows: Section II provides a brief description of official estimates of female labor force participation in Egypt and

Section III provides a brief description of the ILO/CAPMAS Egyptian labor force Methods Test survey. Section IV discusses international recommendations on defining labor force activity as well as on the sensitivity of female labor force estimates to changes in this definition based on ILO/CAPMAS Methods Test survey data. This discussion covers: (a) types of activities that are considered to be labor force activities; (b) length of the reference period used to measure labor force activity; and (c) minimum amount of work-time required for someone to be included in the labor force. Section V discusses three important fieldwork and data collection issues: (a) questionnaire design, (b) respondents, and (c) interviewers. The final section provides a short summary and conclusion.

II. OFFICIAL ESTIMATES OF FEMALE LABOR PARTICIPATION IN EGYPT

Egypt, as other Arab countries in the region, has very low female labor force participation rates according to official government estimates. According to pre-1983 data, only 5–6 percent of Egyptian women were in the labor force (and this included a high proportion of unemployed women, as 1–2 percent of all Egyptian women were reportedly unemployed, thereby implying that only about 3–4 percent of Egyptian women were engaged in a labor force activity that produced an economic good or service). Similarly, very low female labor force participation rates were reported in the 1976 Egyptian population census, in the 1978–1982 annual Egyptian national labor force surveys (Table 1), as well as in the ILO's standardized estimates (ILO, 1986).

Beginning with the 1983 national labor force survey, the official Egyptian estimate of the female labor force participation rate showed a dramatic increase from approximately 6 percent in 1982 to approximately 13 percent in 1983 (although it is worth noting that the rate from the 1986 population census was in between, about 9 percent).

How could estimates of the Egyptian female labor force have changed so dramatically from one year to the next? How could results prior to 1983 have been so consistent if they were so wrong?

There is a good explanation for these two questions. In 1983 the Central Agency for Public Mobilization and Statistics (CAPMAS) made a conscious effort to improve the reporting of female labor force activity. Prior to this, the fact that family-related activities such as work on the family farm were labor force activities had not been emphasized to interviewers. For the 1983 national labor force survey, however, interviewers took a comprehensive course specifically oriented toward increasing the enumeration of female labor force participants. Interviewers were given a separate form that included separate probing questions that they were supposed to use in order to learn more about women's labor force activities. The number of households each interviewer had to cover

Table 1. Female Labor Force Participation Rates in Egypt Based on Population Censuses and National Labor Force Surveys, 1976–1986[a]

Year (1)	*All ages*[b] (2)	*Women 25–29* (3)	*Women 30–49* (4)
1976 (census)	5.5	10.8	6.0[c]
1977	NR	NR	NR
1978	6.0	11.5	6.5
1979	5.4	10.5	5.8
1980	5.7	11.6	6.0
1981	5.9	NR	NR
1982	5.8	NR	NR
1983	12.5	20.6	19.9[d]
1984	13.5	NR	NR
1986 (census)	8.9	NR	NR

Notes: [a] Rates include unemployment rate (which is usually about 1 to 2 percent of all women for 1976–1984 and about 3 percent of all women in 1986).
[b] Only persons aged 6 years or above can be considered to be labor force participants.
[c] Based on ages 30–44.
[d] Based on ages 30–39.
NR = Not reported.

Sources: Based on national labor force surveys for all years except for 1976 and 1986, which are based on population censuses.
ILO, *Yearbook of Labour Statistics* for 1976 and 1978–1983; Central Agency for Public Mobilization and Statistics, for 1984 and 1986.

was reduced from 15 per day in the 1982 survey to 10 per day in the 1983 survey in order to provide them with sufficient time to collect more complete information on female labor force activity. More women interviewers were hired, with their proportion rising from 8 percent in the 1982 survey to 28 percent in the 1983 survey. Moreover, the instruction manual used to train interviewers mentioned explicitly that some unpaid work done for the family, such as work on the family farm, was considered to be labor force activity.

The fact that almost all of the increase in female labor force participants is concentrated in agriculture (Table 2) provides corroborating evidence that the improved measurement of female labor force activity in the 1983 national labor force survey can be traced to the steps taken by CAPMAS.

However, as we shall see below, based on results of the ILO/CAPMAS Methods Test, even these new higher rates of female labor force activity continue to embody a large underestimate.

III. BRIEF DESCRIPTION OF THE ILO/CAPMAS METHODS TEST SURVEY IN RURAL EGYPT

When work began in 1978 on an ILO research project (with UNFPA funding) concerned with interactions between women's economic roles and demographic

Table 2. Distribution of Egyptian Women by Occupation Based on 1982, 1983, and 1984 National Labor Force Surveys

	Percent of women workers [a,b]			*Percent of all women* [d]		
Occupation *(1)*	*1982* [c] *(2)*	*1983* *(3)*	*1984* *(4)*	*1982* [c] *(5)*	*1983* *(6)*	*1984* *(7)*
Agriculture	8.5	40.6	46.7	0.5	5.1	6.3
Professional	39.2	19.7	19.9	2.3	2.5	2.7
Administration/ managerial	3.9	2.0	2.1	0.2	0.3	0.3
Clerical	28.9	14.9	14.6	1.7	1.9	2.0
Sales	5.0	7.7	6.2	0.3	1.0	0.8
Service	6.0	4.1	3.1	0.3	0.5	0.4
Production	7.4	10.8	7.4	0.4	1.4	1.0
Not elsewhere classified	1.0	0.2	0.0	0.1	0.0	0.0
Total	99.9	100.0	100.0	5.8	12.7[e]	13.5

Notes: [a] Unemployment excluded in calculations of percentage distributions.
[b] For purposes of comparison, note that 39.9 and 42.1 percent of male workers were reported to have agriculture as an occupation in the 1982 and 1983 surveys.
[c] Distribution for 1982 is similar to distribution for earlier years.
[d] Percentage distribution estimated by multiplying rates from columns 2, 3 and 4 by participation rate from Table 1. The underlying assumption is that unemployed women are distributed across occupations as in columns 2, 3 and 4.
[e] Total rate for 1983 for all women differs from rate reported in Table 1 due to rounding error.

Source: ILO, 1986; CAPMAS (1987) and unpublished CAPMAS data.

issues, it became obvious that development planning as well as research on women's issues (and relationships between female labor force participation and demographic variables such as fertility and mortality) were greatly hindered by a lack of accurate data on women's participation in the labor force. The true size of women's contributions to development and labor force activity were, to a large extent, invisible, according to official government statistics. In order to help rectify this situation we felt that it was necessary to obtain statistically supported facts as a basis for indicating to statisticians and policymakers the true extent to which women engage in labor force activities, why official estimates of the female labor are often underestimates, and how these underestimates can be reduced or eliminated. In doing this we wanted to avoid the emotionalism, weak observational empiricism and anecdotal evidence that we felt had crept into some of the literature on women's issues.

For the above reasons, methodological surveys on measuring female labor force activity in India and Egypt were carried out in collaboration with Operations Research Group, Baroda, India (ORG, one of the largest survey organizations in the world) and with Central Agency for Public Mobilization and Statistics (CAPMAS, the Egyptian government's statistical office). Four major methodological issues, which were identified in an earlier publication (Anker, 1983), were directly addressed in these methods test surveys.

1. What type of questionnaire provides the most accurate data on female labor force activity? In particular, does a simplified activity schedule or a keyword-based questionnaire provide more accurate data?
2. Does the sex of the interviewer have an effect on the reporting of female labor force activity?
3. Do proxy-respondents (i.e., persons who answer for someone else) provide different responses on female labor force activity as compared to self-respondents?
4. Do the effects of the above three treatment variables on the reporting of female labor force activity vary according to how the labor force is defined?

Approximately 1,600 households were interviewed in rural Uttar Pradesh, India (a state in north India that is predominantly rural and has a population of approximately 130 million persons) and approximately 1,000 households were interviewed in rural Egypt (which included villages in upper, lower, and middle Egypt). Interested readers are referred to other publications that provide detailed descriptions of these studies (Anker, Khan, & Gupta, 1988 for the Indian study, and Anker & Anker, 1988, for the Egyptian study). A brief description of the Egyptian study follows.

In order to observe how questionnaire design affects the reporting of female labor force activity, two questionnaires were used. Questionnaire A contained a simplified activity schedule (which included a list of labor force activities that were read out to respondents), while questionnaire B contained a series of 10 typical (key)worded questions. Half of the interviews used questionnaire A and the other half used questionnaire B. Results are analyzed in two ways in section 5. First, results from the activity schedule questionnaire and from the keyword questionnaire are compared. Second, results from various combinations of keyword questions are compared in order to find out which keyword questions have a greater effect on the reporting of labor force activity.

In order to examine whether the sex of the interviewer affects the reporting of female labor force activity, male interviewers and female interviewers each interviewed equal numbers of respondents in each sample village. Then in the analysis reported below, results from interviews conducted by male interviewers are compared with interviews conducted by female interviewers.

In order to test whether self-respondents and proxy-respondents (proxy-respondents are persons who answer for someone else, and are usually male) report different levels of female labor force activity, it was ensured that half of the respondents were self-respondents and half were proxy-respondents. A comparison of results based on responses of self-respondents and proxy-respondents are also presented in section V.

To ensure that one-half of the sample fell into each of the experimental groups described above, a fully crossed experimental design was used in which half of the interviewers in each village were male and half were female. Each interviewer type (i.e., gender) used questionnaire A for half of the interviews and questionnaire B for the other half. In addition, male (female) interviewers using each questionnaire interviewed proxy-respondents half of the time and self-respondents half of the time. A schematic representation of all completed questionnaires is presented in Figure 1.

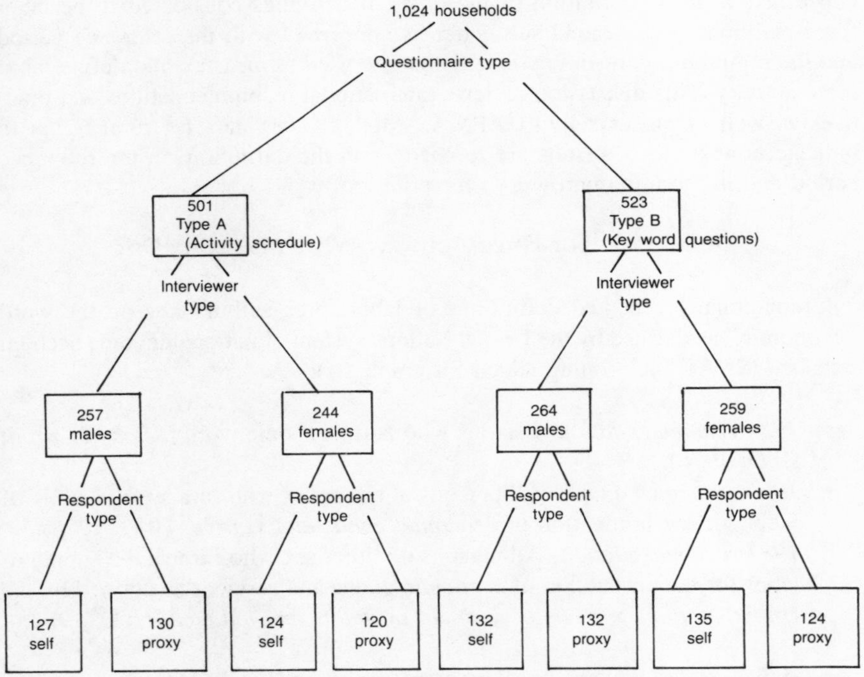

Note: The sample is not quite fully balanced across all treatment factors for two reasons. First, while the sample of households interviewed in the field (which used an age range of 12–64) *was fully balanced*, a subset of these data was used (an age range of 15 years or above) for analytical purposes, so as to be consistent with the sample used in the ILO/ORG Methods Test in rural Uttar Pradesh, India. Second, a small proportion of households were eliminated from the analysis due to missing data.

Figure 1. Schematic Representation of Completed Questionnaires for ILO/ CAPMAS Methods Test Survey for Rural Egypt

IV. DEFINITION OF LABOR FORCE ACTIVITY

The labor force consists of two components: persons who are working/employed and persons who are unemployed.

The present chapter is concerned with issues related to measuring labor force activities that produce economic goods or services. It is not concerned with unemployment or its measurement, because the main problem in developing countries with regard to measurement of the female labor force is not in identifying unemployed women, but rather, in identifying the large number of Third World women who are making important contributions to the development of their countries through their economic/labor force activities.

The remainder of this section is divided into two parts. One subsection is concerned with the definition of the types of activities considered to be labor force activities. The second subsection is concerned with the reference period and the minimum work-time criterion that are used to measure and define labor force activity. This discussion reviews international recommendations and practices as well as presents ILO/CAPMAS Methods Test data for rural Egypt to indicate how sensitive results are to changes in the definition, in the reference period and in the minimum work-time criterion.

Defining Labor Force Activity: What Must She Do?

Internationally accepted definitions of labor force activity key on the word "economic" as defined by the United Nations system of national income account statistics (SNA) (underlining added for emphasis):

- *1954 recommendation:* Persons who perform some work *for pay or profit* (ILO, 1976).
- *1966 recommendation:* All persons of either sex who furnish the supply of labor for the production of *economic goods and services* (ILO, 1976).
- *1982 recommendation:* All persons of either sex who furnish the supply of labor for the production of *economic* goods and services as defined by the *United Nations systems of national accounts and balances* (ILO, 1982b).

Activities related to wage or salary employment and/or market-oriented enterprises are clearly labor force activities. So too are many nonmarket activities such as subsistence agriculture, home construction and improvement, milking animals, and processing food, according to United Nations recommendations of SNA:

> *All production of primary products* should, in principal, be included in gross output [in national income], whether for own account consumption, for barter or for sale for money. It is also desirable to include in gross outputs: (i) the output of producers of other commodities,

> which are consumed in their household and which they also produce for the market and (ii) the *processing of primary commodities by the producers of these items* in order to make such goods as butter, cheese, flour, wine, oil, cloth or furniture for their own use *though they may not sell any of these manufactures.* (United Nations, 1968)

Because of the unavoidable practical and theoretical ambiguities and arbitrariness involved in distinguishing between economic and noneconomic activities as regards own-account activities, the appropriateness of these distinctions for many subsistence activities have been questioned (e.g., Beneria, 1982; Connell & Lipton, 1977; ILO, 1972; Myrdal, 1968). Similarly, a United Nations report concluded that:

> accurate figures on women's economic contribution are almost impossible to attain in most parts of the region. In the non-market sector where most women work, the distinction between economic and non-economic activities is seldom clear and most arbitrarily applied. The work activities of many women have only a weak attachment to the traditionally defined workforce. (United Nations, 1977)

Under such circumstances we feel that there is a need for *several* labor force measures that indicate the type (e.g., paid, not paid) and level (e.g., part-time, full-time, or number of hours) of labor force activity based on different definitions of "economic" activity.

A number of important purposes are served by having several labor force definitions. First, each definition provides information on a different aspect of the labor market. And, as planning needs are varied and multidimensional, so too measures of the labor force need to be in order to assist in such planning. Second, due to inherent ambiguities in defining the labor force, it is in our opinion not possible to have one "correct" labor force definition. By using several definitions, it becomes possible for data collectors and users to be clear about what is being measured by each labor force definition. Third, also due to ambiguities in labor force concepts, it is likely that the broader and more encompassing the labor force definition, the greater will be the inaccuracy with which it is measured. This has particular relevance for the Indian and Egyptian Methods Test surveys, which are concerned with measurement error, as it is especially important for us to know if measurement error is indeed related to the comprehensiveness of labor force definition.

For these reasons, four labor force definitions were developed and used in earlier publications (see Anker, 1983; Anker, Khan, & Gupta, 1987, 1988): paid labor force, market labor force, ILO labor force and extended labor force. All four of these definitions, which provide information on different aspects of the labor market and national income, are defined below and used in the Indian and Egyptian Methods Test surveys. Inclusion of an activity in a specific labor force definition depends on performance of that activity, whether wages or salary payment was received (to qualify for inclusion in the paid labor force), and whether products produced in a family enterprise were sold (to qualify for inclusion in the market labor force). Each successive definition includes all persons and activities included in previous, narrower definitions.

Our four definitions—from the narrowest to the broadest—are as follows:

1. *Paid labor force* includes persons in wage or salary employment for which they are paid in cash or in kind. This definition corresponds fairly closely to the employment status category of "employees" currently in use. There is relatively little ambiguity among labor statisticians and respondents on whether a person working for wages or salary is in the labor force; consequently, it is expected that the paid labor force is relatively easy to measure and so will be subject to less measurement error than broader labor force measures.

2. *Market-oriented labor force* refers to persons in "paid labor force" plus persons engaged in an activity on a family farm or in a family enterprise or business that sells some or all of its products. The following are included in the market labor force: employers; own-account workers; unpaid family workers; and members of producers' cooperatives—but only those who are involved in activities where sales and/or monetary transactions occur. The "market-oriented labor force" covers persons engaged in monetary transactions.

3. *ILO labor force* includes persons engaged in activities whose products or services should be included in the national income accounts statistics according to United States recommendations. This definition of the labor force corresponds to what we consider to be the recommendation of the thirteenth International Conference on Labour Statisticians (ILO, 1982b).[1] Given the difficulty of interpreting and following these international recommendations in rural areas in a country such as Egypt where subsistence production is important, our definition may differ slightly from that of others. However, by being very specific as to which activities we included, our definition is unambiguous. Our "ILO labor force" includes persons engaged in the production of economic goods and services, irrespective of whether these goods or services are sold.

4. *Extended labor force*. In addition to persons in the "ILO labor force," the "extended labor force" includes persons engaged in activities not included in the most recent United Nations recommendations on the SNA, but which nonetheless contribute to meeting their family's basic needs for goods and services which are generally purchased in developed countries. For our particular study, the "extended labor force" includes ILO labor force activities plus gathering and preparing fuel (e.g., gathering sticks and wood, preparing cow dung cake).

The basic rationale underlying the concept of the extended labor force is the usefulness of having data on the satisfaction of basic needs that is comparable across cultural and development levels and of broadening the definition of "economic" activity beyond the often arbitrary distinctions made in the United Nations system of national income accounts statistics (see, e.g., Goldschmidt-Clermont, 1987). There is also the possibility that future SNA statistics on nonmonetary subsistence activities will be expanded (United Nations, 1979), and it would be useful to have a time series of comparable labor force data.

In rural Egypt, the main activities comprising the paid labor force were found to be agricultural activities for nonfamily members and government service, which were done during the past year by 8.7 and 2.1 percent of sample women, respectively. The main activities comprising the market labor force (in addition to the two paid labor force activities mentioned above) were work on a family farm, work with family-owned animals, and work with family-owned poultry, where products were sold. These activities were done by approximately 13, 10 and 11 percent of sample women, respectively.

Results from the ILO/CAPMAS Methods Test survey for Egypt and the ILO/ORG Methods Test survey for India indicate how sensitive the estimated size of the female labor force is to the definition used. Thus, in the Indian Methods Test, adult female activity rates were reported to be approximately 12, 33, and 90 percent for the paid, market, internationally accepted labor force definitions respectively for the past season reference period.

Results from the ILO/CAPMAS Methods Test survey indicate that rural Egyptian women are also quite active (Table 3)—much more active than official government statistics indicate. Reported activity rates range from about 15 percent for the paid labor force, to approximately 40 percent for the market labor force, to approximately 80 to 90 percent for the ILO and extended labor forces in terms of ever performing a relevant activity during the past year, or past three months or past week reference periods (rows 1–3 in Table 3).

For the most part, labor force activity using the broader definitions (ILO and extended labor forces) of the labor force can be characterized by the performance of many different activities, each for a relatively short period of time, whereas the activities that comprise the narrower definitions (paid and market labor forces) tend to be more time intensive. For example, whereas the paid labor force activity rate for the past week reference period (with a 10-hour work-time constraint) was 11.6 percent, its major component, farming for others, had an activity rate of 8.4 percent. For the market labor force (30.0 percent for past week), major components were farming for others (8.4 percent) and farming for family (12.4 percent); both of these activities tended to be done for substantial amounts of time as over two-thirds of the women who performed a farming activity last week did so for more than 20 hours in the week. In contrast, many of the activities done by the majority of extended labor force participants, such as gathering fuel, processing and grinding grain, and so on, usually involved less than 10 hours a week, and it was rare for any one of these activities to be done for more than 20 hours a week. These results imply that it is important to add up time spent in all of the labor force activities that women perform if one is to get a complete picture of the labor force activity of rural women in Egypt and other Third World countries.

Table 3. Activity Rates For Rural Egyptian Women (With and Without Work-Time Criterion) For Four Labor Force Definitions For Past Week, Season, and Year Reference Periods Based on Activity Schedule Results[a]

	LF definition			
	Paid LF	*Market LF*	*ILO LF*	*Extended LF*
Performed at all in past				
(1) year	14.8	41.3	90.2	91.0
(2) season	14.4	40.1	90.0	90.8
(3) week	13.0	39.6	82.0	83.0
Performed for more than minimum work-time in past[b]				
(4) season	10.8	27.3	49.9	53.9
(5) week	11.6	30.0	53.3	56.9

Notes: [a] Information on time was not collected for past year reference period.
[b] Minimum number of work-hours is 10 hours in past week and 130 hours in past three month season. See section 4.2 for discussion on minimum work-hours.
Source: ILO/CAPMAS Methods Test survey for rural Egypt.

Reference Period and Minimum Work-Time Criterion: When and For How Long Must She Do Work?

The two most common conceptual approaches for measuring labor force activity are: (1) the labor force approach, which measures the number of persons currently active in a short reference period of one day or more typically one week; and (2) the gainful worker approach, which measures the number of persons usually in the labor force over a long reference period of past season or past one year. The *current labor force* provides a snapshot picture of the number of persons in the labor force at one point in time; the *usual labor force* provides a measure of the number of persons who are usually in the labor force. These estimates need not be the same and indeed are often quite different; differences are most likely to occur in settings with strong daily, weekly, and seasonal variations in labor force activities. Both measures of the labor force—current and usual labor forces—are important and are used in the ILO/CAPMAS Methods Test survey for Egypt based on past week and past season/past year reference periods, respectively.

There are, of course, international recommendations on the amount of time a person must perform labor force activities to be considered as a labor force participant. These recommendations are complicated, however, by the fact that the recommended minimum work-time cut-off differs according to both the length of the reference period used and the type of activity performed. When a short reference period such as one week is used to measure the current labor force, by far the most common worktime criterion is a minimum of one hour of relevant work during the reference week. In fact, of course, this one-hour rule is so weak a criterion that it is meaningless. This supposition is supported by many studies[2] and is well illustrated by data from the present ILO/CAPMAS Methods Test reported on below (see Table 4). Of course, the main reason for the one-hour work-time criterion for the current labor force is to include in the labor force all persons who engage in *any* labor force activity so that unemployment (which requires the absence of any labor force activity) can be measured.

Further complicating matters is the fact that many countries apply a different minimum work-time criterion for unpaid family work—the most common criterion being a minimum of 15 hours in the reference week (or approximately one-third of normal working hours). This 15-hour rule is a carry-over from the 1954 and 1966 international recommendations that were changed in 1982. According to the 1982 recommendations, only activities involving the production or processing of primary products for own or household consumption should be treated differently in terms of the minimum work-time requirement; to be considered as a labor force activity, such activities should "comprise an important contribution to total consumption of the household" (ILO, 1982a).

Obviously, this new criterion is impractical and unimplementable. (For example, what is "important"? How should total consumption be measured? Does this "important" rule apply to each activity separately or to all relevant activities taken together?) For this reason, it is not surprising that many countries continue to rely on the earlier, more practical work-time criterion, which is time based.

This practice is incorrect, however, as long as a distinction is made between unpaid family workers and own-account workers. According to current international recommendations, the "important contribution to household consumption" rule should apply to all subsistence labor force activities and there should not be any distinction between self-employed/own-account workers and unpaid family workers; otherwise, a strong gender bias would be built into labor force statistics, because in practice men are much more likely to be designated as own-account workers, while women are much more likely to be designated as unpaid family workers.

For measuring the usual labor force based on the gainful worker approach, a number of different types of minimum work-time criteria have been used in surveys and censuses (Mehran, 1986b). This is hardly surprising, because international recommendations on the usual labor force do not include a specific minimum work-time criterion. In many instances, this has involved use of a majority time criterion—that is, labor force activity has to be for at least half of the weeks or for half of the days in the reference period (e.g., activity in 26 different weeks or in 183 different days in a one year reference period). Other possibilities include, among others, a majority of work-time (in weeks or in days or in hours) in one season during the year in order to capture labor force partici-

Table 4. Female Labor Force Activity Rates in Rural Egypt as a Function of the Reference Period and the Minimum Work-Time Required to be in the Labor Force[a]
(N = 1024)

	Last week						Last season (13 weeks)					
Labor force definition	*No time constraint*	*At least 1 hour*	*At least 4 hours*	*At least 7 hours*	*At least 10 hours*	*At least 15 hours*	*No time constraint*	*At least 13 hours*	*At least 52 hours*	*At least 91 hours*	*At least 130 hours*	*At least 195 hours*
Paid	11.9	11.9	11.3	11.0	10.7	9.3	12.9	12.2	11.2	10.8	10.3	7.9
Market	37.0	36.9	34.5	33.3	29.2	23.7	38.5	36.6	33.4	31.9	26.5	21.0
ILO	79.8	79.0	70.7	66.7	54.2	42.3	87.3	77.8	69.8	65.2	51.0	39.5
Extended	81.1	80.1	72.6	68.4	57.7	47.4	88.5	79.4	71.9	67.3	54.3	44.7

Notes: [a] Information was not collected on amount of work-time for the past one year reference period. Therefore the above breakdown cannot be provided for a one year reference period.

For description of each labor force definition see section 4.

Source: ILO/CAPMAS Methods Test survey for rural Egypt.

pants who work in only one season; or a work-time rule that is chosen so as to obtain an estimate of the usual labor force that is similar to that for the current labor force, in order to provide an estimate of the average labor force.

For the ILO/CAPMAS Methods Test survey, we wanted a minimum work-time criterion that eliminated marginal labor force participants so that we did not get a false impression of the importance of observed biases in the reporting of female labor force activity associated with methods test treatment factors such as questionnaire design. At the same time, we did not want this minimum work-time criterion to be so high as to eliminate too many women who were clearly quite active in the labor force. Also, for simplicity of presentation and interpretation, the use of similar criteria for all four of our labor force definitions and both of our reference periods made sense.

Based on these considerations, we decided to use 10 hours per week as the minimum work-time criterion. (This implied a minimum of 130 hours for the season.) This criterion, which was chosen on an ad hoc basis, is high enough to eliminate marginal labor force participants but not so high as to eliminate too many active women. It is a compromise between use of the very low one-hour criterion and what we felt was the too high 15-hour, or one-third, criterion.

In order to observe what difference the reference period and the minimum work-time criterion have on measured female labor force activity rates, ILO/CAPMAS Methods Test data are tabulated in Table 4 by number of work-hours (none, 1, 4, 7, 10, and 15 hours per week) for each of two reference periods (last week, last season). These data are presented for each of four definitions of the labor force (see the last subsection for details on these definitions).

The first striking aspect of these data is the *close correspondence* between activity rates for both the *last week* and the *last season* reference periods when equivalent minimum work-time criteria are used—although there is a tendency for rates to be slightly higher for last season as compared to last week for the zero-hour and one-hour work-time constraints (as indeed they must because it is only possible for an individual to do more, not fewer, activities in the past season as compared to the past week) and to be slightly lower for the 4, 7, 10 and 15 hour per week work-time constraints for the past season as compared to the past week. The similarity of these results implies that rural Egyptian women follow a fairly regular routine across the season.

A second striking aspect of these data is that, as expected, the one hour per week work-time criterion has almost no effect on estimates of the current labor force, although its equivalent (13 hours in past season) has somewhat of an effect on estimates of the usual labor force. This result adds new evidence to common-sense observation and previous studies that the one hour work-time criterion is more or less equivalent to no criterion at all when the reference period is the past week.

Third, the narrower the labor force definition, the less sensitive labor force estimates are to the minimum work-time criterion—both in absolute and relative terms. For example, whereas estimates of the paid and market labor forces for a one week reference period decrease by only 1.2 and 7.8 absolute percentage points respectively when one moves from no work-time criterion to a 10-hour per week criterion, there are 25.6 and 23.4 absolute percentage point reductions respectively in the ILO and extended labor forces. One implication of this result is that singling out paid and market labor force activities for having a lower minimum work-time cut-off—as suggested by current international recommendations—does not make that large a difference in their labor force estimates.

Fourth, the longer the reference period, the more sensitive labor force estimates are to the minimum work-time criterion. Notice that whereas labor force activity rates are higher for the past week than for the past when there is no work-time criterion, the opposite is true when a 15-hours per week criterion is applied.

V. FIELDWORK AND DATA COLLECTION ISSUES

Questionnaire Design: How are the questions being asked?

Labor force questionnaires typically rely on keywords or phrases, such as "main activity," "secondary activity," "work," "economic," "pay or profit," which are embedded in questions. Examples of keyword questions from the 1961, 1971 and 1981 Indian censuses are given below (as cited in Anker, Khan and Gupta, 1988); underlining added for emphasis.

- *1961 Indian census.* Are you *working* as a cultivator, agricultural laborer, working at household industries or working under any category other than the three mentioned?
- *1971 Indian census.* What is your *main activity?* What is your *other (secondary) activity?*
- *1981 Indian census.* *Worked* any time last year? *Main activity* last year? Any other *work* any time last year?

Given the ambiguities in international definitions and the strong market and wage connotation of the usual keywords, it is hardly surprising that respondents often misunderstand keyword questions and so often do not mention activities performed on the family farm or other unpaid labor force activities. For example, results from a 1974 national economic-demographic survey in Kenya of about 3,000 households found an adult female labor force activity rate of about 90 percent based on a keyword question that used the word "work" and an activity rate of about 20 percent based on a keyword question that used the word "job" (Anker & Knowles, 1978). Inspection of these data indicated that "jobs" consisted almost exclusively of wage and salary employment while "work" included many time consuming activities required for family survival.

Results from the ILO/ORG Methods Test survey in India, which used two types of questionnaires: (a) a keyword questionnaire that included a nested set of keyword questions that began with a very general question on "main activity" and got progressively more specific with follow-up keyword questions on: "secondary activity," "work," "help on a family farm or business," "helping family by caring for livestock, processing food for storage, cooking for hired laborers, gathering fuel, sewing clothes"; and (b) an activity schedule that included a list of 14 specific activities also indicate how sensitive activity rates are to the questions being asked. There were enormous differences in the Indian survey between questionnaire types in reported female labor force activity when only a few keyword questions were used. (See Figure 2 for a graphical presentation of results from the ILO/ORG Methods Test survey for Uttar Pradesh, India.) And, the broader the definition of the labor force involved, the more keyword questions that needed to be asked to get activity rates, which were insignificantly different from those obtained using the activity schedule.

The same two basic types of labor force questionnaire were also used in the ILO/CAPMAS Methods Test survey for rural Egypt. Questionnaire A used a simplified activity/time schedule. Questionnaire B used a series of increasingly specific keyword questions in a "nested" design, so that with each additional question a new questionnaire could be considered to have been completed as indicated in schematic form in Figure 3. This nested design serves a very useful purpose: it allows us to ascertain how many additional women are identified as labor force participants by each additional keyword question, and consequently, how many keyword questions are required to obtain an accurate estimate of the female labor force.

Table 5 presents results for all combinations of keyword questions and Table 6 compares results from the keyword questionnaire to results from the activity schedule. We are concerned here with two main issues: (1) whether the activity schedule questionnaire type is superior to the keyword questionnaire type in that it elicits a more complete enumeration of female labor force activity; (2) if not, how many keyword questions need to be asked to obtain similar responses to those obtained using an activity schedule.

For the most part (see Table 5), only keyword questions *B1* ("main activity"), *B2* ("next most important activity"), and *B8* (which specifically mentions eight separate activities) have large effects on the reporting of female labor force activity, although some small but significant increases are observed when *B3* ("work for earnings") and *B6* (on "agricultural work for family") are asked. Estimates of the paid labor force change very little after question *B1* (on "main activity") and *B2* (on "second most important activity") are asked. Question *B3* on "work for earnings" also adds significantly to reported activity rates for the other three labor force definitions. Question *B8,* which mentions specific activities, has a major and significant impact on activity rates for the three broader definitions. This increase is especially large for the ILO and extended labor force definitions where female activity rates nearly double.

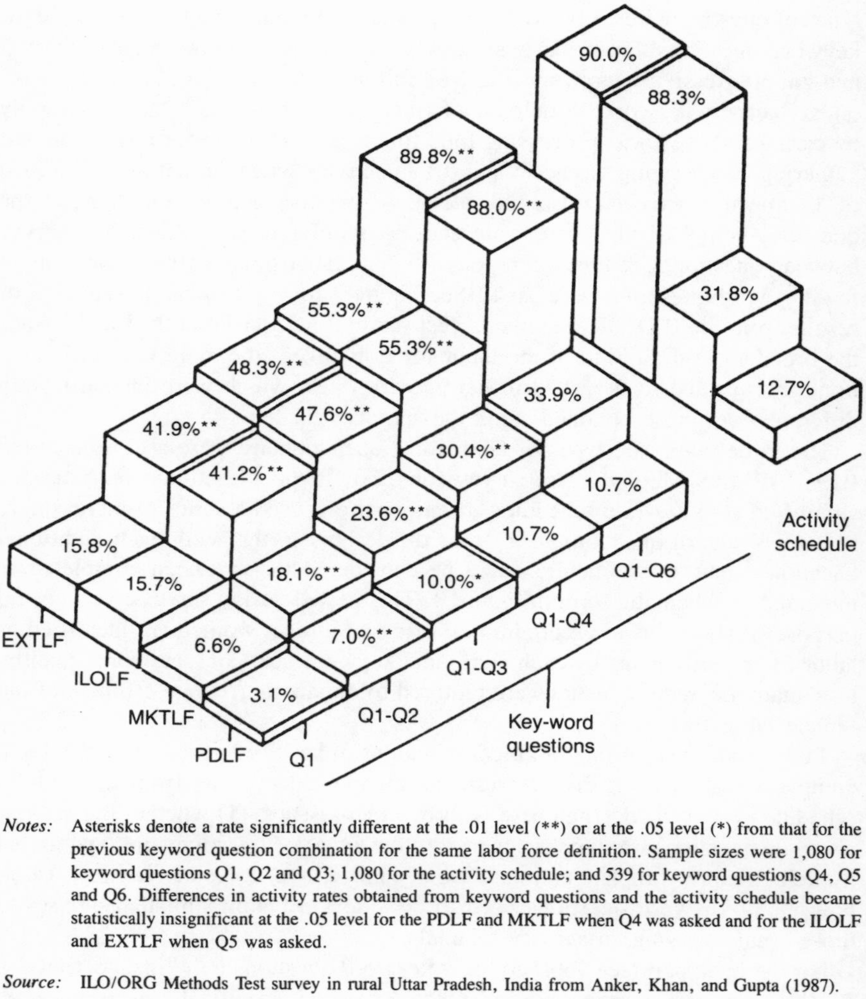

Notes: Asterisks denote a rate significantly different at the .01 level (**) or at the .05 level (*) from that for the previous keyword question combination for the same labor force definition. Sample sizes were 1,080 for keyword questions Q1, Q2 and Q3; 1,080 for the activity schedule; and 539 for keyword questions Q4, Q5 and Q6. Differences in activity rates obtained from keyword questions and the activity schedule became statistically insignificant at the .05 level for the PDLF and MKTLF when Q4 was asked and for the ILOLF and EXTLF when Q5 was asked.

Source: ILO/ORG Methods Test survey in rural Uttar Pradesh, India from Anker, Khan, and Gupta (1987).

Figure 2. Indian Methods Test study: Estimates of female labor force activity rate by questionnaire type for four labor force definitions (In Percent)

Now turning our attention to Table 6 and comparisons of results from the keyword questions to results from the activity schedule, we find that in the ILO/CAPMAS Methods Test that activity rates based on these two questionnaire types are quite similar when a "sufficient" number of keyword questions are asked—with the number of questions required related to the type of activity performed and the specificity of the keyword questions being asked. (A similar

B1	Main activity?	B1
B2	Next most important activity?	B1 to B2
B3	Worked for earnings?	B1 to B3
B4	Worked in family business/ trade in a constant place?	B1 to B4
B5	Worked in family business/ trade in a non-constant place?	B1 to B5
B6	Agricultural work on family farm?	B1 to B6
B7	Worked for payment inside home?	B1 to B7
B8	Engaged specifically in:	B1 to B8
	sewing, basket/rug making?	
	animal husbandry?	
	poultry caring?	
	gathering fuel?	
	making cow dung cakes?	
	fetching water?	
	processing food for preservation?	
	processing/grinding grain?	
B9	Any other activity for income?	B1 to B9
B10	Any other important activity in terms of time?	B1 to B10

Note: For each activity performed, information was collected on: employment status, sales of products produced, time in past week and time in past season.

Figure 3. Schematic Representation of Questionnaire B ("nested" Keyword Questionnaire) Used in ILO/CAPMAS Methods Test Survey for Rural Egypt According to Keywords Used

Table 5. Rural Egyptian Female Labor Force Activity Rates For Four Labor Force Definitions Based on Responses to Keyword Questions For Past Season and Past Week With Minimum Work-Time Criterion[c] (N = 523)

Reference period/ labor force definition	*Keyword questions*									
	B1	*B1 to B2*	*B1 to B3*	*B1 to B4*	*B1 to B5*	*B1 to B6*	*B1 to B7*	*B1 to B8*	*B1 to B9*	*B1 to B10*
Last season										
Extended	15.7	27.0[a]	28.9[a]	28.9	28.9	29.3	29.3	54.6[a]	54.6	54.8
ILO	15.7	26.8[a]	28.7[a]	28.7	28.7	29.1	29.1	52.0[a]	52.0	52.2
Market	14.0	22.0[a]	23.1[b]	23.1	23.1	23.5	23.5	25.8[a]	26.0	26.2
Paid	6.9	8.6[a]	9.2	9.2	9.2	9.2	9.2	9.4	9.8	9.8
Last week										
Extended	16.4	28.1[a]	30.6[a]	30.6	30.8	31.5[b]	31.5	58.5[a]	58.7	58.8
ILO	16.4	27.9[a]	30.4[a]	30.4	30.6	31.4[b]	31.4	54.9[a]	55.1	55.3
Market	14.7	22.8[a]	24.1[a]	24.1	24.3	25.0[b]	25.0	27.9[a]	28.3	28.5
Paid	6.9	8.6[a]	9.2	9.2	9.2	9.2	9.2	9.4	9.8	9.8

Notes: [a] Statistically different at the .01 level compared to the previous question combination (which is immediately to its left).
[b] Statistically different at the .05 level compared to the previous question combination (which is immediately to its left).
[c] Women were considered to be in the labor force if they worked at least 10 hours during the last week or 130 hours during the last three month season.
Significance estimated using one-tailed paired t-test.

Source: ILO/CAPMAS Methods Test survey for rural Egypt.

Table 6. Comparison of Rural Egyptian Female Labor Force Activity Rates For Four Aggregate Labor Force Definition Based on Keyword Questions and Activity Schedule For Past Year, Past Season, and Past Week

		Activity rate (no time constraint)		*Activity rate (minimum 10 hours per week time constraint)*		*Keyword questions for which activity rate based on activity schedule is significantly different from activity rate based on keyword questions*[a]	
Reference period (1)	*Labor force definition (2)*	*Activity schedule (3)*	*Keyword questions B1 to B10 (4)*	*Activity schedule (5)*	*Keyword questions B1 to B10 (6)*	*No time constraint (7)*	*Minimum time constraint (10 hours last week or 130 hours last season) (8)*
Last year	Paid	14.8	11.3	NA	NA	B1 to B7[b]	NA
	Market	41.3	36.7	NA	NA	B1 to B7	NA
	ILO	90.2	85.1	NA	NA	B1 to B10	NA
	Extended	91.0	86.8	NA	NA	B1 to B10	NA
Last season	Paid	14.4	11.3	10.8	9.8	B1 to B6[b]	B1
	Market	39.3	35.9	26.7	26.2	B1 to B9[b]	B1 to B7
	ILO	90.0	84.3	49.9	52.0	B1 to B10	B1 to B7
	Extended	90.8	85.7	53.9	54.5	B1 to B10	B1 to B7
Last week	Paid	13.0	10.7	11.6	9.8	B1	B1
	Market	39.5	34.6	29.0	28.5	B1 to B7	B1 to B5
	ILO	82.0	77.4	53.3	55.1	B1 to B7	B1 to B7
	Extended	83.0	78.8	56.9	58.5	B1 to B7	B1 to B7

Notes: N is equal to 501 for activity schedule and 523 for keyword questions.

[a] Significance is at .05 level based on a two-tailed t-test.

[b] The increase in labor force participation rates which would result from including results from the next keyword question is less than 1 percentage point; nonetheless, when the next additional keyword questionnaire is counted, the difference between the activity questionnaire and the cumulative keyword questions is no longer significant.

NA = Not applicable as data on time were not collected for past one year reference period.

Source: ILO/CAPMAS Methods Test survey for rural Egypt.

result was found in the ILO/ORG Indian Methods Test survey.) The broader the labor force definition and the longer the reference period involved, the more keyword questions which need to be asked to obtain responses which are similar (i.e., insignificantly different) to those obtained using the activity schedule. Thus, for example, the performance of paid labor force activities in the past week is fully reported when *B1* ("main activity") and *B2* ("next most important activity") are asked, whereas seven keyword questions must be asked when the reference period is the past season, and eight keyword questions must be asked when the reference period is the past year. For the reporting of the market labor force activities, it is necessary to ask the very specific keyword question *B8* to get results which are insignificantly different from those of the activity schedule. The performance of activities included in the broader definitions (i.e., ILO and extended labor forces) during the past week are identified after asking the specific keyword question *B8* (although not for the last season and last year reference periods).

We would like to draw the reader's attention to four important implications that can be drawn from these results and discussions. First, whereas the activity schedule is significantly better at identifying the performance of the less obvious labor force activities included in the ILO and extended labor forces, it is not significantly better at identifying women who engage in such activities for more than 10 hours in the past week or 130 hours in the past season.

Second, keyword questions must be very specific—to the point of mentioning particular activities—if nonwage, nonagricultural activities are to be identified, even including some activities that result in the earning of cash income. General keyword questions that use phrases such as "main activity," "next most important activity," and "work" are not sufficient for identifying anything but the paid labor force (i.e., wage or salary earners).

Third, it appears that including an activity schedule and/or a series of specific keyword questions in the questionnaire had a major effect on responses to general keyword questions such as on "main activity" and "next most important activity." This supposition is supported by the fact that based on only these two general keyword questions, activity rates for the paid, market labor force and ILO labor forces far exceed those obtained on Egypt's population census and national labor force survey. The implication is that considerably improved female labor force data would result if interviewers were forced to become aware of what are relevant labor force activities by a questionnaire which includes specific mention of important labor force activities.

Fourth, it is important to collect information on all (or many) of the multiple labor force activities women perform. It is not sufficient to stop collecting these data when one (or even two) labor force activities have been identified, because many women (and many men for that matter) in the Third World engage in multiple labor force activities, each for a relatively small amount of time (especially activities done for the family). For example, in the ILO/CAPMAS

Methods Test (based on results from the activity schedule) 89, 76, 65 and 68 percent of sample women who engaged in a paid, market, ILO or extended labor force activity respectively did so for more than 10 hours in the past week; in contrast, only 5, 13, 14, 15, 18, 24, 33, 43, and 57 percent of sample women who engaged in processing food for storage, making cow dung cakes, constructing houses, grinding grains, gathering fuel, caring for poultry, sewing, animal husbandry, vegetable trading, respectively, did so for more than 10 hours in the past week.

Respondent: Who is Providing the Answers?

The usual instruction given to interviewers in Third World countries is to interview the "head of household" and to collect information on all household members from him or her. This procedure may result in the underreporting of female labor force activity. First, because a male member of the household is usually identified as the head of household, respondents are usually male. This, in turn, would cause the female labor force to be underreported, if male respondents are more likely to have a preconceived belief that women should be housewives. Also, in some countries such as Egypt, male household members may be hesitant to report female labor force activity by female household members as they may feel that this would negatively affect their family's status (e.g., Dixon, 1982; Pittin, 1982; United Nations, 1980). Second, as a proxy-respondent, the head of household may not be knowledgeable about the activities of other household members; this may include activities performed by female household members.

The recent 1986 Egyptian national labor force envisaged these problems and so mentioned in its interviewer instructions that "stress is to be placed on completing the labor force information in the various tables of the questionnaire by interviewing each individual in person." It will be very interesting to learn how frequently it was possible to follow this instruction (and whether doing so affected responses), since most interviews in rural areas of the Third World occur in the presence of other persons (e.g., in the Indian and Egyptian methods tests, 97 and 89 percent of interviews in these surveys took place with someone else present).

Despite the above discussion and the widespread belief about the effect particular types of respondents have on the reporting of female labor force activity (especially the possible negative effect associated with male respondents), there is little hard evidence to support this belief in the research literature. Indeed, results from the ILO/ORG Methods Test in India found virtually no differences in the responses of male and female respondents or in the responses of (mostly male) proxy-respondents and (female) self-respondents as regards women's performance of labor force activities.

In order to observe whether self-respondents and proxy-respondents in rural

Egypt report different rates of female labor force activity (in particular, whether proxy-respondents, who are mostly males, report lower rates of female labor force activity as compared to self-respondents, who are all female), ILO/CAPMAS data were tabulated by the type of respondent. Table 7 reports labor force activity rates for both respondent types, for our four labor force definitions for all three reference periods, with and without minimum work-time constraints.

Self-respondents reported significantly greater paid (i.e., wage or salary) labor force activity than proxy-respondents, and this result was similar for each questionnaire type regardless of the reference period or the minimum work-time criterion being used. Based on results for the activity schedule, for example, we find that whereas self-respondents indicated that 18.7 percent of sample women were in the paid labor force during the past year, only 10.8 percent of proxy-respondents reported this. Similar results for the paid labor force were also observed for the other reference periods (i.e., past week and past season). These differences in the reporting of the paid labor force (of approximately eight absolute percentage points) between self-respondents and proxy-respondents carry over to estimates of the market labor force, causing self-respondents to again report significantly lower market labor force activity rates (e.g., 46.6 percent compared to 36.0 percent for proxy-respondents for the past year). For the two broader measures of the labor force (i.e., ILO and extended labor forces), differences between self-respondents and proxy-respondents narrow greatly and become statistically insignificant (except for the past week reference period with a minimum work-time constraint).

Because it is possible that the additional women, whom self-respondents identified as paid and market labor force participants, were marginal participants, we also investigated whether these additional rural Egyptian women reported to be labor force participants worked only a few hours. (Alternatively, the opposite could be true as there could be a common tendency for proxy-respondents to underreport the performance of paid and market labor force activities as well as to underestimate the number of work-hours participants put in.) The number of hours worked by female labor force participants in rural Egypt according to self-respondents and proxy-respondents tended to be similar for the paid and market labor forces as none of the 24 comparisons we made was significant at the .05 level.

These results from the Egyptian Methods Test are different from those for the Indian Methods Test where there were no significant differences between the responses provided by self-respondents and proxy-respondents in the reporting of either the performance of labor force activities or the reporting of the number of work-hours engaged in by labor force participants. These differences in the Egyptian and Indian Methods Test results imply that the effect of this gender-related aspect on the reporting of female labor force activity is quite country and culture specific.

Table 7. Comparison of Female Activity Rates For Rural Egypt Reported by Self-Respondents and Proxy-Respondents For Four Labor Force Definitions

Labor force measure/ questionnaire	*Last year*		*Last 3 months*				*Last week*			
	No minimum time[c]		*No minimum time*		*At least 130 hours last 3 months*		*No minimum time*		*At least 10 hours last week*	
	Self	*Proxy*	*Self*	*Proxy*	*Self*	*Proxy*	*Self*	*Proxy*	*Self*	*Proxy*
Paid LF										
B1	9.7	5.1[b]	9.7	5.1[b]	9.4	4.3[b]	9.4	5.1	9.0	4.7
B1 to B2	12.7	6.6[b]	12.7	6.6[b]	11.6	5.5[b]	12.4	6.3[b]	11.2	5.9[b]
B1 to B3	12.7	7.7[b]	12.7	7.4[b]	12.0	6.3[b]	12.4	7.0[b]	11.6	6.6[b]
B1 to B8	13.5	8.2	13.5	8.2	12.0	6.6[b]	12.7	7.8	11.6	7.0
B1 to B10	14.2	8.2[b]	14.2	8.2[b]	12.7	6.6[b]	13.5	7.8[b]	12.4	7.0[b]
Activity schedule	18.7	10.8[b]	18.3	10.4[b]	13.5	8.0[b]	17.1	8.8[b]	15.1	8.0[b]
Market LF										
B1	18.7	16.8	18.4	16.8	14.2	13.7	17.2	16.8	15.0	14.5
B1 to B2	31.1	25.8	30.3	25.4	24.7	19.1	29.2	25.0	24.3	21.1
B1 to B3	32.6	27.3	31.8	27.0	26.2	19.9	31.1	26.6	26.2	21.9
B1 to B8	40.8	31.6[b]	39.7	31.3[b]	28.8	22.7	37.5	30.9	29.2	26.6
B1 to B10	41.2	32.0[b]	40.1	31.6[b]	29.6	22.7	37.8	31.3	30.0	27.0
Activity schedule	46.6	36.0[b]	43.8	34.8[b]	29.4	24.0	45.4	33.6[a]	34.3	25.6[b]
ILO LF										
B1	21.7	19.5	21.7	19.5	15.7	15.6	20.2	19.1	16.5	16.4
B1 to B2	41.2	38.3	41.2	37.9	29.6	23.8	39.0	35.9	29.6	26.2
B1 to B3	43.4	40.6	43.4	40.2	31.8	25.4	41.6	38.7	32.6	28.1
B1 to B8	85.8	84.4	84.6	84.0	53.9	49.6	79.0	75.8	57.3	52.0
B1 to B10	85.8	84.4	84.6	84.0	54.3	49.6	79.0	75.8	57.7	52.3
Activity schedule	91.6	88.8	91.6	88.4	52.6	47.2	82.4	81.7	58.2	48.4[b]
Extended LF										
B1	21.7	19.5	21.7	19.5	15.7	15.6	20.2	19.1	16.5	16.4
B1 to B2	41.6	38.7	41.6	38.3	29.6	24.2	39.3	36.3	29.6	26.6
B1 to B3	43.8	41.0	43.8	40.6	31.8	25.8	41.9	39.1	32.6	28.5
B1 to B8	88.0	85.5	86.1	85.2	56.2	52.3	80.1	77.3	61.0	55.1
B1 to B10	88.0	85.5	86.1	85.2	56.6	52.3	80.1	77.3	61.4	55.5
Activity schedule	92.0	90.0	92.0	89.6	57.8	50.0	82.5	83.6	62.9	50.8[a]

Notes: B1, B2, . . . , B10 are keyword questions used in questionnaire B.

[a] Differences between self-respondents and proxy-respondents significant at .01 level using two-tailed *t*-test.

[b] Differences between self-respondents and proxy-respondents significant at .05 level using two-tailed *t*-test.

[c] Information on time was not collected for last year reference period.

Source: ILO/CAPMAS Methods Test survey for rural Egypt.

Interviewer: Who is Asking the Questions?

It is widely believed that one reason why female labor force activity is underreported in the Third World is that most interviewers are men. This downward in the reporting of female labor force activity is caused, according to this view, by prevailing male attitudes toward women that they are, or at least should be, "housewives" (Baster, 1981; Lattes & Wainerman, 1979; Slatter, 1982; United Nations, 1980).

On the other hand, there is little statistical evidence to support or to reject this widely held view. Results of the ILO/ORG Methods Test survey in rural India, for example, do not provide strong support or counterfactual evidence on the effect gender of the interviewer has on the reporting of female labor force activity. Whereas female interviewers in this Indian survey tended to record significantly higher female labor force activity than male interviewers when general keyword questions (such as *B1, B2* and *B3*) were used, the opposite was true when specific keyword questions (such as *B8*) or an activity schedule was used.

In order to observe whether the reporting of women's labor force activity in rural Egypt is affected by the gender of the interviewer (i.e., in particular whether there is a bias whereby women's labor force activity rates are lower when men do the interviewing as compared to when women do the interviewing), ILO/CAPMAS Methods Test data are tabulated by gender of the interviewer in Table 8. Male and female interviewers in the ILO/CAPMAS Methods Test tended to elicit similar responses. Of the 120 comparisons for male and female interviewers made in Table 8, only 8 comparisons were significant at the .05 level. In short, there is virtually no evidence from the ILO/CAPMAS Methods Test that male interviewers cause the reporting of female labor force activity to be underreported in rural Egypt (indeed, the tendency, albeit insignificant, is for male interviewers to elicit higher female labor force activity rates as compared to female interviewers). Of course, this result must be interpreted with great caution, since only eight male and eight female interviewers took part in the Egyptian study; nonetheless this result should be reassuring for Egyptian survey organizations.

Because these results are somewhat different from results of the Indian Methods Test survey, and because so few interviewers were involved in the Indian and Egyptian studies (a total of 14 female and 15 male interviewers), one must remain very cautious about generalizing on the effect the interviewer's gender has on the reporting of female labor force activity in the Third World. One must also keep in mind that in normal field work (and as indicated by Indian and Egyptian methods test data) that the gender of the interviewers helps determine the gender of the respondent (i.e., male interviewers tend to interview male respondents and female interviewers tend to interview female respondents) and that this relationship could itself affect the reporting of female labor force activity even if there were no ceteris paribus effect due to the gender of the interviewer.

Table 8. Comparison of Rural Egyptian Female Labor Force Activity Rates as Reported to Male and Female Interviewers For Four Labor Force Definitions

Labor force definition/ questionnaire	*Last year*		*Last 3 months*				*Last week*			
	No minimum time[c]		*No minimum time*		*At least 130 hours last 3 months*		*No minimum time*		*At least 10 hours last week*	
	Male	*Female*	*Male*	*Female*	*Male*	*Female*	*Male*	*Female*	*Male*	*Female*
Paid labor force										
B1	9.5	5.8	9.1	5.8	8.7	5.0	9.1	5.7	8.7	5.0
B1 to B2	11.0	8.5	11.0	8.5	9.8	7.3	11.0	7.7	9.8	7.3
B1 to B3	11.4	8.9	11.4	8.9	10.6	7.7	11.4	8.1	10.6	7.7
B1 to B8	11.7	10.0	11.7	10.0	11.0	7.7	11.7	8.9	11.0	7.7
B1 to B10	12.5	10.0	12.5	10.0	11.7	7.7	12.5	8.9	11.7	7.7
Activity schedule	14.4	15.2	14.0	14.8	9.7	11.9	12.5	13.5	11.7	11.5
Market labor force										
B1	20.5	15.1	20.5	14.7	16.7	11.2	20.5	13.5[b]	17.4	12.0
B1 to B2	30.3	26.6	29.9	25.9	23.5	20.5	29.2	25.1	24.6	20.8
B1 to B3	30.3	29.7	29.9	29.0	24.2	22.0	29.5	28.2	25.4	22.8
B1 to B8	37.5	35.1	37.1	34.0	28.0	23.6	36.0	32.4	30.3	25.4
B1 to B10	37.9	35.5	37.5	33.4	28.4	23.9	36.4	32.8	30.7	26.3
Activity schedule	42.4	40.2	40.5	38.1	26.5	27.0	40.9	38.1	30.3	29.5
ILO labor force										
B1	27.7	18.5	22.7	18.5	18.6	12.7	22.8	16.6	19.3	13.5
B1 to B2	41.7	37.8	41.3	37.8	27.3	26.3	39.4	35.5	29.2	26.6
B1 to B3	43.2	40.9	42.8	40.9	28.8	28.6	41.3	39.0	31.1	29.7
B1 to B8	87.5	82.6	87.5	81.1[b]	53.8	49.8	80.3	74.5	57.2	52.1
B1 to B10	87.5	82.6	87.5	81.1[b]	53.8	50.2	80.3	74.5	57.2	52.9
Activity schedule	91.1	89.3	90.7	89.3	52.1	47.5	82.9	81.1	54.5	52.0
Extended labor force										
B1	22.7	18.5	22.7	18.5	18.6	12.7	22.7	16.6	19.3	13.5
B1 to B2	42.4	37.8	42.0	37.8	27.7	26.3	40.2	35.5	29.5	26.6
B1 to B3	43.9	40.9	43.5	40.9	29.2	28.6	42.0	39.0	31.4	29.7
B1 to B8	89.4	84.2	89.0	82.2	57.6	51.0	81.4	76.1	61.7	54.4
B1 to B10	89.4	84.2	89.0	82.2	57.6	51.4	81.4	76.1	61.7	55.2
Activity schedule	91.1	91.1	90.7	91.0	54.8	52.9	82.9	83.2	58.4	55.3

Notes: B1, B2, . . . , B10 refer to keyword questions.

[a] Difference between responses to males and females significant at .01 level using two-tailed t-tests.

[b] Difference between responses to males and females significant at .05 level using two-tailed t-tests.

[c] Information on time was not collected for last year reference period.

Source: ILO/CAPMAS Methods Test survey for rural Egypt.

VI. SUMMARY

This paper has been concerned with the measurement of women's participation in the labor force and, in particular, identifying the main reasons for (and possible solutions for rectifying) its frequent underestimate in the Third World. This discussion has concentrated on *nonbehavioral* factors that might be contributing to this underestimate, factors such as the definition of labor force activity and the fieldwork techniques used to collect these data, including choice of questionnaire design for how to ask the questions, choice of respondent for answering the questions, and choice of interviewer for asking the questions. This discussion purposely ignored conceptual and empirical issues associated with socio-economic-demographic behavior and the determinants and consequences of female labor force participation, which are addressed in other papers in this volume. Also ignored were issues related to the measurement of unemployment, because the main need with respect to female labor force data in the Third World is in improving the measurement of women's labor force activity and their contributions to development and not in measuring the extent to which women are unemployed.

Discussion in this paper was based to a large extent on the situation in Egypt and, in particular, on results from a 1983 methodological survey of approximately 1,000 households in rural areas of Upper, Lower and Middle Egypt on the measurement of women's participation in the labor force that was conducted by the Central Agency for Public Mobilization and Statistics (CAPMAS), the Egyptian government's statistical office, in collaboration with the ILO. This methodological survey used a randomized, fully-crossed experimental design to ensure that half of the interviews used a questionnaire that contained a list of possible labor force activities and that the other half of the interviews used a series of 10 questions (typically used on labor force surveys) that relied on keywords and phrases such as "main activity," "next most important activity" and "work for earning"; half of the interviews were conducted by male interviewers and half were conducted by female interviewers; half of the respondents were proxy-respondents who provided information on a female household member and half of the respondents were self-respondent women who provided information about themselves. Four definitions of the labor force were used, ranging from the paid labor force (wage or salary employees), to the market labor force (activities involving monetary transactions), to the ILO labor force (internationally recommended definition) and to an even broader definition (the extended labor force). This Egyptian Methods Test survey used virtually the same study design as a comparison methods test survey, which was carried out in rural areas of Uttar Pradesh, India in collaboration with the Operations Research Group, Baroda (ORG).

Section II provided background information on the Egyptian government's official estimates of the female labor force. According to these data, female labor force participants in Egypt are somewhat unusual. Prior to 1983, only about 5 percent of Egyptian women were in the labor force according to official government statistics. In 1983 the official female participation rate more than doubled to about 13 percent due to a concerted effort by CAPMAS to increase the enumeration of female labor on the 1983 national labor force survey; the proportion of female interviewers was increased from 8 to 28 percent and the need to improve the identification of women-workers, particularly those working in agriculture, was stressed in interviewer training sessions.

Still, as data from the ILO/CAPMAS Methods Test survey indicate, even these higher official female labor force participation rates continue to embody large underestimates as approximately 12, 37, 80 and 81 percent of adult rural Egyptian women were reported to have engaged in a paid, market, ILO or extended labor force activity respectively in the week before this ILO/CAPMAS Methods Test survey. These methods test data also indicate how sensitive female labor force estimates are to the specific types of activities included in them. A further indication of the sensitivity of female labor force estimates from the ILO/CAPMAS Methods Test is provided by the fact that female activity rates for the paid, market, ILO and extended labor forces change from 12 to 11 (9) percent, 37 to 29 (24) percent, 80 to 54 (42) percent and 81 to 58 (47) percent respectively when a minimum work-time criterion of 10 (15) hours in the past week is applied. Also, the sensitivity of labor force estimates is related to the narrowness/broadness of the definition itself, as the paid and market labor force estimates are much less sensitive to the imposition of a minimum work-time criterion than are estimates of the ILO and extended labor forces; each individual paid and market labor force activity is much more time-intensive as compared to ILO and extended labor force activities. On the other hand, reported female activity rates from the ILO/CAPMAS Methods Test survey are not very sensitive to a change in the reference period from the past week to the past season, due it seems to women's fairly regular work patterns throughout the season.

Three other measurement issues believed to be important by the research literature—type of questionnaire, gender of interviewer, type of respondent—were then investigated in Section V, again using data from the ILO/CAPMAS Methods Test survey which was purposely designed to investigate these issues. It was found that the reporting of female labor force activity was not affected by the gender of the interviewer, that is, male and female interviewers elicited similar responses.

The other gender-related factor, respondent type, was, however, found to have a significant effect on responses. Female self-respondents reported significantly higher paid labor force activity rates as compared to (mostly male) proxy-respondents. These data indicate that, as argued in the research literature, rural Egyptian men are reluctant to mention to a stranger (i.e., interviewer) that a female household member is working as a wage or salary employee. However, this particular result is at variance with results from the Indian Methods Test study, where self-respondents and proxy-respondents provided similar estimates of female labor force activity. Obviously, the effect of the respondent's knowledge and gender on the reporting of female labor force activity is country- and culture-specific.

Major differences in female activity rates were caused by changes in the questions used to elicit responses. These results are similar in both the Indian and Egyptian Methods Test surveys. When typical keyword questions on "main activity," "second most important activity," "work" were used, female activity rates were greatly underreported, except for paid (i.e., wage and salary) labor force activities. In order to obtain accurate estimates of other labor force activities, it was necessary to ask additional questions that become so specific as to actually mention specific labor force activities (or alternatively, an activity list can be used). The important point is that respondents do not provide anything near a complete accounting of female labor force activity (except for wage or salary employment) unless they are asked very specific questions that mention important labor force activities. This situation is hardly surprising, since the international recommendations on labor force activity are ambiguous and sometimes even inconsistent when it comes to subsistence and family-oriented activities.

This paper on measurement issues and the reasons for the underreporting of female labor activity has indicated some of the shortcomings of these data as well as ways for improving them. By being very clear and specific about what is to be measured on an upcoming labor force survey (for survey organizations, interviewers and respondents) and about what was measured on a past labor force survey (for policymakers and researchers), it should be possible to greatly improve female labor force statistics and therefore analyses based on them.

ACKNOWLEDGMENTS

I would like to thank CAPMAS, ILO and UNFPA for their support of the work on which this paper is based, although the opinions contained in this paper are, of course, my own. In particular, I would like to thank Dr. Halouda, Mr. Shalaby, Dr. Eissa, and Mr. Ibrahim in CAPMUS; Dr. Nizamuddin of UNFPA; and Eddy Lee and Farhad Mehran in ILO. Special thanks are also due to my wife Martha, who not only read and commented on all of the various drafts of this paper, but who was also responsible for the processing and analysis of the Egyptian survey data; as well as to Eva Mueller, since the idea to use a controlled experimental survey design came out of discussions with her.

NOTES

1. For a thorough and illuminating discussion of the recommendations of the Thirteenth International Conference of Labour Statisticians and its implications, see Mehran, 1986a.

2. "The data from surveys which do not make exceptions for unpaid family workers show that the proportion of persons working a few hours a week is not substantial. Where the required data are available, it is usually found that the proportion of persons working, for example, less than five hours a week does not exceed a few percentage points of total employment. This means that raising the one-hour criterion of the definition of employment by a few hours is in practice not likely to change the resulting employment statistics substantially" (Dupre, Hussmans, & Mehran, 1987).

REFERENCES

Anker, R. (1983, November–December). Female labour force participation in developing countries: A critique of current definitions and data collection methods. *International Labour Review, 122*(6). (Geneva, ILO).

Anker, R., & Anker, M. (1988). *Improving the measurement of women's participation in the Egyptian labour force: Results of a methodological survey.* Population labour policies (Working Paper No. 163). Geneva: ILO.

Anker, R., & Knowles, J. C. (1978). A micro analysis of female labour force participation in Kenya. In G. Standing & G. Sheehan (Eds.), *Labour force participation in low income countries.* Geneva: ILO.

Anker, R., Khan, M. E., & Gupta, R. B. (1987, March–April). Biases in measuring the labour force: Results of a methods test survey in Uttar Pradesh, India. *International Labour Review 126*(2). (Geneva, ILO).

———. (1988). Women in the labour force: A methods test in India for improving its measurement. In *Women, Work and Development* (Series No. 16). Geneva: ILO.

Baster, N. (1981). *The measurement of women's participation in development: The use of census data* (Discussion Paper No. 159). Sussex: IDS.

Beneria, L. (1982). Accounting for women's work. In L. Beneria (Ed.), *Women and development.* New York: Praeger.

Central Agency for Public Mobilization and Statistics. (1986) *Population, housing and establishment census, 1986. Preliminary results for 1986.* Cairo: CAPMAS.

———. (1987). Unpublished data for 1984 *National Labor Force Survey* Unpublished data for 1984.

Connell, J., & Lipton, M. (1977). *Assessing village labour situations in developing countries.* Delhi: Oxford University Press.

Dixon, R. (1982). Women in agriculture: Counting the labour force in developing countries. *Population and Development Review, 8*(3), 539–566.

Dixon-Mueller, R. (1985). *Women's work in third world agriculture: Concepts and indicators.* Geneva: ILO.

Dupre, M. T., Hussmans, R., & Mehran, F. (1987). *The concept and boundary of economic activity for the measurement of the economically active population.* Geneva: ILO (mimeographed).

Goldschmidt-Clermont, L. (1987). *Economic evaluations of unpaid household work: Africa, Asia, Latin America and Oceania.* Geneva: ILO.

ILO. (Various years). *Yearbook of labour statistics.* Geneva: ILO.

———. (1972). *Employment, incomes and inequality. A strategy for increasing productive employment in Kenya.* Report of an interagency team financed by the United Nations Development Programme and organized by the International Labour Office. Geneva.

———. (1976, October). *Labour force, employment and unemployment and underemployment.* Report prepared for the Thirteenth International Conference of Labour Statistics, Geneva.

———. (1982a, June). *Revision of the international guidelines on labour statistics.* Paper prepared for OECD Working Party on Employment and Unemployment Statistics.

———. (1982b) *Amended draft resolution concerning statistics of the economically active population, employment, unemployment and underemployment.* Thirteenth International Conference of Labour Statisticians (mimeographed).

———. (1986). *Economically active population: Estimates and projections*. Geneva: ILO.

Lattes, A. Recchini de, & Wainerman, C. H. (1979). *Data from census and household surveys for the analysis of female labour force in Latin America and the Caribbean: Appraisals of deficiencies and recommendations for dealing with it in the United Nations Economic and Social Commission*. Santiago: United Nations Economic and Social Commission and Economic Commission for Latin America and the Caribbean (doc. E/CEPAL/L.206).

Mehran, F. (1986a). *Surveys of the economically active population*. Geneva: ILO (mimeographed).

———. (1986b). *The usually active population*. Geneva: ILO (mimeographed).

Myrdal, G. (1968). *Asian drama: An inquiry into the poverty of nations* (Vol. 3). New York: Pantheon.

Pittin, R. (1982). *Documentation of women's work in Nigeria: Problems and solutions* (Population and labour policies Working Paper No. 125). Geneva: ILO.

Slatter, C. (1982, April). *Women in the labour force in the Pacific*. Document prepared for ILO InterCountry Workshop in Employment and Human Resources, Venuatu (mimeographed).

United Nations. (1980). *Sex-based stereotypes, sex biases and national data systems*. New York: (doc. ST/ESA/STAT/99)

United Nations, APCWD. (1977, December). *The critical needs of women*. Expert Group Meeting on the Identification of the Basic Needs of Women of Asia and the Pacific and on the Formulation of a Programme of Work, Tehran.

United Nations, Statistical Office. (1979, November) GDP as a measure of output: Problems and possible solutions. Annex A of *Future directions for work on the United Nations system of national accounts* (Draft Report of Expert Group Meeting). New York: Author. (doc. ESA/STAT/AC.9/1)

MAKING FEMALE LABOR FORCE PARTICIPATION COUNT IN POPULATION CENSUSES:
EVIDENCE FROM PARAGUAY

Catalina H. Wainerman

I. INTRODUCTION

The inaccuracy of female labor force statistics, especially in developing countries, has already been found to be commonplace by experts in the field. Population censuses underenumerate the females' economic contribution. This is the result of the specific ways that women are inserted in the labor market, and of the characteristics of the census procedures, both dependent on the cultural assumptions concerning the sexual division of labor.

The study partially summarized here attempted to improve the accuracy of the census measurement of the female labor force. Its ultimate aim was to grant female workers the same chances of being counted in labor statistics as men have. This implies the acceptance—because of technical, not ideological or

Research in Human Capital and Development, Vol. 6, pages 59–85.

ISBN: 1-55938-032-2

theoretical reasons—of the official definition of the concepts "economic activity" and "labor force."

The research was conducted in two Latin American countries, Argentina and Paraguay, with a twofold aim. First, to test the effects on the reporting of female workers by: (1) the types of procedures of data collection (basically types of questionnaire and interviewers' training); (2) the length of the reference period; and (3) the length of the minimum working-time requirement. Second, to test the adequacy of alternative census instruments designed to record the economic activity of the population after the recommendations of the ILO (1983). Although the study centered on women, men were also studied because the comparison between sexes throws additional light on the resulting pictures, and also because some sectors of the male population are also underreported by current census statistics.

This paper reports on the results of the Paraguayan survey, carried out with the collaboration of the Bureau of Statistics of Paraguay in 1986. The paper begins by summarizing the major conceptual and technical problems which have been identified. Some empirical evidence of the inaccuracy of the census measurement originated by those problems is shown. A review of international recommendations on the labor force measurement precedes the description of the Paraguayan research and its results. It ends with an assessment of its consequences for future population censuses.

Conceptual and Technical Problems

Although population censuses make no sex differences when defining the labor force activity (i.e., the same questions on activity condition are used for women and men), the quality of its recording is sex-differentiated. Ultimately, this is due to cultural reasons, and more specifically, to the socially shared ideas about the sexual division of labor. They are embedded in the conceptual definitions of labor force, in their operational translation into instruments (questionnaires and interviewers' training), in the characteristics of the labor behavior of women, and in their own perceptions of the nature of their activities. It is important to stress that women are not the only underenumerated sector of the labor force. The economic activity of the youngest and the oldest sectors of the population, irrespective of sex, also tends to be ignored.

Due to the need to articulate the reproductive and the productive roles, and because of the fewer opportunities for formal education and training for the world of "productive" work, it is more frequent for women to work part-time or seasonally; in activities that are difficult to differentiate from domestic ones; in the more traditional sectors of the economy; in family enterprises without pay or on own-account basis; and/or inside the household or family unit. Other difficulties are added in the rural areas, especially in the agricultural sector. These difficulties derive from the very characteristics of the agricultural activities—the work is conducted in household units that integrate consumption and production, often difficult to distinguish. It should be added that in most societies where the sexual division of labor assigns the leadership of production to men and the reproduction to women, the activity of women engaged in production is seen as marginal and subsidiary. This leads many women to perceive their work not as economic activity as such, but as part of the homemaker's duties or of the *help* they owe to other productive members of the household, whether they are their fathers or their husbands. Hence, in certain sectors, although performing the same activities, women see themselves as homemakers (economically inactive according to the censuses), whereas men perceive themselves as workers (economically active according to the censuses).

From the perspective of censuses, there are various factors that contribute to the low quality of the enumeration of the female labor force. The main factor concerns the definition of "economic activity" and "labor force"; other factors deal with aspects of the data collection procedure. Let us start with the definition.

Experts agree that until the 1980s, international recommendations have defined "work" and "economic activity" by following the model of developed economies and the behavior of salaried, stable, full-time workers. It is also agreed that international standards are difficult to apply to developing countries where laborers are more likely to work seasonally rather than all the year-round, to be unemployed rather than formally employed, and to engage in a fluid pattern of diverse and shifting economic activities. Finally, there is a consensus that this definition lacks conceptual clarity (Anker, 1983b; Beneria, 1982; Hauser, 1974; Blacker, 1978, 1980; Dixon, 1982; Horstman, 1977; PREALC-ILO, 1979; Seltzer, 1978). The distinction between economic and domestic activities is not based on a clear criterion but on a set of arbitrary, nonrational conventions, established by the economists to estimate the national income. It could be asked, for instance, why the production of the raw material used for cooking is considered economic but the preparation and elaboration of the same raw material for consumption is not. According to some authors, the division is not arbitrary, but based on the evidence of the socially shared ideas regarding the sexual division of labor.

Blacker (1980) suggests that the criteria applied to determine the character of the activities leading to the production of a loaf of bread is not their intrinsic nature but whether they are performed by "housewives"—that is, by female, unpaid family workers. Anker (1983b) points out that those activities typically done by women (like subsistence livestock, food processing) are usually considered noneconomic, "almost as if the criteria were made on the basis of existing knowledge on male and female activity patterns" (p. 714).

The length of the reference period, and of the minimum working-time required for a person to be considered economically active are also aspects of the definition of labor force. The use of a short reference period (one week) and the requirement of a large minimum working-time (most of the week) contribute to the underenumeration of female workers who, more often than their male counterparts, move in and out the labor market and work part-time or less. Evidence of the sex-differential effects of these factors can be found in Mueller (1974), Durand (1975), Horstmann (1977), PREALC-ILO (1979), ECLAC (1982), Dixon (1982), De Vries Bastiaans (1983), Pitten (1983).

Regarding the question of data collection procedures, in many developing countries censists are badly trained, poorly remunerated, have little or no motivation at all, and are reluctant to study or even read the instruction manual. They are barely supervised and, last but not least, they take preconceptions (shared by the interviewees themselves) to the interviews about the suitability of certain activities for women and men, which lead them to classify married women as housewives and young and old people as students or retired, that is, as economically inactive, without further investigation.

As far as the questionnaires are concerned, many censuses use what seems to be one single item to collect information on the activity condition of the population, consisting of one question followed by a set of response alternatives. The format makes the interviewer read them all together, directing the interviewees to *choose* one alternative. Because most censuses ask solely for the *main* activity, married women, young students, and retired people engaged in economic activities tend to declare themselves as economically inactive (Lopes, 1981). Other problems concerning the questionnaires derive from the use of terms like "job," "employment," and "paid work," which make interviewees equate economic activity with formal, full-time, remunerated economic activity. This question has been extensively discussed by Anker & Knowles (1978) and by Anker (1983b).

For the 1970 round of Latin American population censuses there is abundant empirical evidence of the sex-selective underenumeration of the labor force. The evidence was produced by comparing the activity rates obtained by censuses and by (more valid) household surveys collected about the same time in various countries, using the same conceptual definition of labor force, the same length of the reference period, and the same minimum working-time requirement. The census underenumeration, high among women and low among men, is higher among workers in the agricultural sector, unpaid family workers, the less educated, and so forth (Recchini de Lattes & Wainerman, 1986; Wainerman & Moreno, 1987; Wainerman & Recchini de Lattes, 1981). To give a few examples, the 1970 population census of Sao Paulo (the most developed region of Brazil), underenumerated 18 percent of female workers but only 3 percent of male workers, more among women occupied in agricultural activities (60 percent) than in all other activities (10 percent), more among unpaid family workers (84 percent) than among salaried women (9 percent). In the Northeast region (the most backward of Brazil), the same census underenumerated 52 percent of female workers but a bare 4 percent of male workers. Again, the female underenumeration was higher among agricultural workers (63 percent) than among the rest (44 percent), among unpaid (88 percent) than among salaried workers (29 percent). Similarly, the 1974 Guayaquil (Ecuador) census underenumerated 27 percent of all female workers but only 7 percent of male workers, and much more among females with primary education or less (34 percent) than among those with the highest educational level (16 percent). Also in Colombia, the 1973 census underenumerated 12 percent of all female workers—32 percent among rural residents and 7 percent among urban ones—but not one single male worker.

The low quality of the measurement of the female labor force and some of its causes were already acknowledged some time ago (Bancroft, 1958), but it was not until the last decade that the awareness expanded (Anker, 1983b; Baster, 1981; Beneria, 1982; Dixon, 1982; D'Souza, 1980; Durand, 1975; Fong, 1980; Hamad, 1984; Hauser, 1974; Leon, 1985; Safilios-Rothschild, 1982; Standing, 1978; Wainerman & Recchini de Lattes, 1981; Zurayk, 1983). It has been the central topic of the agenda of several seminars and conferences. In Latin America, researchers from PREALC (ILO), and ECLAC, among others, have especially concentrated on the measurement of employment in rural areas and in the urban informal sector. (For rural employment, see Buvinic, 1982; Deere & Leon de Leal, 1982; ECLAC, 1982; Klein, 1983; Paraguay DGES, 1979; Pisoni, 1983; PREALC-ILO, 1979; Torrado, 1978, 1981; Wainerman, Moreno, & Geldstein, 1985). For the measurement of the informal sector, see Arizpe, 1976; Kritz & Ramos, 1976; Marulanda, 1979; Pina Riquelme, 1981; PREALC-ILO, 1978; Raczynski, 1979; Souza & Tokman, 1976; Tokman, 1977).

The wide recognition of the conceptual and technical inaccuracy of population censuses and the need to review and enlarge current norms and recommendations was taken up at the 13th International Conference of Labour Statisticians (ILO, 1982). The report prepared for the Conference recognized the need to reexamine the existing concepts and methods so as to improve the conceptualization and measurement of the economic participation of women both in and outside the home (par. 12). With respect to the measurement, it was suggested that "it is important not only to control available stereotypes and sex biases but also to conduct, wherever necessary, specialized surveys to identify objectively the size, nature and sources of biases involved and to develop appropriate methods of reducing them" (par. 230).

The recommendations that emerged from the Conference modify the definition of labor force used up to the 1980s in a number of aspects. The major recommendations are: (1) the explicit inclusion of self-consumption producers within the labor force (whenever this activity makes "an important contribution to the total consumption of the household"); (2) the elimination of the minimum working-time criterion for everybody, including unpaid family workers, and the adoption of just one hour of activity to qualify as active; and (3) the use of two reference periods (one week and one year) to collect information on the "current" and the "usual" active population.[1] Even though these modifications improve the conceptual definition of labor force, there is a vagueness as regards a number of aspects such as the criterion to distinguish economic and noneconomic activities and the making of the meaning of an "important" contribution to the household's consumption clear. These questions, as well as the lack of recommendations for the operationalization of concepts, may become sources of invalidity in future registers of the labor force.

So far, attempts to improve the census recording of the female labor force have been conspicuously scarce, so only a few exceptions can be mentioned. Two exceptions come from the ILO, one from the Bureau of Statistics (Mehran, 1985; Trigueros Mejia, 1986), the other from the World Employment Programme (Anker, 1987; Anker, Khan, & Gupta, 1987). The third exception is partly summarized in this paper.

II. THE DESIGN OF THE STUDY

Context, Samples and Surveys

The research in Paraguay was conducted in Asuncion, the country's capital city, and in the rural area of the Piribebuy district. According to the 1982 census, the metropolitan area of Asuncion had 800,000 inhabitants. Being a capital city, the main economic activities are related to the tertiary sector, that is, services—mostly government services—and commerce. The latter has been the most dynamic sector in recent years; its development being linked to the import and export commerce, as well as to the petty trade. Manufacturing and construction are secondary activities in Asuncion.

The Piribebuy district is predominantly rural: 73 percent of its population was rural according to the 1982 census. It has a mild climate, with little variations during the year. It is an area of old settlements with a prevalence of small landholdings (*minifundios*) and subsistence economy. The typical productive unit does not go beyond 18 acres, but more than half do not reach 10 acres. The small size allows the demand for labor to be met by the family unit. The economy of Piribebuy is based on agriculture, mainly maize, cotton, *mandioca,* and sugar cane. There is also some manufacturing of agricultural products—honey cane, honey sugar, mandioca starch—but in very small productive units. The diversified nature of the agricultural activity, where the production of sugar cane is combined with cotton and with subsistence production, requires labor throughout the year, except from mid-July to mid-September, which is a period devoted to maintenance activities.

Fieldwork was carried out between August and September, the period of low labor demand in Piribebuy, which we chose to make our test stronger and because of its relative closeness to the 1982 census collection date (July). We conducted three methodological surveys (field experiments) in each locality on statistically representative, comparable, household samples (see Appendix and Footnote 4).

One of the surveys (the "CENSAL survey") reproduced the census. In the other two, we put an alternative data collection procedure in practice, establishing a short reference period in one case, the "CENEP-week survey," and a long one in the other, the "CENEP-year survey." There are three explanatory variables whose effects on the enumeration of the labor force we studied: type of procedure of data collection (CENSAL and CENEP); length of the reference period (one week and one year); and length of time worked during the reference period (short—1 to 19 hours per week, or less than 6 months per year; part-time—20 to 34 hours per week, or about six months per year; and full-time—35 or more hours per week, or 12 months per year). The first two variables were manipulated when creating the experimental groups; the third one was investigated during the interviews.

We interviewed a total of 1,400 active-age persons (12 years of age and over) of both sexes in 365 households in Asuncion, and about 3,600 persons of the same age in 1,152 households in Piribebuy.

Conceptual and Operational Labor Force Definition

The three surveys used the same conceptual definition of labor force, following the 1982 ILO definition quite closely, but with some modifications. The first modification is that we focused on the enumeration of one part of self-consumption laborers considered active by the ILO: the producers of primary products (vegetable cultivation, sowing, poultry and animal caring, which are mostly feminine activities). We did not place any stress on, but we did not explicitly exclude, people processing primary products produced by themselves, or producers of fixed assets like houses, boats or canoes. In the case of the former, the reason is that it is extremely difficult to draw the line between making cheese, butter or fat and cooking for one's own consumption (considered noneconomic by the ILO); thus, we preferred to run the risk of losing some of the producers rather than to decrease the validity of the measurement.

Another modification is that we did not limit the definition of self-consumption producers to those whose activity makes an *important contribution* to the total consumption of the household. This was due to the conceptual and operational difficulties involved in determining what is "important" (For what kind of household structure? For which consumption level? According to objectives or subjective parameters?, etc.). Nevertheless, using the length of working time during the reference period as a proxy, it is possible to calculate activity rates that take the "importance" of the activity into account. We did not set any minimum requirement of working time in any of the three surveys. Summing up, the population of both sexes aged 12 years or more was classified as economically active or inactive, and the former as employed or unemployed in this study.

The CENSAL survey reproduced the procedure (schedule and interviewers' training) used by the 1982 Paraguayan census (and by most 1970 and 1980 Latin

American population censuses) to investigate the activity condition of the population during the previous week. One single question followed by a set of pre-coded response alternatives was applied by interviewers with an average of two-hours training. Its format was:

Q.7 What did you do last week?
Worked.
Did not work but had a job.
Looked for work.
Engaged in household activities.
Studied.
Is retired, pensioned or rentier.
Is sick or invalid.
Other situation, which one

The CENEP-week and CENEP-year surveys used a group of questions and two-days interviewers' training. The former set the previous week as the reference period, the latter the previous year. The three surveys collected information on sociodemographic and economic variables such as sex, age, marital, educational and household status, occupation, industry, employment status, place of work, time worked, destination of the agricultural production (mostly for the market or for self-consumption).

The CENEP questionnaire contains a group of seven questions when the reference period is one week and five questions when it is one year. Its design transmits the principle "you are active unless you prove otherwise," and it was applied to every person aged 12 years and over. In fact, it displays the response alternatives of the single CENSAL question into a set of four questions (Q7, Q9, Q10, Q12), to which three are added. One of these (Q8) makes the definition of work and economic activity explicit by giving examples of activities chosen among those that are generally invisible to interviewees and to interviewers (carried out *inside* the household, for a *short* time, *helping* another worker, similar to domestic chores, and so on). A second one (Q11) reiterates the question on job seeking. The third question (Q13), called the "self-consumption module," emphasizes the elicitation of self-consumption producers. We presented it at the end of the household interview to every member (of all rural units and of those urban units with a plot of land that allowed growing vegetables, raising chickens, and so on) and who had been classified as economically inactive by their responses to the previous questions. It was included in another schedule, not in the central one, though we present it here below Q12 to make the point clear. The phrasing of all questions required a yes or no answer before proceeding to the next one, as follows:

Q.7 During last week, did you work at anything?
yes – no

Q.8 And during that week, did you do or *help* to do any activity, paid or *unpaid, inside* or outside your household, if only for *a few* hours? For instance: helping in a grocery store or kiosk; selling crafts, food, vegetables, newspapers, lottery tickets or cosmetics; planting, harvesting, or raising chickens *to be sold,* washing, ironing, or sewing clothes *for others;* making confitures, cheeses, or knitting *to sell;* taking care of children or old people *for pay.*
yes – no

Q.9 During last week, did you not work because of illness, leave, strike, bad weather conditions, or any other temporary reason, even though you had a job or an occupation?
yes – no

Q.10 During that week, did you look for a job or any activity by talking to friends, offering yourself in a firm, advertising or answering ads, or in any other way?
yes – no

Q.11 During that week, did you *stop looking* for a job or an occupation because either you or a family member were sick, because of bad weather conditions, or for any other reasons?
yes –no

Q.12 And during that week,
Were you a housewife and did you not work?
Were you a student and did you not work?
Were you retired, pensioned or rentier and did you not work?
Were you chronically sick or invalid and did you not work?
Were you in another situation?
yes – no

Q.13 Although you've already said that you didn't carry out any activity, during last week, did you work in the family farm or did you raise chickens for your own or your family consumption, even if only for a few hours?
yes – no

The CENEP-year questionnaire was identical except for the reference period— "the last twelve months"—and for the elimination of Q9 and Q11, which were meaningless for such a long reference period.

It should be borne in mind that CENEP questionnaires operationalize a set of theoretical criteria. They were not meant to be applied in all details in its current design in future censuses. The format of the set of questions allowed us to determine the capacity of each one to identify labor force members and, at the same time, to identify the factors that make for greater improvement in the counting of workers.

As regards the interviewers' training, the CENSAL procedure was the usual: brief, completed in one session lasting two or three hours, devoted to handling the questions and the definition of their categories. The CENEP procedure comprised four sessions lasting two days. It included two sections. One was devoted to handling (conceptually and technically) the questionnaire and included role-playing and evaluating the trainees. The other was devoted to sensitizing data collectors to the socially-shared ideas about the sexual division of labor in order to make them aware of groups of the population (women, young and old people) who are liable to be defined as inactive without further investigation and on the exclusive basis of sex and age characteristics. This section of CENEP's training was not meant to be used in population censuses; it was designed to assess the extent to which sex biases are present among interviewees.[2]

We collected information in the three surveys on the amount of time each employed person had worked during the reference period in order to test the effect of varying the minimum working-time requirement. The question was posed in quantitative terms and reiterated in qualitative terms for respondents unable to answer otherwise. For the weekly period, time was requested (quantitatively) in number of hours or (qualitatively) in terms of three predetermined categories: "the whole day," "about half day," "short time," day by day, seven days of the week. The categories used in the analysis reflected the total time worked per week; they were: 1–19 hours (short time), 20–34 hours (part time), and 35 hours and over (full time). For the yearly period, time was qualitatively requested in terms of: "twelve months," "at least six months," and "at least one month."

Whenever possible, we requested interviewees to answer by themselves in the three surveys in both areas. The three questionnaires were worded in Spanish and in *j'opara* (coloquial Guarani). The interviewers, all bilingual, used either language, according to the needs of the interviewees.

III. RESULTS

The High CENSAL Underenumeration of Females, the Low CENSAL Underenumeration of Males

It is important to stress at the beginning that we were highly successful in setting up a census-type operation in both Paraguayan localities, as shown by the statistically significant similarity between the activity rates obtained by the CENEP-week survey and by the 1982 population census (see Table 1). This gives more weight to the results of this study.

The CENEP surveys enumerate significantly many more workers than the CENSAL survey in both areas. This greater enumeration is clearly different according to sex and to the area of residence (see Table 1 and Figure 1). The CENSAL survey underenumerates as much as 84 percent of the rural women—at a time of *low* labor demand—and 42 percent of the urban women counted by the CENEP-week survey, but only 10 and 14 percent of rural and urban males, respectively. In other words, the proportion of the working women who do not

Table 1. Economic Activity Rates According to Data Collection Procedures and Length of the Reference Period, By Sex and Locality

Data collection procedures	*Asuncion*		*Piribebuy*	
	Women	*Men*	*Women*	*Men*
CENSAL (1)	34.2	71.7	13.7	83.6
CENEP-week (2)	59.0	83.6	87.6	92.8
CENEP-year (3)	69.2	86.6	91.2	95.6
1982 population census (4)	37.0	75.2	14.3	88.2
CENSAL undereport: (2–1)/2	42.0	14.2	84.4	9.9

Note: All differences between rates 1 and 2, 1 and 3, and 2 and 3 for both sexes, in both localities, are statistically significant at the .05 level with only one exception, that between Asuncion male rates 2 and 3. All differences between rates 1 and 4 for both sexes, in both localities, are not statistically significant at the .05 level with only one exception: that between Piribebuy men.

perceive and do not declare themselves to be workers but as economically inactive (mostly "housewives"), and who remain invisible in the usual census statistics, amounts to five-sixths in Piribebuy and to close to one-half of the female labor force in Asuncion. With a longer reference period, the CENEP-year survey also enumerates significantly more workers than the CENEP-week survey (except among Asuncion males), though less than was expected.

As a consequence of the greater recording of female workers by the CENEP procedure in the rural area, most women as well as most men (about 90 percent) appear to be supplying their labor to the economy. This result is consistent with what is known of poor small land-holding agricultural areas, where the family unit survives on the labor supply of all of its members, whether they are old, young, women or men. However, it openly contradicts most labor force statistics in Latin America, which overwhelmingly record a very low economic participation of rural women, much lower than among urban females (Elizaga & Mellon, 1971).

The Sensitivity of CENEP Questionnaire to Elicit Female and Male Labor Force Data

What are the reasons for the greater sensitivity of CENEP procedure, that is, of its appropriateness for eliciting labor force data? As we said before, the CENEP differs from the CENSAL procedure in two aspects: the questionnaire and the training of interviewers. We will show below that the greater sensitivity responds primarily to the questionnaire and secondarily to the training of interviewers.

Let us begin by examining the capacity of CENEP's questions to record the labor force. The focus is on the employed population, because unemployment is

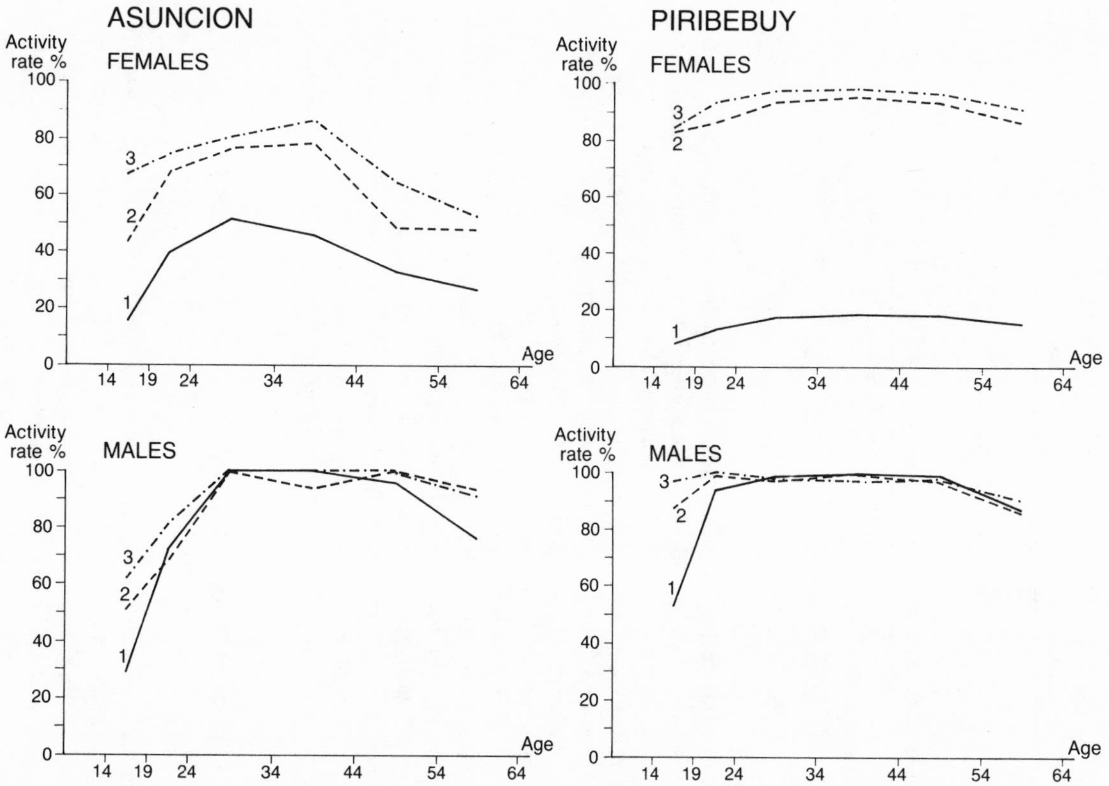

Note: 1: CENSAL; 2: CENEP-week; 3: CENEP-year.

Figure 1. Asuncion and Piribebuy. Female and Male Economic Activity Profiles according to the CENSAL and CENEP Surveys

virtually nonexistent in the rural locality—as it is in any subsistence economy—and does not surpass 6 percent in the urban one. Data vary significantly by sex (see Table 2). In both localities, about 90 percent of the employed male labor force counted by CENEP-week is elicited by Q7 ("During . . . , did you do any work?"), and no more than 6 percent by Q8 and Q13. CENEP-year reproduces CENEP-week's findings in Asuncion and Piribebuy. It should be recalled that Q8 reiterated the content of Q7, conveying to the interviewees the meaning of "work" through concrete activities chosen among those less visible as economic. Q13—the self-consumption module—made explicit, again through concrete examples, that certain activities whose products do not go to the market but are consumed within the household are also to be considered "work."

These results make it plain that, as far as men are concerned, one single question phrased such as Q7 is adequate enough to register most of the labor force participation, either in the urban or in the rural locality. Indeed, if the workers registered by CENEP-week Q8 and Q13 are excluded, the male activity rates only decrease (not significantly) from 83.6 to 79.2 percent in the urban area and from 92.8 to 86.8 percent in the rural one. Similar figures are found for CENEP-year survey, as shown in Table 3.

However, Q7 proves quite inadequate when applied in the CENEP-week survey among women, especially in the rural locality, where it elicits only one-third of the employed labor force (see Table 2). In the urban locality it is more efficient, as nearly two-thirds are elicited by it. Most of the remaining employed

Table 2. Economically Active Population Recorded By Each Question of the CENEP Questionnaires, By Sex and Locality (In Percent)

	Asuncion		*Piribebuy*	
Questions	*Women*	*Men*	*Women*	*Men*
CENEP—Week	(144)	(153)	(502)	(500)
Employed	93.8	95.4	99.2	99.8
Q 7	62.9	90.4	32.8	93.6
Q 8	9.0	3.5	2.0	0.4
Q 9	6.7	4.1	0.0	0.0
Q 13	21.4	2.0	65.2	6.0
Unemployed (Q10 + Q11)	6.2	4.6	0.8	0.2
CENEP—Year	(180)	(160)	(518)	(561)
Employed	94.5	95.6	99.6	99.7
Q 7	70.6	94.1	35.0	92.3
Q 8	13.5	4.0	15.0	0.0
Q 13	15.9	1.9	50.0	7.7
Unemployed (Q10)	5.5	4.4	0.4	0.3

Note: All differences between the female and male activity figures for CENEP-week and CENEP-year, in both localities, are significant at the .05 level.

Table 3. Activity Rates According to the CENSAL and CENEP Surveys With and Without Workers Elicited By Q8 and Q13, By Sex and Locality

	Asuncion		*Piribebuy*	
Activity Rates	*Women*	*Men*	*Women*	*Men*
CENEP-Week				
Total (1)	59.0	83.6	87.6	92.8
Minus Q8 and Q13 (2)	42.2	79.2	29.1	86.8
CENSAL (3)	34.2	71.7	13.7	83.6
CENEP-Year				
Total (4)	69.2	86.6	91.2	95.6
Minus Q8 and Q13 (5)	50.0	81.6	32.2	88.2

Note: All differences between rates 1 and 2, 4 and 5 for females, obtained by CENEP-week and CENEP-year, in both localities, are statistically significant at the .05 level. Those for men are not statistically significant at the .05 level. The differences between rates 2 and 3 for both sexes in both localities (except for rural women) are not statistically significant at the .05 level.

women are elicited firstly by Q13, especially in Piribebuy, and secondly by Q8. The CENEP-year survey closely reproduces the CENEP-week findings. The relatively minor recording capacity of Q8 was totally unexpected; we had expected a much higher capacity and a much lower for Q7.[3] The overwhelming capacity of Q13 among rural women went much beyond our expectations instead. For people unfamiliar with urban settings in developing societies, the relatively high percentage of women engaged in production for self-consumption in the capital city of Paraguay may be surprising. Indeed, the mixture of social areas is extremely high in Asuncion. It is not infrequent to find the modern house of a surgeon side by side with the precarious house of a water seller who grows vegetables or raises chickens for his own consumption in the backyard, only 10–15 minutes from downtown.

These results show plainly that, contrary to the situation of the men, one single item such as Q7 is not adequate to register most of the female labor, especially rural, but also urban. In the Paraguayan rural locality studied—and also in the urban locality—had it not been made explicit to women that self-consumption production is considered "work," as Q13 did, the measurement of its labor force activity would have been quite deficient. This also would have occurred, though to a lesser degree, if the meaning of "work" through concrete examples had not been conveyed to them, as Q8 had.

As shown in Table 3, if the female workers elicited by Q8 and Q13 of CENEP-week questionnaire are excluded, the urban activity rates significantly decrease from 59.0 to 42.2 percent, and the rural rates from 87.6 to 29.1 percent. This decrease would cut down the differences with respect to the CENSAL rates to the point of their becoming statistically nonsignificant in the urban, although not in the rural area. A similar trend is reproduced in the CENEP-year survey for the urban and rural rates.

What type of workers did not perceive themselves as being engaged in an activity that deserves to be qualified as "work," and which were "rescued" as economically active by Q8 and Q13? First, they are mostly women, as we said before. In Table 4 some occupational characteristics of the females "rescued" by Q8 and Q13 are compared with those of the total of employed women enumerated by all CENEP questions. In Asuncion they are clearly "secondary" workers, most of whom have worked for a short time during the previous week, or part-time or less during the previous year, mainly at home, on their own-account basis or without pay, helping in a family enterprise. Full-time workers who have a formal relationship with the world of production as employers or employees in an establishment are more frequent among those elicited by Q7 and Q9. There are minor or no differences at all between the women brought in by Q8 and Q13 and by the rest of the questions in terms of these aspects in Piribebuy, where production for self-consumption predominates. The majority of them work full-time, within the family household, on their own-account basis, or as unpaid family workers, with few exceptions. Hence, on the basis of the information at hand, it is not possible to say why these women did not perceive and did not declare themselves as economically active. But what is absolutely clear is that most women engaged in production for self-consumption—even if working full-time—do not perceive themselves as workers, and that their visibility to labor statistics depends on a special effort, something that men do not need.

The activity rates of the CENSAL and the CENEP-week surveys include the effects of the type of questionnaire and those of interviewers' training. It is impossible to explain how much of the CENEP enumeration is due to the questionnaire and how much to the training with the available information. One reason is because a better questionnaire leads to a better application. There is some evidence, however, that both had effects, but that those of the questionnaire were greater.[4] One piece of evidence is that the differences between the CENSAL and the CENEP-week rates excluding workers enumerated by Q8 and Q13 is substantially smaller than those with respect to the total CENEP-week rates, that is, including workers enumerated by Q8 and Q13 (see Table 3). This is true for women and men. Because both the CENEP-week rates were obtained with the same type of interviewers' training, it can be hypothesized that the effect of the latter is less than the effect of the questionnaire.

The greater enumerating capacity of the CENEP questionnaire can be attributed to several reasons. First, by displaying the response alternatives of the CENSAL item in a set of questions to be read (and answered) *one by one,* interviewers and interviewees are compelled to read them one at a time before proceeding to the next. In the CENSAL survey, however, many interviewers read the response alternatives all at once (as many data collectors in population censuses do, in spite of being instructed to do otherwise). In doing so, inter-

Table 4. Economically Active Female Population Elicited By Q8 and Q13 According to the CENEP Surveys and Occupational Characteristics, By Locality

	Asuncion				*Piribebuy*			
	CENEP-week		*CENEP-year*		*CENEP-week*		*CENEP-year*	
Occupational Characteristics	*Total (135)*	*Q8 + Q13 (41)*	*Total (170)*	*Q8 + Q13 (50)*	*Total (497)*	*Q8 + Q13 (335)*	*Total (516)*	*Q8 + Q13 (329)*
Time Worked								
Short-time	32.1	68.3*	12.4	20.0*	19.1	21.5	12.7	32.2*
Part-time	23.9	22.0*	19.4	34.0*	32.0	32.5	15.9	11.8*
Full-time	44.0	9.7*	68.2	46.0*	48.9	46.0	71.4	56.0*
Place of Work								
Establishment	24.4	0.0*	25.3	4.0*	2.6	0.0*	1.6	0.0
Employer's home	23.7	4.9*	24.7	0.0	2.6	0.3*	1.4	0.6
Street or route	11.1	2.4*	8.2	8.0*	3.6	0.3*	2.6	1.5
Own home	40.7	92.7*	41.8	88.0*	91.0	99.4*	94.6	97.9
Employment Status								
Employer + employee	44.4	0.0*	47.1	0.0*	4.4	0.0*	1.9	0.3*
Own-account + unpaid family	55.6	100.0*	52.9	100.0*	95.6	100.0*	98.1	99.7*

Notes: For CENEP-week: short-time = 1–19 hours.; part-time = 20–34 hours; full-time = 35+ hours.
For CENEP-year: short-time = less than six months; part-time = 6 months or more; full-time = twelve months.
*denotes differences between the female enumerated by the total questionnaire and by Q8 plus Q13 that are statistically significant at the .05 level.

viewees learn about all the alternatives and are directed toward *choosing* answering either to have worked, or to have looked for a job, or to have been engaged in household chores, and so on. In this situation it is not surprising that many women engaged in some kind of economic activity, *in addition* to domestic chores, declare themselves "housewives" because they consider this role to be the main one in terms of social acceptability or because of the time devoted to it. The same happens with retired people or with students who also carried out some economic activity during the reference period, and who choose to define themselves as economically inactive, thus violating the "priority rule" of international recommendations according to which the condition of "active" has to have precedence over the condition of "inactive."

The Greater Sensitivity of the CENSAL Survey to Full-Time Workers and of CENEP-Week to Part-Time Workers

We did not set any working-time requirement for people to be considered active in any of the surveys, but we investigated the amount of time actually worked during the reference period by every employed person. Assuming that the time actually worked corresponds to minimum requirements, we calculated different activity (employment) rates. They allow the assessing of the degree of elasticity of the CENSAL and the CENEP-week procedures (both having set a weekly reference period) to varying time requirements (see Table 5).

What is worth highlighting is that the increment of the employment rates that results from diminishing the time requirement from full-time ("most of the

Table 5. Activity Rates for Different Working-Time Requirements According to the CENSAL and CENEP-Week Surveys, By Sex and Locality

	Asuncion		*Piribebuy*	
Weekly Activity Rates	*Women*	*Men*	*Women*	*Men*
		CENSAL		
Full-time	23.9	56.1	9.7	59.2
Part-time	31.3	66.8	11.4	77.5
Short time	33.5	67.7	12.7	79.0
Full-time vs. Short-time	40.2*	20.7*	30.9	33.4*
		CENEP–Week		
Full-time	24.2	58.5	42.4	61.8
Part-time	36.5	67.8	70.2	85.7
Short-time	54.9	77.6	86.7	91.7
Full-time vs. Short-time	126.9*	32.6*	104.5*	48.4*

Notes: See note, Table 4.
*denotes differences that are statistically significant at the .05 level.

week" or "at least 35 hours") to short time ("at least one hour") is much lower for the CENSAL than for the CENEP-week survey and for men than for women. In fact, the CENEP rate for Asuncion women significantly increases 126.9 percent, whereas the CENSAL rate increases only 40.2 percent, a figure that barely reaches significance. There is a similar increment among the Piribebuy women in CENEP rate (104.5 percent), whereas the CENSAL rate shows only 30.9 percent increase, which does not reach statistical significance. The trends are reproduced among men, though much less intensely and with much higher rates than among women.

These findings show the greater sensitivity of the CENSAL survey to register full-time, weekly workers. They also show the greater proneness of male workers to work (or to report to have worked) on a full-time basis, whatever the procedure of data gathering. In other words, these findings prove that the census procedure is inadequate to register part-time labor, a mode that is much more frequent among women than among men.

The Identity of Female Workers Made Visible by the CENEP procedure

Is there any difference between the economically active population enumerated by CENEP-week and by the CENSAL survey, apart from sheer size? Who are the workers who do not perceive and do not declare themselves as such unless a special effort is made to detect them? The answers to these questions give some indication of the groups that need special attention in order to be more adequately registered.

In Asuncion, the capital city of Paraguay, the CENEP-week survey enumerates about three-quarters more female workers than the CENSAL procedure. Both surveys give portraits of the female labor force that do not differ significantly in terms of age, marital status, position in the household or educational level. They differ, however, in their modalities of insertion in the labor market. These clearly reveal which are the workers that are most invisible to the usual census statistics (see Table 6). CENEP enumerates more informal workers, self-employed or family aids than the CENSAL survey (55.6 versus 35.9 percent). As a consequence, CENEP detects more females working in their homes than the CENSAL survey, where owners and salaried women prevail, most of them working outside, in an establishment, and only a few inside their own homes. More female workers in the CENEP than in the CENSAL survey devote only a short time a week to working (one-third of the CENEP workers compared with only 7 percent of the CENSAL workers invest less than 19 hours a week), and less than one-half work full-time, a figure that rises to 71 percent among the CENSAL workers (see Table 6).

The differences between both pictures of the female labor force are only partially due to the (29) self-consumption producers rescued by Q13, all of

Table 6. Asuncion. Economically Active Population Enumerated by the CENSAL and CENEP–week Surveys According to Sociodemographic Characteristics By Sex (In Percent)

	Women		*Men*	
Sociodemographic characteristics	*CENSAL*	*CENEP week*	*CENSAL*	*CENEP week*
Age group	(93)	(144)	(160)	(153)
12–19	9.7	20.8	9.4	11.1
20–54	80.6	67.4	77.5	71.3
55+	9.7	11.8	13.1	17.6
Marital status	(93)	(144)	(160)	(153)
Without spouse	67.7	55.5	30.0	35.3
With spouse	32.3	44.5	70.0	64.7
Position in household	(79)	(126)	(157)	(151)
Head	20.3	9.5	61.1	62.3
Wife/husband	31.6	47.6	0.6	0.0
Daughter/son	34.2	30.2	27.4	28.5
Other	13.9	12.7	10.8	9.3
Educational level	(92)	(143)	(160)	(153)
Incomplete primary or less	21.8	30.8	18.1	20.2
Complete primary	31.5	35.0	23.8	32.7
Incomplete secondary or more	46.7	34.3	58.1	47.1
Occupational category	(92)	(135)*	(151)	(142)
Professional, technical workers	27.2	15.6	23.9	20.5
Business and sales	28.3	17.8	8.1	12.3
Service workers	35.9	33.3	6.5	6.8
Farm laborers	0.0	21.5	4.5	3.4
Nonfarm laborers	8.7	11.9	47.1	56.8
Employment status	(92)	(135)*	(151)	(142)
Employer + employee	64.1	44.4	63.6	62.7
Own-account + unpaid family	35.9	55.6	36.4	37.3
Place of work	(91)	(135)*	(150)	(139)*
Establishment	47.3	24.4	70.7	60.4
Employer's home	19.8	23.7	1.4	4.3
Street, route	10.9	11.1	14.6	27.4
Own home	22.0	40.7	13.3	7.9
Time worked	(91)	(135)	(151)*	(142)*
1–19 hours	6.6	32.1	1.3	12.0
20–34 hours	22.0	23.9	15.9	12.7
35+ hours	71.4	44.0	82.8	75.4

Note: * denotes differences between surveys' rates that are statistically significant at the .05 level.

Table 7. Piribebuy. Economically Active Population Enumerated by the CENSAL and CENEP–week Surveys According to Sociodemographic Characteristics By Sex (In Percent)

Sociodemographic characteristics	*Women*		*Men*	
	CENSAL	*CENEP week*	*CENSAL*	*CENEP week*
Age group	(95)	(502)*	(558)	(499)*
12–19	16.8	29.1	14.9	21.6
20–54	69.5	57.2	70.7	67.0
55+	13.7	13.7	14.4	11.4
Marital status	(95)	(502)*	(558)	(498)
Without spouse	64.3	46.6	44.5	44.6
With spouse	35.7	53.4	55.5	55.4
Position in household	(94)	(502)*	(557)	(498)
Head	25.5	9.6	57.0	58.6
Wife/husband	34.0	50.0	0.0	0.0
Daughter/son	36.2	35.1	38.2	38.4
Other	4.3	5.4	4.6	4.6
Educational level	(95)	(499)	(556)	(497)*
Incomplete primary or less	59.0	66.7	52.7	63.0
Complete primary	35.8	28.7	40.5	28.6
Incomplete secondary or more	5.3	4.6	6.8	8.5
Occupational category	(90)	(498)*	(528)	(499)
Business and sales	27.8	5.8	1.7	4.4
Service workers	7.8	4.6	0.2	0.6
Farm laborers	44.4	81.9	81.9	84.6
Nonfarm laborers	17.8	7.0	14.1	9.8
Other	2.2	0.6	2.1	0.6
Employment status	(90)	(498)*	(528)	(498)
Employer + employee	10.0	4.4	15.0	16.3
Own-account + unpaid family	90.0	95.6	85.0	83.7
Destination agricultural Production	(40)	(406)*	(402)	(422)
Mostly market	30.0	7.1	19.7	25.2
Mostly self consumption	70.0	92.9	80.3	74.8
Place of work	(90)	(498)*	(528)	(499)
Establishment	2.2	2.6	13.6	15.8
Employer's home	7.8	2.6	3.0	2.6
Street, route	13.3	3.6	6.6	4.4
Own home	76.6	91.0	76.7	77.2
Time worked	(88)	(497)*	(527)	(494)
1–19 hours	10.2	19.1	1.9	6.5
20–34 hours	13.6	32.0	23.1	26.1
35+ hours	76.1	48.9	75.0	67.4

Note: * denotes differences between surveys' rates that are statistically significant at the .05 level.

whom are agricultural laborers who contribute without pay to the household production, for only a short time a week. They are also only partially due to the few (12) workers rescued by Q8, most of whom work a short time a week, inside their homes, on their own basis or as unpaid family workers (see Table 4). Among the remaining workers brought in by the other CENEP-week questions (Q7 and Q9), it is also more frequent than among the CENSAL workers to find own-account, unpaid family workers, whose working place is other than an establishment. There is something built in the CENSAL procedure that makes it more sensitive to enumerate formal female workers; conversely, there is something in the CENEP procedure that makes it more sensitive to female workers with lower (cultural) probabilities of participating in the labor market and, when the occasion comes, to do it in the informal sector.

The female labor force of Piribebuy registered by the CENEP-week questionnaire is five times greater than the one registered by the CENSAL survey, mostly made up of the huge number of self-consumption producers rescued by Q13 (325 out of 497). The former differs significantly from the latter in most of the characteristics analyzed even more than in Asuncion. It is a younger population, where married wives of the head of the household are more frequent than in the CENSAL population. Very few are occupied outside the agricultural sector, whereas among the CENSAL labor force more than half are. Those women from the CENEP survey engaged in subsistence production are more than in the CENSAL survey (92.9 versus 70.0 percent). Although the majority works on a full-time basis, an important sector is on a part-time basis. There are no significant differences among them, however, regarding the extremely low educational level of the majority (see Table 7).

As in Asuncion, the self-consumption module contributes to enumerating producers that otherwise define themselves as "homemakers." The rest of the questions contribute toward enumerating agricultural workers that produce mainly for the market. Both sections of the CENEP-week questionnaire are more sensitive than the CENSAL one to enumerate women that devote part of their time or less to working (see Table 4).

These results make it plain that in an urban area as well as in a rural one, the usual population censuses are more sensitive to enumerate women with a greater propensity to work, who perceive themselves and are perceived as members of the labor force.

IV. SUMMARY AND CONCLUSIONS

In spite of the consensus that exists among experts that a great share of the female contribution to the economy remains invisible to labor statistics, therefore to planners, policymakers, researchers, and the society in general, there have been few systematic attempts to modify the situation.

This paper has been concerned with improving the counting of the female labor force in population censuses. It is based on the results of three highly controlled experimental surveys. The three were carried out on comparable samples of the female and male population of two areas. One is a rural locality based on subsistence economy, the other is the largest urban area of Paraguay, a country that ranks among the least developed of Latin America. One of the surveys reproduced the 1982 Paraguayan census (CENSAL), the other two, alternative procedures that may be used with some adaptations in future censuses (CENEP-week and CENEP-year).

The study consistently produced evidence that the usual Latin American censuses give a fairly valid portrait of the male labor force, but a quite invalid one of the female labor force.

As compared with CENEP-week, and using the same "official" conceptual definition of "economic activity," the CENSAL procedure underenumerated as much as five-sixths of the rural female workers—mostly self-consumption producers—and close to one-half of their urban counterparts. Only about one-tenth of the male workers, either urban or rural were victims of a similar censal invisibility. The CENSAL procedure proved to be more sensitive to full-time workers, who are more frequent among men, whereas the CENEP procedure was more sensitive to part-time workers, who are more frequent among women.

The urban female workers recorded by CENEP differ from those recorded by the CENSAL procedure. The former enumerates more frequently "secondary workers," engaged in informal activities as self-employed or unpaid family aids, who work at home part-time or less, that is, labor force members with a low visibility. In the rural area, the CENEP female workers are younger than the CENSAL ones and are more frequently wives of the household head. They work no less than part-time and most of them work full-time, producing for their own consumption. The similarity between the male labor force recorded by the CENSAL and the CENEP procedures shows the adequacy of the usual population censuses to register the male labor force. It provides evidence that, contrary to women, men tend to perceive themselves, and consequently to declare themselves, as workers, whatever the activity and the amount of time they devote to it.

The evidence is conclusive regarding the need to reexamine the current concepts and methods to improve the measurement of the female participation in economic activity. The international organizations have taken some steps in this direction. Indeed, the new recommendations issued by the ILO-UN for the coming 1990 round of censuses, if put into practice, will have a marked effect on the measurement of the female labor force, perhaps much more so than on the male population. In particular, we single out the explicit inclusion of self-consumption producers within the labor force, the elimination of a minimum working-time criterion, including unpaid family workers, and the acceptance that only one-hour's work qualified as economically active. Nevertheless, attempts to translate the concepts into reliable measurement procedures have been absent so far.

On the basis of the study conducted in Paraguay, it seems highly advisable to drop the use of a single census item to investigate the activity condition of the population and to incorporate, instead, a set of questions to be read one at a time, thus eliminating the possibility of a choice among alternatives. It also seems advisable to transmit the meaning of "work" by means of concrete examples chosen for their relevance in each society, and to stress that self-consumption production is also "work." While lowering the working-time requirement to a minimum of one-hour, it seems advisable to collect information on the actual time worked during the reference period. This information allows different measures of the labor force for different requirements to be obtained.

The empirical evidence is here. It points out the urgency with which this task must be faced. If not done, the coming population censuses will keep producing a most inadequate view of women's contribution to the economy, and therefore of the total labor force.

APPENDIX

The size of the samples was determined as a function of the average number of members per household, the index of masculinity (both figures taken from the 1982 population census), and the female activity rates (from the 1982 census for the CENSAL survey and from the 1982 household survey for the CENEP surveys), plus the requirements of the analysis (a minimum average of 20 household units per cell for up to 10-cell tables). Evidence of the comparability of the three samples of each locality in terms of its age-structure by sex is contained in Table A.

Table A. Comparison By Age-Structure of the Active-Age Population of the CENSAL and CENEP Surveys, By Sex and Locality (In Percent)

	Women			*Men*		
Age groups	*CENSAL*	*CENEP week*	*CENEP year*	*CENSAL*	*CENEP week*	*CENEP year*
			Asuncion			
12–25	35.3	41.4	38.1	37.6	32.2	37.3
25–34	23.2	20.5	19.2	20.2	23.5	22.2
35–54	24.6	23.4	27.3	25.6	27.3	27.6
55+	16.9	14.8	15.4	16.6	16.9	13.0
(N = 1,367)	(272)	(244)	(260)	(223)	(183)	(185)

(*continued*)

Table A. (Continued)

	Women			Men		
Age groups	*CENSAL*	*CENEP week*	*CENEP year*	*CENSAL*	*CENEP week*	*CENEP year*
			Piribebuy			
12–24	39.4	40.3	35.0	38.0	36.3	39.9
25–34	18.3	17.1	17.3	19.7	16.9	17.9
35–54	27.1	27.4	29.4	26.3	32.7	26.4
55+	15.3	15.2	18.3	16.1	14.1	15.8
(N = 3,627)	(694)	(573)	(568)	(666)	(539)	(587)

Note: The twelve comparisons, CENSAL vs. CENEP-week rates, CENSAL vs. CENEP-year rates, and CENEP-week vs. CENEP-year rates, obtained for women and men in Asuncion and Piribebuy, are not statistically significant at the .05 level.

ACKNOWLEDGMENTS

This paper is based on part of the results of a study carried out by the author with the cooperation of Martin Moreno and financial support from the Ford Foundation (1985–1987). It is the last stage of a research project on the censal measurement of the female labor force, which was initiated jointly with Zulma Recchini de Lattes under contract with the Economic Commission for Latin America and the Caribbean, in 1979. At other stages the project was funded by The Population Council. Work for this paper was done by the author as a senior researcher of the National Council of Scientific and Technical Research (CONICET) at the Center for Population Studies (CENEP) in Argentina.

NOTES

1. A clear statement of the concepts and limits of economic activity adopted by the 1982 ILO resolution and its relation with the national accounts criteria is contained in Rao and Mehran (1984).
2. The results of this test are contained in Wainerman and Moreno (1986).
3. It could be hypothesized that the result was a spurious consequence of some interviewees having learned the content of Q8 (either because they have attended to, or have answered on behalf of other household members that had gone through that question). A careful analysis of CENEP-week data for Asuncion showed that, out of the 85 women classified as active on the basis of Q7, 44 have been interviewed *after* another household member had gone through Q8. (This analysis was made possible because the order of interviewing of the household's members was known.) Of those 44 women that had chances of being acquainted with Q8, most were adults who had worked every day, 20 or more hours a week, half of them as salaried domestic servants living in their employer's home, hence visible as members of the labor force. In other words, they had a high probability of perceiving themselves as workers, hence, a low probability of responding not having worked to Q7. Only four women out of the 44 had the opposite characteristics. Two were street vendors, one was seamstress and one was a washerwoman who had worked only a few hours the previous week, down the street or at home. These were the only ones who could have answered affirmatively to Q7 because of having learned the meaning of "work." On the basis of this analysis, the hypothesis of learning was rejected and with it, the spuriousness of the results.

4. The research included two other surveys. One used the CENSAL training and the CENEP questionnaire, the other the CENEP training and the CENSAL questionnaire. They were included with the aim of testing the effect of the questionnaire (the training) while keeping the training (questionnaire) under control. Much too late we realized that the personality of the interviewers was a relevant factor, confounded with the type of training. The relatively low number of interviewees that participated in each survey did not allow to randomize this factor; therefore, we failed to assess the separate effect of the questionnaire and the training.

REFERENCES

Anker, R. (1983a). *The effect on reported levels of female labour force participation in developing countries of questionnaire design, sex of interviewer and sex/proxy status of respondent: Description of a methodological field experiment* (Working paper). Geneva: ILO, World Employment Programme.

———. (1983b, November–December). Female labour force participation in developing countries: A critique of current definitions and data collection methods. *International Labour Review, 133*(6), 709–723.

Anker, R., & Knowles, J. C. (1978). A micro-analysis of female labour force participation in Africa. In G. Standing & G. Sheehan (Eds.), *Labour force participation in low-income countries*. Geneva: ILO.

Anker, R., Khan, M. E., & Gupta, R. B. (1987, March–April). Biases in measuring the labour force. *International Labour Review, 126*(2), 151–167.

Arizpe, L. (1977). Women in the informal labor sector: The case of Mexico City. *Signs, 3*(1).

Bancroft, G. (1958). *The American labor force: Its growth and changing composition*. New York: Wiley.

Baster, M. (1981). *The measurement of women's participation in development: The use of census data*. (Discussion Paper No. 159). Brighton: University of Sussex, Institute of Development Studies.

Beneria, L. (1982). Accounting for women's work. In L. Beneria (Ed.), *Women and development: The sexual division of labor in rural societies*. New York: Praeger.

Blacker, J. G. C. (1978, June). A critique of the international definitions of economic activity and employment status and their applicability in population censuses in Africa and the Middle East. *Population Bulletin of the Economic Commission for Western Asia, 14* (Beirut), 47–54.

———. (1980, December). Further thoughts on the definitions of economic activity and employment status. *Population Bulletin of the Economic Commission for Western Asia, 19* (Beirut), 69–80.

Buvinic, M. (1982). La productora invisible en el agro centroamericano: un estudio de caso en Honduras [The invisible female producer in Central American agriculture: A case study of Honduras]. In M. Leon Magdalena (Ed.), *Las trabajadoras del agro* (Vol. 2). Bogota: ACEP.

DeVries Bastiaans, W. (1983). Census data and the economic activity of women. In C. Oppong (Ed.), *Sex Roles, Population and Development*. Winchester, MA: Allen & Unwin.

Deere, C. D. & Leon de Leal, M. (1982). *Women in Andean Agriculture*. Ginebra: ILO.

Dixon, R. (1982). Women in agriculture: Counting the labour force in developing countries. *Population and Development Review, 8*(3), 539–566.

D'Souza, S. (1980). *Sex-based stereotypes, sex biases and national data systems*. New York: United Nations. [ST/ESA/STAT 99]

Durand, J. D. (1975). *The Labour Force in Economic Development*. Princeton, NJ: Princeton University Press.

ECLAC. (1982). *Medicion del empleo y de los ingresos rurales* [Measurement of rural employment and income]. Santiago: Estudios e Informes de la CEPAL. [E/CEPAL/G.1226]

Elizaga, J. C., & Mellon, R. (1971). *Aspectos demograficos de la mano de obra en America Latina* [Demographic aspects of manpower in Latin America]. Santiago: CELADE.

Fong, M. (1980). Victims of old-fashioned statistics. *Ceres FAO Review on Agriculture and Development, 13*(3), 29–32.

Hamad, A. M. (1984). *Conditions of the Sudanese Women. Some evidence of undercount of urban female labour in the Sudan* (Research Report No. 1). Khartoum: Development Studies and Research Centre, Faculty of Economic and Social Studies, University of Khartoum.

Hauser, P. (1974, April). The measurement of labour utilization. *The Malayan Economic Review, 19*(1).

Horstmann, K. (1977, May). *Ascertaining data on economic activity for population censuses*. Bangkok: Economic and Social Commission for Asia and the Pacific (ESCAP), Working Group on the Regional Programme for Organizing the 1980 Censuses of Population and Housing. [STAT/WG/CPH/1]

ILO. (1982, October). *Statistics of labour force, employment, unemployment and underemployment* (Report No. 2). Report prepared for the Thirteenth International Conference of Labour Statisticians. Geneva: ILO. [ICLS/13/II)

———. (1983). *Report of the Conference*. Thirteenth International Conference of Labour Statisticians. Geneva: ILO.

Klein, E. (1983, December). Problemas metodologicos de una encuesta rural en Chile y estructura del empleo [Methodological problems of a rural survey in Chile and the structure of employment]. In *Cuadernos de Economia* (No. 61, pp. 127–140). Santiago: Pontificia Universidad Catolica de Chile.

Kritz, E., & Ramos, J. (1976, January–February). Medicion del subempleo urbano. Informe sobre tres encuestas experimentales [Measurement of urban underemployment. Report from three experimental surveys]. *Revista Internacional del Trabajo, 93*(1), 127–140.

Lopes, V. (1981, April). Los censos de poblacion y habitacion: criticas y sugerencias [Population and housing censuses: Critics and suggestions]. *Notas de Poblacion, 9*(25), 69–92.

Leon, M. (1985). La medicion del trabajo femenino en America Latina: problemas teoricos y metodologicos [Measurement of female work in Latin America: Theoretical and methodological problems]. In E. Bonilla (Ed.), *Mujer y familia en Colombia*. Bogota, Colombia: ACEP-UNICEF, Plaza y Janes.

Marulanda, O. (1979). Sector informal: Algunas reflexiones surgidas a la luz de un estudio sobre la economia urbana de Bogota [Informal sector: Some reflections emerging from a study on the urban economy of Bogota]. In V. Tokman & E. Klein (Eds.), *El subempleo en America Latina*. Buenos Aires: El Cid Editor-CLASCO.

Mehran, F. (1985). *Methodological survey on the measurement of employment, unemployment, underemployment and income. 1983-84. Costa Rica, June-October 1983, Basic Tables, Questionnaire C*. Geneva: ILO/DGEC (mimeo).

Mueller, E. (1974, November). Design of employment surveys in less developed countries. In J. Brown, W. Marczewski, D. Miller, D. Roberts, & W. Scott (Eds.), *Multi-purpose household surveys in developing countries*. Proceedings and paper of the study session by OCDE, Development Centre, Paris.

Paraguay, Direccion General de Estadistica y Censos. (1979). *La mujer rural en el paraguay. Dimension socioeconomica* [The rural women in Paraguay. Socioeconomic dimension]. Asuncion: DGEC.

Pina Requelme, C. (1981). *Sector informal: estrategias occupacionales y orentaciones ideologicas* [Informal sector: Occupational strategies and ideological orientations]. Santiago: PREALC-ILO (Monograph No. 20). (mimeo).

Pisoni, R. (1983, September). *El trabajo de las mujeres usualmente consideradas como economicamente inactivas* [The work of women who are usually considered economically inactive]. Paper presented at the 8th National Demographic Seminar, San Jose, Costa Rica.

Pittin, R. (1983). Documentation of women's work in Nigeria: Problems and solutions. In C. Oppong (Ed.), *Female and Male in West Africa*. Winchester, MA: Allen & Unwin.

PREALC-ILO. (1978). *Sector informal, funcionamiento y politicas* [Informal sector, functions and policies]. Santiago: PREALC-ILO.

———. (1979). *Diagnostico de las estadisticas y bibliografia sobre el empleo rural en America Latina y Panama* [Diagnostic of statistics and bibliography on rural employment in Latin America and Panama] (Working paper 174). Santiago: PREALC-ILO.

Raczynski, D. (1979). Sector informal urbano: algunos problemas conceptuales [Urban informal sector: Some conceptual issues]. In V. Tokman, & E. Klein (Eds.), *El subempleo en America Latina*. Buenos Aires: El Cid Editor-CLASCO.

Rao, M. V. S., & Mehran, F. (1984). Salient features of the new international standards on statistics of the economically active population. *Bulletin of Labour Statistics, 4*, IX–XIX.

Recchini de Lattes, Z., & Wainerman, C. H. (1986). Unreliable account of women's work: Evidence from Latin American census statistics. *Signs, 11*(4), 740–750.

Safilios-Rothschild, C. (1982). *The persistence of women's invisibility in agriculture: Theoretical and policy lessons from Lesotho and Sierra Leone* (Working Paper No. 88). New York: The Population Council, Center for Policy Studies.

Seltzer, W. (1978, June). A reply. *Population Bulletin of ECWA, 14*, 55–56.

Souza, P. R., & Tokman, V. E. (1976, November–December). El sector informal urbano en America Latina [Urban informal sector in Latin America]. *Revista Internacional del Trabajo, 94*(3), 385–397.

Standing, G. (1978). *Labor Force Participation and Development*. Geneva: ILO.

Tokman, V. E. (1977). *Dinamica del mercado de trabajo urbano: el sector informal urbano en America Latina* [Dynamics of urban labor markets: the urban informal sector in Latin America] (Occasional Paper No. 13). Santiago: PREALC-ILO (mimeo).

Torrado, S. (1978). Algunas reflexiones sobre los censos de 1980 en la perspectiva de la investigacion sociodemografica y las politicas de poblacion en America Latina [Some reflections on the 1980 census in the perspective of sociodemographic research and population policies in Latin America]. In *Informacion e investigacion sociodemografica en America Latina*. Santiago: PISPAL-CLACSO.

———. (1981). Los censos de poblacion y vivienda en America Latina durante el periodo 1970–1980: recommendacions y practicas [Population and housing censuses in Latin America during 1970–1980: recommendations and practices]. In S. Torrado (Ed.), *Investigacion e informacion sociodemografica* (Vol. 2). Buenos Aires: CLACSO.

Trigueros Mejia, R. (1986). ILO methodological survey on the measurement of employment, unemployment and underemployment in Costa Rica. *Bulletin of Labour Statistics, 1*, pp. IX–XX.

Wainerman, C. H., & Recchini de Lattes, Z. (1981). *El trabajo femenino en el banquillo de los acusados. La medicion censal en America Latina y el Caribe* [Female work on trial. Census measurements in Latin America and the Caribean]. Mexico: Editorial Terra Nova-The Population Council.

Wainerman, C. H., & Moreno, M. (1986). Sensibilizando a los censistas a los sesgos sexuales: un ejercicio de entrenamiento [Sensitizing census takers to gender biases: A training exercise]. In INDEC/CENEP/CELADE, *Los censos del 90. Caracteristicas economicas de la poblacion* (INDES Study No. 8). Buenos Aires: INDEC.

Wainerman, C. H., Moreno, M., & Geldstein, R. (1985). La medicion censal de la participacion economica: una evaluacion con especial referencia a las mujeres [Census measurement of economic participation: An evaluation with special reference to women]. In Argentina, INDEC, *Los censos de poblacion del 80. Taller de analisis y evaluacion,* (INDEC Study No. 2). Buenos Aires: INDEC.

———. (1987). Incorporando las trabajadoras agricolas a los censos de poblacion [Incorporating female agriculture workers to population censuses]. *Desarrollo Economico, 27*(107), 347–376.

Zurayk, H. (1983, November). *Women's economic participation*. West Asia and North Africa, The Population Council, Regional Papers.

PART II

FEMALE LABOR FORCE PARTICIPATION IN DEVELOPED SOCIETIES

REFERENCE GROUPS, OCCUPATIONAL CLASS AND MARRIED WOMEN'S LABOR FORCE PARTICIPATION

Susan Elster and Mark S. Kamlet

I. INTRODUCTION

Married women have been the fastest growing labor force participants in this century, especially since World War II. Their rate of labor force participation nearly quadrupled between 1940 and 1985. In contrast, participation rates of all women increased only about twofold (U.S. Department of Commerce, 1986, p. 398).[1] These changing patterns extend even to married mothers of very young children: half of wives with children one year or younger worked in 1985 compared to 31% just 10 years before (Hayghe, 1986).[2]

The literature in economics has modeled married women's labor force participation decisions to be a function of husband's income, household characteristics (e.g., number of children), and variables measuring the human capital

Research in Human Capital and Development, Vol. 6, pages 89–123.

ISBN: 1-55938-032-2

and potential wage of the wife (e.g., her education). The economics studies have become increasingly sophisticated in both theory and methodology; however, the best models have been unable to account fully for recent increases in wives' labor force participation. In contrast, the sociological literature has focused on the role of changing attitudes and cultural norms in prompting married women to work. The results of this sociological research have been mixed. Moreover, even in cases where a link has been demonstrated between attitudes and wives' labor force participation decisions, there has been controversy over the nature of the causality between the two.

More important for our present purposes, neither literature has examined to any significant degree potential differences that may exist across social groups (defined on the basis of socioeconomic class, occupational groupings, and so forth) in the influence of the so-called "traditional economic" variables (such as children, education, and others) on wives' labor force participation decisions. This neglect in the economics literature is perhaps not unexpected; class distinctions have not typically played a central role in neoclassical economic theory. Even from a sociological perspective, the neglect may be understandable, despite the traditional importance of class-based behavior differences in sociological theory. Sociological work has seldom consistently controlled for traditional economic influences on wives' labor force participation decisions, being more concerned with attitudes and cultural norms; nor has it kept fully apace with econometric advances in estimation techniques. As such, it may be less surprising than at first glance that sociological work has also not attempted to distinguish the impact of traditional economic influences on wives' labor force participation decisions across social groups.

Still, there may be much to gain from unifying the concerns of these two disciplines and analyzing differences across social groups in the influence of "traditional economic" variables on wives' labor force participation. As we argue below, there are important reasons to suggest that such differences may exist. Moreover, analyses of the impact of traditional economic variables across social groups can, we argue, shed important, if indirect, light on the role of attitudes and social norms on married women's decision to engage in market work. This can be done in a context in which issues of causality are less problematic. The first purpose of this paper, then, is to examine differences across social groups, defined in terms of broad occupation and age groupings, in the influences on wives' labor force participation decisions.

A second, and related purpose of this paper, is to examine differences across social groups in the particular impact of family "income aspirations" on wives' labor force decisions. Neither the economics nor the sociology literatures has examined the possible role of measures of relative income, such as income aspirations, on labor force behavior. In an earlier paper (see Elster & Kamlet, 1988), we hypothesized that a wife's decision to enter the labor force is influenced not only by her husband's current level, but also by the relationship between the household's current and its "aspired" income.

To examine this hypothesis, we used microdata from the decennial census for the Pittsburgh SMSA in 1970 and 1980. Using a variety of measures of "income aspirations," our empirical results strongly supported our hypothesis that income aspirations influence wives' labor force participation decisions. This influence was found to be as strong as the influence of the household's actual income level on the wife's labor force participation decision. Such a finding is of particular importance given our still incomplete understanding of the causes of recent increases in the labor force participation of married women.

Our focus on income aspirations introduces centrally into the analysis of married women's labor force participation the notion of "reference group." This notion is often associated with a sociological perspective, although demographers, such as Easterlin and others, have also employed reference group theory in studies of family fertility behavior. For us, aspirations for income were assumed to be influenced by the income that could be earned by a worker with given characteristics (age, education, occupation and industry group) in a prior time period (e.g., 10 years before). Thus, the reference group was postulated to consist of individuals of comparable age, education, and so on, in a prior time period and aspired income was defined as the average wage income of members of the reference group.

While embodying a sociological concern with reference groups, our analysis remained firmly rooted within the economics paradigm in its assumption that individuals in different groups form income aspirations in the same way. We did not entertain the possibility that, for example, different occupational or age groups could form income aspirations in different manners, or that the impact of income aspirations on wives' labor force participation decisions could vary across such groups. Examining differences across groups in the influence of income aspirations on wives' labor force participation rates is then the second purpose of this paper.

To summarize, a primary purpose of this paper is to examine whether "traditional economic" variables have a differential influence across social groups (defined here by broad occupation and age classifications). A second, and related purpose of the paper is to examine whether "income aspirations" have a differential influence across these same social groups.

We begin in Section II with a brief review of the several relevant literatures. Section III discusses the data used and Section IV presents a first set of empirical results, looking at some basic patterns in the data. Section V presents a logit model specification for examining more formally the influences on women's labor force participation decisions. Section VI reports and discusses four sets of estimation results. First, drawing from Elster and Kamlet (1988) as a benchmark, results for the whole sample of married women are reported. Second, the sample is divided into three groups based on broad occupational groupings. Third, the sample is divided into two groups based on husband's age. Fourth and finally, results are reported from disaggregating the data by age and occupational group. We conclude in Section VII.

II. LITERATURE REVIEW

Labor Economics

Labor economics has traditionally viewed individuals as maximizing their consumption of leisure time and other goods subject to an income constraint. Time allocation decisions are seen as a choice between hours spent in leisure and labor. Consumers, responding to rising wages, find that the opportunity cost of consuming leisure increases, and choose to supply more labor to the market (the substitution effect). Similarly, as wages continue to rise and a certain level of income is attained, the individual will consume more leisure, and his/her labor supply curve will bend backwards (the income effect). Wage rate increases are thus expected to exhibit both substitution and income effects in terms of their influence on labor supply.

Early empirical analyses of wage effects on labor supply tended to indicate that the income effect was stronger than the substitution effect, and thus higher wages were seen, on the average, to lower labor force participation (Mincer, 1962, pp. 99–100). This conclusion was particularly problematic for the analysis of married women's labor force participation. It seemed to contradict the experience of the 1950's, in which married women's labor force participation rates increased concurrent with rapid gains in husband's real income.

In an effort to resolve this and other problems, advances were made in both basic theory and in estimation methods. For example, in a revision of the traditional theoretical perspective, Mincer (1962) pointed out that wives typically allocate time over market work, leisure time *and* home work. The relevant "income maximizer" became seen not as the individual, but the husband and wife jointly. Income is pooled by family members, and a wife's response to her own wage rate is both a reflection of the value to her family of her home work and the ease with which substitutions for home work can be made.

Following Mincer's lead, a large literature began to further identify important characteristics associated with married women's labor supply (see, for example, Bowen & Finegan, 1969; Cain, 1966). The variables identified in this literature may be subdivided into two broad groups. First are a series of measures related to a woman's "stock" of human capital, including her work experience, education, and health; second are a number of personal and family characteristics that are also associated with wives' labor supply, including race, age, number and age of children, husband/family income, assets, and tastes and preferences. Of the key variables associated with wives' labor force participation, the economics literature finds rising wages to be the most salient explanation for the rising labor force participation rates of married women.[3]

Other advances focused on estimation techniques. Most of the early empirical analyses relied upon regression analysis using ordinary least squares estimation procedures. In critiquing many of these studies—representative of what they label "first generation research"—Heckman, Killingsworth, and Macurdy (1981, p. 80) note that "the empirical results . . . are not particularly encouraging, and often raise more questions than they answer." For example, reported own-wage substitution effects (expressed as an elasticity) for women ranged from −.05 to +2.00, and income effects ranged from 0 to −.40. a new set of methodological tools were developed that took better account of the limited dependent variables that appeared in many models.

Additional contributions addressed specification issues involving the unobservability of wage rate for women who do not work, and resolved the confounding influence of a variety of selection effects. This "second generation" of research, then, has attempted to correct for some of the methodological shortcomings of earlier studies. These revisions have led to elasticity estimates that are much closer to the levels anticipated in theoretical work (Heckman, et al., 1981, p. 108).

Despite the contributions of the recent literature (upon which we draw in this paper), the existing models cannot fully explain the increase of married women into the labor force, particularly during the last 15 years, when growth in own-wages was slow or nonexistent. Additionally, the possible role played by social groups in labor supply decisions is, as in the earlier literature, not addressed. Finally, the possible role of "income aspirations," as compared to absolute levels of income, on labor force participation has also not been considered.

Sociological Studies of Married Women's Labor Force Participation

In contrast to work in economics, research in sociology has focused on the role of changing attitudes and cultural norms in prompting married women's labor force participation. In this view, husbands' growing acceptance of wives' market work and women's changing expectations about work result in rising female participation rates. Ferber (1982), reporting results from a 1968–1972 longitudinal survey of couples married in 1968, claims that attitudes are the key determinant of subsequent employment behavior. Gerson (1985, p. 10) argues that recent labor force changes are due to the entrance of younger cohorts of women with behaviors altered by their having "reached adulthood during a period of accelerated social change."

A variant of this emphasis on changing attitudes and cultural norms suggest that an individual's position in the economy, as represented by, say, socioeconomic status, gives rise to particular attitudes, values, or "class consciousness." Centers (1949, pp. 28–29, cited in Jackman & Jackman, 1983) hypothesizes, for example, that

> a person's status and role with respect to the economic process of society imposes upon him certain attitudes, values and interests relating to his role and status in the political and economic sphere . . . and that the status and role of the individual in relation to the means of production and exchange of goods and services gives rise in him to a consciousness of membership in some social class which shares those attitudes, values and interests.

In response to work on the role of changing attitudes and cultural norms, other studies, while not disputing that attitudes are linked to employment behavior, suggest however, that attitude changes follow employment changes. Molm (1978), using the 1970 Equal Employment Opportunity Survey, which reinterviewed 30-year olds who were high school sophomores in 1955, concludes that attitudes are "self descriptions of overt behavior" (p. 523). Economist Victor Fuchs (1985) notes that the 1960's feminist writings *followed* the rise in age at marriage, growth of married women's labor force participation, and declines in birth rates, and suggests that these writings will likely be understood "primarily as a rationale and a rhetoric for changes that were already occurring for other reasons" (p. 128). These researchers posit that our attitudes are often formed as a consequence of or as a rationalization for particular life experiences.

The methodological approaches adopted in many sociological studies make it hard to resolve this debate. Traditional economic variables influencing wives' labor force participation decisions have not been systematically controlled for in the analyses. By not controlling for these factors, such studies are subject to the criticism that the influence of attitudes on employment is spurious and/or noncausal. Critiques, such as those of Molm and Fuchs, cannot be easily refuted by existing analysis.

Insofar as sociological analyses have not consistently controlled for traditional economic factors or incorporated its methodological advances, it follows that they also have not examined differences in the impact of these traditional economic factors across social, age, or occupational groups. At the same time, there is certainly reason to think that such differences may exist. Strumpel (1972), for instance, finds important differences across broad occupational groups in the family head's ranking of job characteristics, personal goals, levels of satisfaction with job, income, standard of living, and education across the five groups. Such differences might easily translate into differences across social groupings in the determinants of wives' employment decisions.

The lack of attention in the sociological literature to possible differences across social, occupational, and age groups in the factors influencing wives' employment decisions is doubly ironic. First, it is ironic because of the traditional importance given to class and social group in sociological theory. Second, it is ironic because an examination of differences across groups in the role of traditional economic factors may represent a powerful, if indirect, way to address the very issue with which the sociological literature has been concerned, namely the importance of cultural norms and attitudes.

Suppose cultural norms and attitudes *do* causally affect wives' labor force participation decisions and that these norms and attitudes vary across social, age, or occupational groups. This may well be manifested by differences across social groups in the impact of traditional economic influences on wives' labor force participation decisions. Indeed, if found, such differences would seem directly to reflect systematic differences in attitudes across groups. Interpreting "attitudes" broadly, such differences would almost definitionally mean that preferences and/or beliefs on matters relevant to wives' labor force participation differ as a function of social group. Thus, insofar as the sociological literature has been concerned with showing a causal link between attitudes and labor force behavior, it may have overlooked an indirect but powerful way to examine this link.

Income Aspirations and Labor Force Participation

Quite apart from the debate over the role of traditional economic influences versus social attitudes and norms on wives' labor force participation, neither the economics nor sociological literatures has devoted much attention to the impact that "aspirations" and "expectations" about family income may play on wives' labor force participation decisions. There is, however, substantial work in social psychology and in demography emphasizing the role of "reference groups" on behavior. Because exploring this influence is a secondary goal of this paper, the relevant literature is briefly discussed.

Two early reference groups theorists, Merton and Rossi (1968, p. 35), state that, "reference group theory aims to systematize the determinants and consequences of those processes of evaluation and self-appraisal in which the individual takes the values or standards of other individuals and groups as a comparative frame of reference." Underlying this concept is the notion that an individual's values, tastes, preferences and aspirations are functions of the values, tastes and preferences of some reference group (Runciman, 1968, p. 69).

Most directly related to our purpose here is work on family fertility behavior in demography. Central to the development of this research is the work of Easterlin (1961, 1968, 1978, 1980), who argues that adult consumption expectations are formed during an individual's adolescence by the standard of living characterizing the parents' home (see also Freedman & Thornton, 1982; Johnson & Lean, 1985). If, as an adult, the standard of living improves on (falls short of) that experienced during adolescence, the individual is likely to consider herself relatively well off (worse off), and to make behavioral adjustments in marriage, work and childbearing decisions accordingly.

At its core, Easterlin's research postulates that material well-being is not adequately reflected in absolute measures of income—that there is a subjective component to individual or family evaluations of well-being that matters when explaining such family economic behavior as fertility. These fertility studies can be related to the aforementioned work on reference group theory. Easterlin's subjective understanding of income relies on the sociological concept of "reference groups." Although reference groups may consist of one's friends, neighbors, education, cohort, and so on, Easterlin's subjective understanding of income relies on the family as reference group, and in particular, its values and standard of living during that individual's adolescence.

To explain the upsurge in fertility following World War II that resulted in the baby boom, Easterlin points out that the parents of this cohort grew up during the Depression, and consequently developed modest consumption expectations (see also Elder, 1974). Finding themselves to be relatively well off during the prosperous 1950s, and experiencing high wages due to supply and demand effects associated with their relatively small cohort size, they chose to marry younger and have more children than any previous cohort in the twentieth century. Easterlin similarly explains the delayed marriages and reduced fertility of the baby boom cohort: growing up in relatively affluent homes, they came to expect a standard of living that their cohort size and the economic conditions of the 1970s and 1980s did not permit them to attain.[4]

That individual actions are based on comparisons—of, for example, their economic well-being in one period versus another, or of their economic well-being relative to that of others—is a central supposition in other literatures as well. Studies in "distributive justice," for example, deal specifically with the question of income distribution and individual satisfaction with monetary rewards. Central to this literature is the notion that individuals evaluate the fairness of monetary rewards by comparing themselves with others (see Alwin, 1987). Messick and Thorngate (1967) report work on relative gain maximization and show that individuals are likely to maximize their gain (in simulated settings) relative to that of others even if the resulting outcome means a lower absolute gain. Brickman and Campbell (1971) examine the phenomenon of decreasing satisfaction with a given standard of living and note that individuals tend to compare their economic level over time and among reference groups.

Sociology and demography are not alone in considering the importance of comparisons over time or across groups. Precedents in the economics literature date at least to the permanent income work of Freidman (1957) and Ando and Modigliani (1963), who propose that income expectations for period $t+1$ depend on actual income in period t. Duesenberry (1949) suggested that the consumption aspirations of a given income group are more likely to emulate those of the next higher income group if the higher income group is large relative to the given income group.

The most complete application of reference group theory to family labor supply is provided by Oppenheimer (1982) in the demographic literature. Her study emphasizes the importance of family consumption expectations and current income in wives' labor supply. She views such expectations as related to a family's occupation and income reference group as well as to the family's "stage" in the life cycle. Oppenheimer constructs a measure of relative income, which is the ratio between the husband's current earnings and the earnings of "others in the same general occupational reference group and at approximately the same stage of the career cycle" (p. 216). However, her analysis is unable to separate the influences of absolute and relative income levels on wives' labor force participation, which we believe to be critical to an examination of the role of relative versus absolute income on labor force participation decisions.

Elster and Kamlet (1988) is the only other work of which we are aware that examines the impact of income aspirations of wives' labor force participation decisions. This work is reviewed in greater detail below. However, it assumed that income aspirations were formed in the same way by all families and that such aspirations affected wives' labor force participation to the same extent regardless of social group. It thus also fails to address the issue of differences across social groups in the factors influencing wives' labor force participation rates.

Summary

To briefly summarize the relevant literatures, the economics literature has focused on a particular set of influences on wives' labor force participation rates. Preferring to view differences in attitudes, tastes or preferences as randomly distributed across individuals, it has not examined the differential impacts of such influences across social groups. Nor has it examined the role of income aspirations in wives' labor force participation decisions. The sociological literature has focused on the impact of attitudes on wives' labor force participation, with substantial debate remaining as to the causal relationship between attitudes and labor force participation decisions. As in the economics literature, the sociological literature has not devoted effort to examining differences across social groups in the role of traditional economic influences on wives' labor force participation. Examining such differences, however, may in fact be a powerful, if indirect, way to examine the impact of attitudes on married women's labor force participation decisions.

Finally, neither the economics nor sociological literatures has devoted significant effort to examining the role of measures of relative income, such as income aspirations, in wives' labor force participation decisions. While Elster and Kamlet (1988) examine the impact of income aspiration, that work does not consider differences across age, occupational, or social groups in the effect of income aspirations on wives' labor force participation rates. It is to this lack of attention to differences across social groups in the influences—traditional economic influences and income aspirations—on wives' labor force participation decisions which this paper begins to address.

III. DATA

Data for the study were drawn from the U.S. Bureau of the Census, 1980 Five Percent Public-Use Microdata Sample for the Pittsburgh Standard Metropolitan Statistical Area (SMSA) (1983).[5] Two parallel samples of white married couple families in which spouses are between 20 and 60 years old were constructed. An effort was made to draw a relatively homogeneous sample. For this reason, black married couple families were not included in the sample, due to important differences in the labor supply of black and white women.[6] Families in which husbands were self-employed were also excluded, due to likely difficulties in determining if the wife works off the payroll in her husband's business. Finally, families in which the husband was out the labor force (not employed and not looking for work) were excluded.

The data set offers several advantages. First, the data allow us to examine detailed characteristics of both the husband and wife in 5966 households in 1980. Second, it avoids problems associated with aggregating data at the SMSA level. Previous studies typically either aggregate data at the SMSA level (see for example, Cain, 1966) or use individual data and include dummy variables for SMSA (see Mroz, 1987). The first approach is problematic in that it misses variations in individual behaviors that arise due to differences among SMSA's. In fact, there are important differences in unemployment rates and employment-related costs (such as transportation, clothing, and child care). Stolzenberg and Waite (1984) show that these variations affect women's labor force participation rates. The second approach is also problematic: by including SMSA as a right hand side dummy variable we must assume that SMSA has an additive effect, or that it does not alter the relationship between the labor force participation rate and the other explanatory variables. By examining a single urban labor market, we control for these across-SMSA differences and circumvent problems characteristic of both approaches.

Third, and very important for our purposes here, we are able to construct a parallel 1970 data set that enables us to construct a "reference group" for the families in our sample.[7] Finally, as opposed to the vast majority of econometric research examining wives' labor force participation, which relies on data from the mid-1970s or before, the data are relatively current. This is an important feature in achieving a better understanding of the very rapid increases in wives' labor force participation over the 1970 to 1980 decade.[8]

IV. BASIC EMPIRICAL PATTERNS

Social groups are complex structures in the real world. However, if differences in the behavior of married women are discernible across *broadly* defined groups, then simple divisions will nevertheless support the importance of examining the linkage between social groups and economic behaviors—both in this study and in future research. In this paper we consider several alternative approaches to examining differences across social groups in the influences on married women's labor force participation decisions.

In this section, we present basic patterns in the data indicating differences in two types of social groupings, one based on broad occupational groupings and the other based on age. Specifically, we examine differences among these groups in the relationship between wives' labor force participation and a measure of income aspiration. To provide a base reading, we first use the whole data set; we then follow with results partitioned by social groups.

The initial measure of income aspirations reported here divides the families into groups based on combinations of the husband's education and income. A husband had a medium level of education if he attained a high school degree, and a high or low education if he had more or less than a high school degree. A family was considered to have a medium income if, in the distribution of family wage and salary income (excluding the wife's), it fell in the second or third quartile; it was considered high income if income fell in the highest quartile, or low income if income fell in the lowest quartile.

There are nine possible combinations of education and income. A scale was constructed ranging from 1 to 5 indicating the degree of inconsistency between husband's educational status and the family's wage income. A value of 3 was assigned if the level of husband's income matched the level of his education (e.g., medium education and medium income). Higher (lower) values were assigned for each level of negative (positive) difference between husband's education and his income. For example, a rank of 5 is assigned to a husband with high education and low income and a rank of 1 to a husband with low education and high income.

Loosely speaking, if income aspirations are based in part on educational levels, the scale indicates the income aspirations of the families. Higher (lower) values are associated with the family making less (more) than they aspire to based on the husband's education. If income aspirations influence labor force participation decisions, there should be a positive monotonic relationship between the education/income inconsistency scale and wives' propensity to enter the labor force. As Table 1, taken from Elster and Kamlet (1988), shows, there is a strong monotonic relationship between the proportion of wives working and the rank of the family education/income inconsistency scale.

Of more direct interest for us here is the question of the consistency of this pattern across social groups. We approach this by looking at two ways of grouping families. The first divides the sample into three groups based on the broadly grouped occupation of the husband. We divide the sample into skilled white collar workers (professional, technical, and managerial occupations), lower white collar workers (sales, clerical, and service occupations), and blue collar workers (craft, operative, and laborer occupations). The second way of grouping

Table 1. Percentage of Wives Working, by Family Socioeconomic Group

Socioeconomic Group	*Wives Working (%)*	*Rank*	
High Ed/Low Income	65.3	5	Educ > Income
High Ed/Med Income	53.6	4	
Med Ed/Low Income	52.0	4	
Low Ed/Low Income	45.5	3	Educ = Income
Med Ed/Med Income	41.6	3	
High Ed/High Income	41.6	3	
Med Ed/High Income	40.3	2	Educ < Income
Low Ed/Med Income	38.9	2	
Low Ed/High Income	30.5	1	

Source: Pittsburgh SMSA (1980).

the sample is by the age, dividing families with husbands over 35 years of age from those families with husbands less than or equal to 35. Table 2 shows the results of these partitionings.

Several observations are apparent from examining Table 2. First, each age and occupation group displays the same basic monotonic relationship: the percentage

Table 2. Percentage of Wives Working Within Socioeconomic Groups, by Husband's Occupation Group and Age

Husband's Occupation Group and Age	*Education/Income Rank*					*Sample Size*
	Educ < Inc		*Educ = Inc*	*Educ > Inc*		
	1	*2*	*3*	*4*	*5*	
Skilled White Collar						
20–35 years	*	*	44.4	56.6	68.3	616
36–60 yearsw	*	43.7	44.8	56.5	*	993
All	*	42.6	44.7	56.6	66.9	1609
Lower White Collar						
20–35 years	*	*	42.6	51.7	66.7	345
36–60 years	*	42.3	46.3	53.9	*	727
All	*	42.2	45.5	52.8	62.6	1072
Blue Collar						
20–35 years	*	29.7	37.7	49.8	63.4	1279
36–60 years	27.1	40.1	41.3	51.3	*	2145
All	27.0	38.7	39.9	50.3	*	3424

Note: *Indicates sample size (summing across rows) less than 6%.
Source: Pittsburgh SMSA (1980).

of wives in the labor force increases as the education/income inconsistency rank increases, or as husband's education level outstrips his income level. Second, there are some differences in base participation rates across socioeconomic and age groups. Perhaps most pronounced of the effects, wives of blue collar workers are less likely to participate in the labor force within almost all rankings and for both age groups.

Thus, these basic empirical regularities in the data indicate that income aspirations, as measured by the gap between the husband's income and educational levels, appear to influence married women's labor force participation in a similar fashion across different age and broad occupational groupings. The results leave open the possibility, however, that there are differences among age groups and particularly occupational groups in base levels of married women's labor force participation, controlling for income aspirations. Although suggestive, the above analyses are only partial in nature. Many important variables are not controlled for, such as wife's education, presence of children, and so on. These shortcomings indicated the need for a more complex analysis. We turn to such an analysis in the next section.

V. GENERAL SPECIFICATION USING LOGIT ANALYSIS

Basic Logit Specification

In this section we review a framework, initially presented in Elster and Kamlet (1988), within which to examine the influences on married women's labor force participation in a multivariate setting, controlling for other factors than those considered in the previous analysis. The basic statistical framework presented is that of logit analysis. We posit an unobserved variable, y_i^*, which measures wife i's propensity to enter the labor force. This variable is a function of multiple influences, represented by the vector X_i of observed variables, as well as by an error term ϵ_i, representing unobserved influences.

Assuming linearity between X and y^*, our basic statistical relationship is:

$$y_{\mathrm{i}} = {}^*\beta X_i + \epsilon_i$$

Wife i chooses to work when $y_i^* = 0$. Since ϵ is a random variable, the outcome $y^* = 0$ is a random variable as well. Its probability depends on the distribution of ϵ. Logit analysis assumes that ϵ is distributed logistically. Under these assumptions, the parameters β can be estimated using maximum likelihood techniques with asymptotic standard errors derived from the inverse of the information matrix.

Variables

In our analysis, the equation $y^* = \beta X + \epsilon$ is treated as a reduced form equation. We therefore avoid the self-selection problems associated with direct use of the wage of wives in the sample who work. We include instead factors that influence a wife's wage either by affecting the value of her market work or by affecting the value of her home work.[9] The variable primarily associated with the market wage is wife's education (FEDUC). Education is assumed to vary positively with the wife's expected wage rate and so is expected to increase the probability of participation. We also include an interactive term between education and age, FAGEED, which allows the impact of wife's education on labor force participation to vary as a function of the wife's age.[10]

It is generally expected that children of different ages affect labor supply differently (Gronau, 1973). Good substitutes for maternal care of young children are often costly or simply unavailable at the desired quality, so that the presence of young children (under 6 years of age) increases the value of the wife's home work and therefore reduces her labor force participation; the effect is stronger the more preschool children there are in the home. By contrast, older children may involve greater expense (Oppenheimer, 1976), or, they may be able to contribute to the family's home work, freeing up time for market work among other family members; both effects would tend to raise the value of the wife's market work and increase the probability of her labor force participation.

We include four variables relating to children in the household: FERTBIG, FERTLIT, FERTMIX, and FERTNO. FERTBIG is an estimate of the number of children in the household between ages 6 and 17, conditional upon there being no children in the household below age 6. FERTLIT is a measure of the number of children under 6 in the household, conditional upon there being no children in the household between 6 and 17.[11] FERTMIX is a dummy variable that equals 1 if there are children in the household both below and above age 6. FERTNO is a dummy variable indicating no children in the household. The presence of costly older children is expected to increase the value of the wife's market wage, and so FERTBIG is expected to increase the probability of wives' labor force participation. Similarly, the coefficient for FERTNO should also be positive. Conversely, young children increase the home or reservation wage of the wife. As a result, we would expect the coefficient for FERTLIT to be negative.

Two other socioeconomic variables included in our analysis are the wife's age (FAGE) and whether she has been divorced (DIVORCE). Age is generally negatively related to married women's labor supply. Women's participation rates tend to peak at an earlier age and decline more rapidly than men's. This is no doubt due to several factors, including the fact that a large proportion of older women did not participate in the labor force even as young women (Feinstein, 1983, p. 50). Higher wife's age is therefore expected to reduce the probability of her participation. FAGESQ is included to test the linearity of the age effect. As mentioned above, we also interact age with education, to allow the impact of age on labor force participation to be mediated by the wife's educational status.

The variable DIVORCE is a dummy variable that equals 1 if at least one previous marriage ended in divorce. Recent research indicates that divorce increases wives' labor supply, both in the years preceding the divorce (Johnson & Skinner, 1986) and in subsequent years (Oppenheimer, 1982; Smith, 1979; Sweet 1973, p. 106). Divorce is generally thought to increase the economic burden on wives who must support themselves and often their children. Additionally, previous divorce increases the probability of future divorce and working may therefore provide some protection for the wife from future economic loss.

Other variables include interest and dividend income (TOTDIV) and other nonwage income (OTHRINC), as well as family earned income excluding the wife's (OTHRWAGE). Nonwife earned income and family assets may be thought of as proxies for family economic need, and it is hypothesized that rising income reduces the wife's need to work in the market. Alternatively, husbands and wives may be thought of as gross substitutes for one another in the performance of home work. For this reason a cross-substitution effect acts to increase the importance of the wife's home work (and decrease the probability that she works in the market) as the husband's income increases. For these reasons, TOTDIV, OTHRINC, and OTHRWAGE are expected to reduce the probability of the wife's labor force participation.[12]

Also included with the income variables is our measure of the family's income aspirations, INCASP. INCASP computes the difference between a husband's 1980 wage and salary income (INC80) and the income an individual with the husband's age, education, occupation and industry characteristics could have expected if he worked in 1970.[13] INCASP assumes that individuals look to see what others like them earned in the past when forming their income aspirations. Alternatively, one may imagine that some husbands were actually in the labor force in similar occupations in 1970 and aspired to income levels in 1980 at least equivalent to that of husbands who were 10 years older than they in 1970. For example, let us say a given husband is 40 years old in 1980. We could imagine that, as a 30 year old in 1970, this husband aspired to an income in 1980 (when he turned 40) at least equal to that of 40 year olds in his occupation and industry group and with his level of education in 1970.

To estimate what an individual with the husband's characteristics would have made in 1970, we substitute his characteristics into an equation estimating earned income for husbands in the Pittsburgh SMSA in 1970.[14] INCASP then is negative if the husband's 1980 earnings fall short of his anticipated earnings. As a result, the probability of wives' labor force participation is expected to vary inversely with INCASP.

The equation estimating (with OLS) the 1970 earned income is detailed in Table 3. The wage equation reported in Table 3 indicates that 1970 male wages were higher for professional workers and clerical workers than for blue collar

Table 3. Specification of Model Estimating Husband's Anticipated 1980 Earned Income, Calculated Using 1970 Data

Variable	*Coefficient*	*T-ratio*	*Sign. Level*	*Variable Definition*
INTERCEPT	1395.27	−0.347	0.7289	
COLLAR1	4321.17	8.057	0.0001	Equals 1 if professional technical or managerial
COLLAR2	901.05	1.730	0.0838	Equals 1 if sales, clerical or service
AGE	616.48	3.620	0.0003	Age
AGEEDUC	34.86	6.520	0.0001	Age times education
EDUCSQ	− 37.27	−3.278	0.0011	Education squared
AGESQ	− 11.42	−6.755	0.0001	Age squared
EDLEHS	−1440.68	−1.928	0.0539	Equals 1 if educ is high school or less
EDGECOL	5976.16	6.139	0.0001	Equals 1 if educ is college or more
INDPROD	− 714.63	−1.200	0.2301	Equals 1 if industry is producer services
INDGOOD	4119.33	8.029	0.0001	Equals 1 if industry is goods-producing

Note: Adjusted $R - SQ = 0.2015$.

workers, controlling for age, education and industry group. There is also an influence of age and education on wages. Having a high school diploma or less significantly decreases wages and, expectedly, a college diploma or more increases wages. Industry group also has an influence. Wages were higher for those working in goods producing industries (manufacturing, construction, mining) and lower for those in producer services (business services, finance and real estate) than for those working in consumer services.

VI. LOGIT ESTIMATION RESULTS

In presenting our empirical results, we begin by examining the results for the whole sample, drawing from Elster and Kamlet (1988). This serves as a benchmark from which to proceed to our main interest here, using the model to examine differences across age and occupational groups in married women's labor force participation decisions.

Analysis for Whole Sample

We begin our presentation of empirical results from the logit analysis by reporting the results of the model estimated for the entire sample. Estimating the model using the entire sample assumes that there are no differences across occupational or age groups in the influences on married women's labor force participation decisions.

Consistent with the discussion of the prior section, the independent variables of the model include: variables relating to household income—TOTDIV, OTHRINC, OTHRWAGE and INCASP; variables related to the wife's age and educational characteristics—FEDUC, FAGE, FAGESQ, FAGEED; variables related to number and type of children in the household—FERTLIT, FERTBIG, FERTMIX and FERTNO; and a variable indicating whether the woman has been divorced—DIVORCE. Table 4 includes the complete definitions of these variables.

Results are reported in Table 5. Beginning with our nonincome variables, a wife's age has a nonlinear effect on labor force participation. In addition, there is an interaction between age and education. For a wife with a high school educa-

Table 4. Variable Definitions

Variable Name	*Definition*
Income Variables	
TOTDIV	Husband and wife interest, dividend or net rental income.
OTHRINC	Social security income, public assistance (AFDC, SSI, GA), veteran's payments, workman's compensation cash benefits, payments from estates and trust funds, alimony and child support, nonservice scholarships and fellowships, periodic contributions from people outside the household, receipts from insurance and annuities.
OTHRWAGE	Total family wage income minus wife's income.
INCASP	Difference between husband's 1980 wage income and his expected income (see below)
Wage Variables	
FEDUC	Wife's education: highest grade completed or currently attending (Possible grades range from 0 to 22, with high school = grade 14).
FAGEED	Wife's age times her education.
FERTLIT	Proxy for the number of children under age 6 (equals the number of children ever born if only children under 6 are present in household).
FERTBIG	Proxy for the number of children age 6 to 17 (equals the number of children ever born if only children age 6 to 17 are present in the household).
FERTMIX	Dummy variable: = 1 if there are children present who are both under 6 and between 6 and 17, 0 o/w
FERTNO	Dummy variable: = 1 if no children
Other variables	
FAGE	Wife's age.
AGESQ	Wife's age squared.
DIVORCE	Dummy variable: = 0 if current marriage is first marriage and = 1 if at least one previous marriage ended in divorce.

Table 5. Logit Results For the Whole-Sample Estimation

Variable	*Coefficient*	*Significance Level*
ONE	−5.21020	0.00000
TOTDIV	−0.000000612	0.96204
OTHRINC	−0.000016223	0.32662
OTHRWAGE	−0.000010116	0.01439
INCASP	−0.000028779	0.00000
FAGE	0.127498	0.00009
FEDUC	0.306664	0.00000
FAGESQ	−0.00173987	0.00000
FAGEED	−0.00225530	0.11986
FERTBIG	0.0301981	0.26508
FERTLIT	−0.906607	0.00000
FERTMIX	−1.32511	0.00000
FERTNO	0.778558	0.00000
DIVORCE	0.127162	0.19245

		Predicted	
Actual		0	1
	0	2484	767
	1	1148	1567

Log-Likelihood	−3565.7
Restricted Log-L (Slopes = 0)	−4111.2
Chi-Squared	1091.0
Degrees of Freedom	13
Significance Level	0.32173E−13

tion (FEDUC = 14), the age at which labor force participation is highest is 26.5. Labor force participation is also positively linked to education. In this context, the age and education interaction term indicates that the impact of education on labor force participation is less pronounced the older the woman. This may be due to the fact that the further in the past the education, the less important the influence of a given level of education on potential wages.

The fertility variables indicate that small children are strong negative influences on labor force participation. In contrast, children over age six in the household do not have this pronounced negative effect. If anything, the results suggest that, as expected, the more children over age six in the household, the greater the propensity to be in the labor force. The DIVORCE variable is positive as hypothesized, but not significant.

Turning to the income variables, the coefficients to TOTDIV and OTHRINC have negative signs, but neither is statistically significant. OTHRWAGE is negative and significant, as expected. The relative income measure, INCASP, is also negative and very significant. Its magnitude is substantially larger than the coefficient estimates for OTHRWAGE, TOTDIV and OTHRINC. Clearly, even controlling for absolute levels of non-wife earned income and other family income, income aspirations, as captured by INCASP, play an important role in wives' labor force participation decisions.[15]

To appreciate better the magnitude of the coefficient estimated in the first column of Table 5, we can consider the impact of a change in a given independent variable on the probability of a wife's entering the labor force. When each right hand side variable is measured at its mean, the probability that the wife is in the labor force is .449. If OTHRWAGE is one standard deviation below its mean, this probability increases to .480. If instead, INCASP is one standard deviation below its mean, this probability increases to .516. Thus, consistent with the magnitude of their respective coefficient estimates, income aspirations appear as important as the absolute levels of income in influencing wives' labor force participation rates.

There are several statistical concerns with the estimation of the basic model. One of the biggest concerns is that our measure of family income aspirations, INCASP, does not measure such aspirations perfectly. Clearly, INCASP is a proxy measure and contains measurement error. Elster and Kamlet (1988) perform a variety of diagnostics and corrective measures to deal with the measurement error in INCASP. They find that accounting for measurement error does not fundamentally alter any of the substantive conclusions from the basic logit analysis. The reader is referred to that work for a more detailed discussion of the issue.

A second statistical issue is a specification issue. The basic specification does not distinguish between the influence on a wife's labor force participation of a husband's "permanent" and "transitory" income. Again, Elster and Kamlet (1988) address this issue and conclude that the substantive conclusions from the basic estimation remain valid when this distinction is taken into account.

Two remaining statistical issues have to do with simultaneity effects. The basic specification employed here considers fertility decisions and husband's income to be exogenous. These factors are assumed to influence a wife's decision to enter the work force, but not conversely. A recent analysis by Mroz (1987) examining the link between fertility and labor force participation decisions, fails to find any simultaneity bias. Nonetheless, these may be productive areas of future investigation.

Analysis By Husband's Occupation Groups

With the results of the logit estimation for the whole sample as backdrop, we now turn to the question of the stability of the results across occupational and age groupings. Consistent with the analysis of Section IV, we divide our sample first into three socioeconomic classes based on the husband's broad occupational grouping: professionals, technical and managerial workers (Skilled White Collar); sales, clerical and service workers (Lower White Collar); and craft, operative and laboring workers (Blue Collar). These results are reported in Table 6.

First, we examine base rate of participation across groups—a rate that would indicate whether substantial differences are immediately apparent. We do this by considering a woman with values for each variable equal to the mean for that variable in the sample as a whole. Such a representative individual has a probability of .46 of being in the labor force if she is from a Skilled White Collar family. This probability is .49 from a Lower White Collar family and .45 from a Blue Collar family. These differences are not very large and an underlying similarity across broad occupational groups, controlling for the various influences incorporated in the specification, is suggested. Thus, the differences in base rate level of participation across social groups observed in Section IV can be largely explained by the variables which are controlled for in this Section.

Next, we will focus specifically on the size and significance of the explanatory variables across the three groups. Looking first at the income and income aspiration variables, several differences among occupational groupings are immediately apparent. Other family wage income (OTHRWAGE) has a significant negative coefficient for wives of Skilled White Collar workers, while there is no statistically significant effect of this variable for wives of Lower White Collar or Blue Collar workers.

This result lends itself to either of two interpretations. It may be that Lower White Collar and Blue Collar families are more influenced by income aspirations (compared to nominal income) than Skilled White Collar workers. Or, all of the groups may be influenced to a similar degree by income aspirations but our measure, INCASP, is a less accurate measure for Skilled White Collar families. It is likely, for example, that Skilled White Collar workers are more mobile than other workers; as a result, such workers would be less likely to have enough tenure in a job to make a comparison of income over a longer period of time a reasonable estimate of income aspirations. Without a reasonable estimate for income aspirations, much of its effect is likely to be picked up by the variable measuring the family's actual wage income (OTHRWAGE). In either case, the results indicate an important difference across groups, either in the impact of income aspirations on women's labor force participation decisions or a difference in how these aspirations are determined.

Turning to the variables for age and education (FAGE and FEDUC, FAGESQ and FAGEED), the same basic pattern is reflected for all three groups. The older the woman, the greater the probability that she is in the labor force (controlling for other factors) up to a certain age. After this age, the older the women the less likely she is to be in the labor force. Higher education is associated with higher probability of labor force participation but this effect is dampened the older the woman.

Within this basic pattern, however, there are some reasonably large differences among groups. Education has less of an impact on Skilled White Collar families and the impact of that education is dampened more quickly by age in this group.

Table 6. Logit Results by Husband's Occupation Group

Variable	Professional, Technical, and Managerial Husbands	Sales, Clerical, and Service Husbands	Blue Collar Husbands
INTERCEPT	−3.90472	−9.30020	−6.52012
	(0.03865)	(0.00014)	(0.00002)
TOTDIV	−0.000006	0.000014	−0.0000256
	(0.71624)	(0.62117)	(0.46486)
OTHRINC	−0.000018	0.000008	−0.0000315
	(0.60466)	(0.84667)	(0.18586)
OTHRWAGE	−0.000029	0.0000004	−0.0000008
	(0.00060)	(0.97164)	(0.89008)
INCASP	−0.000004	−0.0000393	−0.0000471
	(0.65760)	(0.00150)	(0.00000)
FAGE	0.078913	0.291754	0.143429
	(0.23045)	(0.00033)	(0.00283)
FEDUC	0.261699	0.448076	0.425502
	(0.01215)	(0.00225)	(0.00001)
FAGESQ	−0.0012234	−0.0030403	−0.0015848
	(0.06388)	(0.00010)	(0.00026)
FAGEED	−0.0008583	−0.0063287	−0.0047618
	(0.73696)	(0.07381)	(0.04093)
FERTBIG	0.0642537	−0.0058947	0.0175032
	(0.22708)	(0.93119)	(0.62752)
FERTLIT	−0.973817	−0.654184	−0.982582
	(0.00000)	(0.00033)	(0.00000)
FERTMIX	−1.05420	−1.53072	−1.41404
	(0.00002)	(0.00000)	(0.00000)
FERTNO	0.923488	0.672752	0.707956
	(0.00001)	(0.01423)	(0.00000)
DIVORCE	−0.015821	−0.108103	0.236231
	(0.94135)	(0.63369)	(0.06066)

	Predicted		*Predicted*		*Predicted*	
Actual	0	1	0	1	0	1
Total	790	795	494	488	2284	1115
0	533	236	331	171	1595	385
1	257	559	163	317	689	730

Log-Likelihood	−933.74	−601.02	−2009.8
Restricted (Slopes = 0) Log-L.	−1097.9	−680.42	−2309.5
Chi-Squared	328.40	158.80	599.44
Degrees of Freedom	13	13	13
Sign. Level	0.32173E−13	0.32173E−13	0.32173E−13

Note: Standard error is in parentheses.

Controlling for education, consider a woman with a high school education. For Skilled White Collar families, age exerts a negative influence on labor force participation after the age of 27. The threshold age after which labor force participation diminishes is higher for Lower White Collar workers, at 33 years of age. The threshold is lower for Blue Collar workers, at 24 years of age. For a woman of age 40 with a high school education, the impact of another year of age on the dependent variable is −.031 for Skilled White Collar, −.046 for Lower White Collar, and −.052 for Blue Collar. Thus, age appears to have a stronger negative impact on wives' labor force participation for Blue Collar families. Age begins to have a negative influence at an earlier age (24 versus 27 and 33 for the other two groups) and by age 40 has a negative influence which is over 50 percent more pronounced than for Skilled White Collar families.

The lower significance of education in increasing the probability of labor force participation for wives of white collar workers than for wives of blue collar workers seems initially to be counterintuitive. However, we can hypothesize that women who choose to marry white collar workers make investments in their education (or come from families who made investments in their education) with less of a purely employment objective than is true in blue collar families. It has been common, particularly among the better off, to attend college as much for its contributions to maturation as for its employment dividends. Additionally, among such social groups, extended social and employment contacts make job search somewhat easier (Granovetter, 1984). For these groups, education, although important, may not be intended primarily to gain employment, or may not be the only means of securing employment. Alternatively, for women in social groups with fewer financial and job search resources, an investment in education is likely to be made with specific employment goals in mind. For such groups higher education is likely to significantly increase the probability of employment.

Turning to the fertility and previous divorce variables, the impact of children is quite similar across all groups. Having children under six years of age (FERTLIT or FERTMIX) significantly decreases, and having no children (FERTNO) significantly increases the probability of participation for wives across all groups. On the other hand, the previous divorce variable differs in its influence across groups. For Blue Collar families, a previous divorce has a significant positive influence on the probability of the wife working, although this is not the case for either white collar category.

There are several ways to interpret the divorce finding. It may be that wives of blue collar workers experience a heightened "economic vulnerability" relative to other wives following a divorce, which would increase the probability of market work in a subsequent marriage. For example, a Blue Collar husband in a previous marriage[16] may have been unable to lend financial support following divorce; or, because the wife lacked work experience, job skills or education, labor force entry was difficult. In either case, it may not be unreasonable to expect such a wife to be in the labor force in a subsequent marriage to prevent the recurrence of financial difficulty, particularly since labor market reentry is costly.

Alternatively, if values, norms and attitudes tend to be more traditional among blue collar families, we can imagine a scenario in which a previous divorce places a woman in an unfavorable light within her community. Perhaps taking one step outside the boundaries of accepted social group behavior (i.e., the divorce), makes it easier to make others, such as choosing, as a woman in a subsequent marriage, to work.

In summary, there is substantial stability across the broad occupational groupings in the base levels of participation and in the influences on wives' labor force participation decisions of the fertility variables. Closer examination of the results, however, does indicate some important differences across groups:

1. Income aspirations, as we have measured them, play an important role for wives of Lower White Collar and Blue Collar husbands but not for wives of Skilled White Collar workers.
2. Education is a less important influence on labor market participation for wives of Skilled White Collar husbands than for wives of Lower White Collar or Blue Collar workers.
3. Age has a weaker positive impact and/or a stronger negative impact on labor force participation for wives of Blue Collar husbands.
4. Previous divorce has a larger impact on labor force participation for wives of Blue Collar husbands.

Analysis by Husband's Age Group

Having examined the influences on wives' labor force participation by broad occupational classification, we now examine possible difference across age groups. As in Section IV, we divide the sample into two groups, one in which the husband is between ages 20 and 35 and the other in which the husband is between ages 36 and 60. The former group includes those born in 1945 or later, and therefore encompasses the entire "baby boom" generation. Characteristics associated with this age group (for example, shared aspirations, cultural experiences, economic conditions) would presumably be reflected in differences between this group and the older age group. In order to eliminate the effects on wives' participation of a retired husband, those families in which the husbands were over 60 years old were excluded from the sample. The results of running logit specifications for these two groups are reported in Table 7.

Turning first to our income and income aspiration variables, we see that although family wage income (OTHRWAGE) has an important and negative influence on the probability of labor force participation for wives in the younger group, it has a smaller and less significant influence on participation in the older

Table 7. Logit Results by Husband's Age Group

Variable	*Husband age 20–35* *Coefficient*	*Husband age 36–60* *Coefficient*
INTERCEPT	−9.27049	−6.40942
	(0.00541)	(0.00059)
TOTDIV	0.000059	−0.000006
	(0.19623)	(0.67578)
OTHRINC	−0.000040	−0.000002
	(0.32707)	(0.91147)
OTHRWAGE	−0.000043	−0.000007
	(0.00164)	(0.12901)
INCASP	0.000002	−0.000032
	(0.87164)	(0.00000)
FAGE	0.443361	0.176150
	(0.00560)	(0.00333)
FEDUC	0.321142	0.296632
	(0.12016)	(0.00575)
FAGESQ	−0.006533	−0.002173
	(0.00429)	(0.00011)
FAGEED	−0.003401	−0.002122
	(0.63587)	(0.36314)
FERTBIG	−0.082714	0.004157
	(0.37611)	(0.89255)
FERTLIT	−0.929832	−0.841729
	(0.00000)	(0.00000)
FERTMIX	−1.64491	−0.982849
	(0.00000)	(0.00000)
FERTNO	1.01597	0.526063
	(0.00000)	(0.00019)
DIVORCE	0.011082	0.193707
	(0.95438)	(0.09001)

		Predicted			*Predicted*		
Actual		0	1	Total	0	1	Total
Total		1197	1005	2202	2506	1258	3764
	0	893	238	1131	1639	481	2120
	1	304	767	1071	867	777	1644

Log-Likelihood	−1152.0	−2395.4
Restricted (Slopes = 0) Log-L.	−1525.5	−2578.8
Chi-Squared	746.97	366.87
Degrees of Freedom	13	13
Significance Level	0.32173E−13	0.32173E−13

Note: Standard error is in parentheses.

group. Conversely, the income aspiration measure (INCASP) significantly reduces the probability of labor force participation for wives in the older group, it has no effect on wives in the younger group. This result is analogous to that of the prior section, where income aspirations were found to be a more important influence, compared to nominal income, for Lower White Collar and Blue Collar families than for Skilled White Collar families. Here, younger families are more influenced by nominal income than income aspirations relative to older families.

Again, this result is consistent with two possible explanations. It may be that younger families are less influenced by income aspirations than older families. Or, it may be that young families are influenced by income aspirations, but that these aspirations are not formed in the same way as those of older families. This latter explanation has particular appeal given that younger workers are less likely to have sufficient tenure in a job to allow over-time comparisons of income to be a realistic measure of their income aspirations, as assumed in our construction of INCASP.

The age variables are somewhat difficult to compare, because the partitioning of groups is so closely related to the wife's age. The importance of wife's education (FEDUC) is similar for both groups (although FEDUC is not significant at conventional levels for the younger group).

Young children affect both groups similarly, with the negative impact on participation probability of having children both under and over six years of age (FERTMIX) being more pronounced for the younger group. Although having no children significantly increases the probability of participation for wives in both groups, the coefficient estimate for FERTNO in the younger group is twice the size of the estimate in the older group. This may be because many women married to younger husbands (who themselves are likely to be in the 20–35 age group) do not have children intentionally in order to pursue employment.

Finally, previous divorce increases the probability of participation only for wives of husbands 36 to 60 years old. We might hypothesize that a divorced woman married to an older husband is likely to have divorced as an older woman herself. For such women, chances may be higher that they did not work in the previous marriage or that they experienced some labor force interruption. Both conditions (especially if added to limited skills) would have made her labor market entry following divorce more difficult.[17] For this reason, an older woman may be more likely than a younger woman to be financially vulnerable following divorce, and so may be more likely to continue working as a kind of insurance in a current marriage.

As with the partitioning of the sample by occupation groups, the partitioning by husbands' age reveals a similar overall pattern of influences on wives' labor force participation rates. At the same time, closer examination reveals some meaningful differences:

1. Income aspirations are a more important influence on the labor force participation of wives of older husbands.

2. Having no children exerts a stronger positive influence on the probability of labor force participation for wives of younger husbands than for wives of older husbands.
3. Having had a previous divorce exerts a more positive influence on the probability of labor force participation for wives of older husbands than for wives of younger husbands.

Analysis by Husband's Age and Occupation Group

Our final set of empirical results stratifies the sample by combining occupation and age groupings. Because the sample sizes become substantially smaller within each category, we necessarily lose some information regarding the coefficient estimates. Despite the smaller sample sizes, however, we are able to refine some of our previous conclusions by identifying the specific source—age or occupation—of our previous findings.

The previous analyses, reported separately for occupation and age groups, suggested that there were important differences across the groups in the impact of income aspirations, education, and divorce. Table 8 indicates that there is a somewhat more complex pattern in the impacts of these variables than was discernible in the earlier results.

Turning first to the impact of income aspirations, our earlier results indicate that income aspirations, as we have measured them, play a more important role for Lower White Collar and Blue Collar families than for Skilled White Collar families. Additionally, income aspirations appear to increase the probability of wives' labor force participation to a greater extent for older families than for younger families. Table 8 enables us to focus this finding somewhat. For three of the six groups, income aspirations (INCASP) have a pronounced impact on wives' labor force participation decisions: older Lower White Collar families, and both young and old Blue Collar families. For the other three groups, INCASP is not a significant influence.

In an admittedly ex post analysis, we will try, as in the earlier sections, to propose possible reasons for the observed patterns. In constructing our relative income measure, INCASP, we suppose that individuals look to the prior experience of workers in a given occupation and industry in the formation of their "wage" reference group. The measure then, requires accepting a key assumption: namely, that the individual has information regarding the wage income of individuals in similar occupations and industries 10 years previously.

Common sense suggests that there are two primary ways in which such wage information is accessible. First, the individual may have substantial tenure in an industry and occupation and, therefore, have first-hand information about the wages of coworkers (see Hall, 1982, for data on job tenure). Second, wage information—past and present—may be readily available in the form of public

Table 8. Logit Results by Husband's Age and Occupation Group

	Skilled White Collar		*Lower White Collar*		*Blue Collar*	
Age	*20–35*	*36–60*	*20–35*	*36–60*	*20–35*	*36–60*
INTERCEPT	−1.18610	−0.568073	−12.2976	−6.72569	−17.5580	−10.6524
	(0.85964)	(0.87233)	(0.13555)	(0.16766)	(0.00082)	(0.00033)
TOTDIV	0.0000310	−0.0000076	0.0001861	−0.0000036	−0.0002315	−0.0000135
	(0.63782)	(0.64706)	(0.12681)	(0.90775)	(0.11652)	(0.69083)
OTHRINC	0.0000612	−0.0000304	−0.0001440	0.0000515	−0.0001022	0.0000008
	(0.42640)	(0.44700)	(0.22856)	(0.33524)	(0.06090)	(0.97682)
OTHRWAGE	−0.0000350	−0.0000301	−0.0000743	0.0000081	−0.0000071	0.0000010
	(0.16788)	(0.00097)	(0.05684)	(0.43392)	(0.77633)	(0.86668)
INCASP	0.0000035	−0.0000035	0.0000322	−0.0000485	−0.0000445	−0.0000496
	(0.89428)	(0.72289)	(0.42098)	(0.00042)	(0.08226)	(0.00000)
FAGE	0.0836754	−0.0678000	0.649208	0.188076	0.734373	0.308660
	(0.78278)	(0.57134)	(0.14212)	(0.22491)	(0.00241)	(0.00047)
FEDUC	−0.0980518	0.254115	0.233227	0.366092	0.889581	0.457823
	(0.79728)	(0.16124)	(0.65316)	(0.18087)	(0.00717)	(0.01283)
FAGESQ	−0.0040788	0.0003655	−0.0094591	−0.0020049	−0.0074325	−0.0031419
	(0.26940)	(0.75136)	(0.22345)	(0.15265)	(0.01419)	(0.00003)
FAGEED	0.0112269	−0.0007363	0.0009257	−0.0049668	−0.0230169	−0.0052704
	(0.39539)	(0.85259)	(0.95951)	(0.39591)	(0.04786)	(0.18327)
FERTBIG	−0.103787	0.0820441	−0.187629	0.0019260	−0.0735132	−0.0370578
	(0.59819)	(0.17267)	(0.45472)	(0.98022)	(0.53816)	(0.36992)
FERTLIT	−1.09933	−0.972488	−0.950358	−0.352612	−0.928307	−1.12520
	(0.00007)	(0.00109)	(0.00169)	(0.24051)	(0.00000)	(0.00016)

(*continued*)

Table 8. (Continued)

	Skilled White Collar				Lower White Collar				Blue Collar			
Age	*20–35*		*36–60*		*20–35*		*36–60*		*20–35*		*36–60*	
FERTMIX	−1.55017		−0.702110		−2.36353		−1.11958		−1.60278		−1.09050	
	(0.00063)		(0.04071)		(0.00005)		(0.00860)		(0.00000)		(0.00001)	
FERTNO	0.958924		0.900502		0.832275		0.590859		1.11202		0.272839	
	(0.01817)		(0.00089)		(0.11647)		(0.08789)		(0.00004)		(0.15599)	
DIVORCE	−0.397689		0.0790212		−0.169636		−0.128200		0.198000		0.309021	
	(0.33113)		(0.76125)		(0.72007)		(0.63012)		(0.43523)		(0.03551)	
	Predicted		*Predicted*		*Predicted*		*Predicted*		*Predicted*		*Predicted*	
Actual	0	1	0	1	0	1	0	1	0	1	0	1
Total	254	350	537	444	153	175	364	290	787	483	1526	603
0	185	75	349	160	115	41	232	114	596	119	1016	249
1	69	275	188	284	38	134	132	176	191	364	510	354
Log-Likelihood	−309.23		−619.05		−168.14		−422.75		−657.22		−1332.2	
Restricted Log-L (Slopes = 0)	−412.80		−679.28		−226.96		−452.21		−870.19		−1437.7	
Chi-Squared	207.13		120.46		117.65		58.92		425.94		211.02	
Degrees of Freedom	13											
Significance Level	0.32173E–13											

Note: Standard error is in parentheses.

wage contracts in the unionized sectors. Both are plausible explanations for the importance of INCASP to older Blue Collar and Lower White Collar workers, and also to Blue Collar workers generally, who in Pittsburgh are largely unionized.

The availability of wage information, however, presumes an interest on the part of the individual in obtaining it. If a husband in our sample had no intentions of remaining in the same occupation and/or industry over any length of time, presumably such information would be less important. We might expect this to be the case for young Lower White Collar workers, because such positions are a major source of entry-level employment. Similarly, those employed in highly mobile positions, typical of Skilled White Collar occupations for both age groups, are less likely to have either long-term tenure in an industry or occupation or interest in obtaining wage information from coworkers.

Our explanations clearly assume that were the desire for wage information or more stable job tenure present, Skilled White Collar workers and young Lower White Collar workers would have demonstrated similarly significant income aspirations. While these explanations seem to us intuitively appealing, we cannot rule out the possibility that the measure is simply not an accurate depiction of the process by which Skilled White Collar and young Lower White Collar families form income aspirations. Nevertheless, regardless of the explanation, the findings do indicate that there are differences across these social groups in the impact of this important variable on wives' market work.

Interpreting the education and divorce findings is much more straightforward and consistent with our discussions in earlier sections. Previously we saw that education was a more important influence on labor force participation for wives of Blue Collar and older workers than for those in other groups. These findings are consistent with those of Table 8, which indicates that education is very significant for wives of both younger and older Blue Collar workers.

Finally, for reasons primarily focusing on financial vulnerability, we found in Tables 6 and 7 that previous divorce among wives of older workers and wives of blue collar workers significantly increased their probability of participation. Consistent with these findings, Table 8 shows that wives of older Blue Collar workers are significantly more likely to perform market work than are wives of other workers.

VII. CONCLUSIONS

At first, one is struck by the similarity in the broad pattern of determinants of married women's labor force participation decisions across social groups. The labor force participation probabilities of wives of husbands in both age and occupation groups respond similarly to fertility choices, with young children being a strong negative influence and older children or no children a positive influence. In addition, we see similar positive responses to wife's age and education. Finally, controlling for the explanatory variables in our empirical specification, there is substantial similarity across groups in the base level participation probabilities.

Close examination reveals that these broad similarities are only part of the picture. There are substantial and important differences across groups in such influences as education, past marital history, and income aspirations. Moreover, our final age by occupation table indicates that age cohort alone does not, as has been suggested (see, for example, Gerson, 1985, cited earlier), explain the increasing labor force participation of married women, or likely, of women in general.

Our findings may be summarized as follows:

1. Income aspirations, as we have measured them, play an important role for wives of older Lower White Collar and Blue Collar husbands but not for wives of Skilled White Collar workers.
2. Education is a less important influence on labor market participation for wives of Skilled White Collar husbands than for wives of Lower White Collar or Blue Collar husbands.
3. Age has a weaker positive impact and/or a stronger negative impact on labor force participation for wives of Blue Collar husbands.
4. Having no children exerts a stronger positive influence on the probability of a wife's labor force participation for wives of younger husbands than for wives of older husbands.
5. Previous divorce has the largest impact on labor force participation of wives married to older Blue Collar workers.

Because our purpose here, being more exploratory, was not to rigorously test hypotheses regarding social group differences, the explanations for our results are indirect. It seems reasonable to point to differences in job characteristics, such as stability, tenure or mobility, to understand group responses to income aspirations. Likewise, economic vulnerability and social pressures may help to explain our divorce findings. More direct evidence, however, awaits more structured research.

Nevertheless, this work clearly indicates that social groups *do* matter. This conclusion is at variance with the perspective adopted in economic research on women's labor force participation that, controlling for traditional variables, differences across individuals are purely random, without systematic relation to social class. In fact, it appears that differences among individuals are systematically related to both age and occupational group.

Our conclusions also shed light on the role of attitudes and social norms on wives' labor force participation decisions. As we have indicated, this has been a central issue in the sociological literature on wives' labor force participation. Our results indicate that individuals' response to particular influences—for example, education, age, past marital history, fertility, and income aspirations—differs across social groups. It would seem to follow almost definitionally from this that there are differences in attitudes and norms that are related to social group and that influence married women's labor force participation behavior. Although this conclusion is indirect, it seems hard to refute, at least if the terms "attitudes" and "social norms" are used in any general sense. Moreover, it is not clear how concerns with causality between attitudes and behavior can explain this conclusion away.

A variety of further research may be recommended. The social groups used here are extremely broad constructions; larger samples would enable finer occupation and perhaps also industry distinctions. In addition, our data were confined to married couple families residing in the Pittsburgh labor market. There are many ways in which Pittsburgh differs from other major metropolitan areas. For our purposes, however, its relative homogeneity—an over-representation of blue collar workers and fairly pervasive traditional cultural values—may serve to "dampen" distinctions among social groups. Although this characteristic served to strengthen our results, differences among social groups, and the reasons for such differences, may be more easily discernible using a larger and more diverse data set.

NOTES

1. Married women's labor force participation rates were 14.7% in 1940 and 54.2% in 1985 (an increase of 269%); comparable rates for all women were 27.4% in 1940 and 54.5% in 1985.

2. Of those who worked in 1985, half worked full time.

3. Nevertheless, wages, and wages acting through reduced fertility, account for only about 60% of the increase in married women's labor supply since 1950 and provide an even more incomplete explanation for above-average growth rates on female labor force participation during the 1970–1980 decade when wage growth was below normal (see Smith & Ward, 1985, p. S90, footnote 28; see also Fuchs, 1983, p. 132).

4. It should be noted that there is disagreement concerning the effect of cohort size on wages. Although many agree that cohort size has a wage-depressing effect (see, for example, Berger 1985; Welch, 1979), others find economic conditions of the period the more salient explanation (see England & Farkas, 1986).

5. Counties included in the 1980 definition of th SMSA are: Allegheny, Beaver, Washington, and Westmoreland.

6. Race is an important variable in the study of female labor supply (see Hoffman, 1982). Nonwhite women have historically higher labor force participation rates across the life-cycle and do not reduce their work rates with childbirth to the same extent as white women. Bowen and Finegan (1969) hypothesize that this may be a protective response to above average rates of marital dissolution in black families, or it may be that an extended family structure makes market work possible even when young children are present. Questor and Green (1985), however, show that black and white women's behavior has been converging in this regard in recent years, particularly since 1980.

7. 1970 data were drawn from the Census' 1970 Five Percent Public-Use Microdata Sample for

the Pittsburgh SMSA. Because occupations were recoded to match the Standard Occupational Classification (SOC) issued in 1977 by the Office of Federal Statistical Policy and Standards, we constructed new codes so that occupations in 1970 and 1980 could be compared (see U.S. Department of Commerce, 1980, P.K–30). All variables measured in dollars have been adjusted for inflation using the Consumer Price Index and are reported in 1980 dollars.

8. In an important exception, Smith and Ward (1985) use 1980 Current Population Survey data. However, most other econometric studies using recent data contain limited populations of married women or a narrowly defined labor supply subtopic. For example, Berger (1983) uses the 1978 Current Population Survey; his study has limited use for our purposes, however, as it focuses on the effect of disability on 35 to 64 year old spouses' labor force participation; Shapiro and Shaw (1982) use the 1978 National Longitudinal Survey, but examine only the labor supply of 30 to 34 year old wives. Leuthold (1985) uses the 1980 Michigan Survey of Income Dynamics, but examines statistical problems posed by including taxes in models of labor supply.

9. Several authors have demonstrated that significant sample selection biases result from including in analyses only working women, or assigning nonworking women a wage of zero (Heckman, 1974; Heckman & Willis, 1977; Schultz, 1980). Such biases have been addressed by formulating equations to estimate the potential market wage of those women who are not working. Heckman (1974) postulated that a married woman has both an offered wage (market wage) and an asking wage (home wage of "shadow price of her time"). Her asking wage reflects the value to her family of her home work. As such, she will not work until her offered wage equals her asking wage. Using this perspective, he developed a model to estimate the potential wage for working and nonworking married women that corrects the selection bias (Heckman & Willis, 1977; Schultz, 1980).

10. In addition to education, a wife's wage is also likely to be related to her labor market experience. Work experience is hypothesized as influencing labor force participation because, in most occupations, increasing job tenure is associated with greater skill and greater wages. Furthermore, withdrawal from the labor force entails potential future wage losses associated with deteriorating human capital (Mincer & Ofek, 1982). The importance of work experience may also indicate that there are significant start-up costs associated with working (job search costs, clothing costs, child care searches, and others), and therefore a desire to avoid withdrawal and reentry into the labor market (Heckman & Willis, 1977; Nakamura & Nakamura, 1985). Unfortunately, although the census recorded the year last worked by a respondent, no information was collected on the *extent* of previous labor market experience, and so a measure of experience was necessarily excluded from our empirical model.

11. FERTBIG and FERTLIT estimate the number of children in the household conditional on there being no younger/older children using the Census variable giving the total number of children ever born. Although there will be errors in families in which there are both children under 6 and over 17 (with none in between) and in families in which some children have died, we believe FERTBIG and FERTLIT are reasonable estimates of the joint impact of both the age and number of children in the household.

12. Unfortunately, the census excludes questions on household income tax payments. Ideally, some accounting of the impact of tax rates on household income would be included as other researchers have demonstrated the importance of taxes on labor supply (see, for example, Arrufat & Zabalza, 1986; Leuthold, 1984, 1985; Rosen, 1976; Stelcner & Breslaw, 1985).

13. All income information reported in both the 1980 and 1970 censuses refers to incomes in 1979 and 1969, respectively.

14. Incomes are measured in 1980 dollars.

15. We also ran an analysis in which we examined whether the impact of INCASP on labor force participation is symmetric for positive and negative values. This allowed for the possibility of "threshold" effects, where income aspirations are a more important influence on labor force participation if the family falls short of its aspirations than if it exceeds its aspirations. We found,

however, that the impact of INCASP is quite similar for negative and positive values, with the difference not being close to statistical significance.

16. Here we have to assume that a woman is likely to choose marriage partners from among similar social groups over time. In other words, if she married a blue collar worker in her current marriage (recorded in our data set), she was likely to have married a blue collar worker in her previous marriage.

17. It is possible that the woman held a job during her previous marriage. The divorce may have heightened her need for the income in that job; however, this would be a similar predicament for both the wife of a 20–35 or a 36–60 year old husband, and would, therefore not help us to explain the differences observed in the data.

REFERENCES

Alwin, D. F. (1987, February). Distributive justice and satisfaction with material well-being. *American Sociological Review, 52*(1).

Ando, A., & Modigliani, F. (1963, March). The life cycle hypothesis of saving: Aggregate implications and tests. *American Economic Review, 53*.

Arrufat, J. L., & Zabalza, A. (1986, June). Female labor supply with taxation, random preferences, and optimization errors. *Econometrica, 54*(1).

Berger, M. C. (1983, September). Labor supply and spouse's health: The effect of illness, disability, and mortality. *Social Science Quarterly, 64*(3).

———. (1985). The effect of cohort size on earnings growth: A reexamination of the evidence. *Journal of Political Economy, 93*(3).

Bowen, W. G., & Finegan, T. A. (1969). *The economics of labor force participation*. Princeton, NJ: Princeton University Press.

Brickman, P. & Campbell, D. T. (1971). "Hedonic relativism and planning the good society" in M. H. Appley (ed.), *Adaptation-Level Theory: A Symposium*. New York: Academic Press.

Cain, G. G. (1966). *Married women in the labor force*. Chicago: University of Chicago Press.

Centers, R. (1949). *The psychology of social class*. Princeton, NJ: Princeton University Press.

Duesenberry, J. S. (1949). *Income, saving, and the theory of consumer behavior*. Cambridge, MA: Harvard University Press.

Easterlin, R. (1961). The American baby boom in historical perspective. *American Economic Review, 51*.

———. (1968). *Population, labor force and long swings in economic growth*. New York: Columbia University Press.

———. (1978). What will 1984 be like? Socioeconomic implications of recent twists in age structure. *Demography, 15*(4).

———. (1980). *Birth and fortune: The impact of numbers on personal welfare*. New York: Basic.

Elder, G. H., Jr. (1974). *Children of the depression: Social change in life experience*. Chicago: University of Chicago Press.

Elster, S. & Kamlet, M. S. (1988, January). *Income aspirations and married women's labor force participation* (Working paper 88–16). Carnegie Mellon University, School of Urban and Public Affairs Working Paper Series.

England, P. & Farkas, G. (1986). *Households, employment, and gender: A social, economic, and demographic view*. New York: Aldine.

Feinstein, K. W. (1983). *Home work or market work: Time allocation decisions among married women with children under three*. Doctoral Dissertation, Brandeis University.

Ferber, M. (1982). Labor market participation of young married women: Causes and effects. *Journal of Marriage and the Family, 44*.

Freedman, D. S., & Thornton, A, (1982, February). Income and fertility: The elusive relationship. *Demography, 19*(1).

Friedman, M. (1957). *A theory of the consumption function*. Princeton: Princeton University Press for National Bureau of Economic Research.

Fuchs, V. R. (1983). *How we live*. Cambridge, MA: Harvard University Press.

Gerson, K. (1985). *Hard choices: How women decide about work, career, and motherhood*. Berkeley, CA: University of California Press.

Granovetter, M. S. (1974). *Getting a job: A study of contact and careers*. Cambridge, MA: Harvard University Press.

Gronau, R. (1973, March–April). The effect of children on the housewife's value of time. *Journal of Political Economy, 81*, (2, part 2).

Hall, R. E. (1982, September) The importance of lifetime jobs in the U.S. economy. *American Economic Review, 72*(4).

Hayghe, H. (1986, February). Rise in mothers' labor force activity includes those with infants. *Monthly Labor Review*.

Heckman, J. J. (1974, July). Shadow prices, market wages, and labor supply. *Econometrica, 42*(4).

Heckman, J. J., Killingsworth, M. R., & MaCurdy, T. (1981, September). *The economics of the labour market*. Proceedings of a Conference on the Labour Market, sponsored by Her Majesty's Treasury, The Department of Employment and the Manpower Services Commission, at Magdalen College, Oxford. London: Her Majesty's Stationary Office.

Heckman, J. J., & Willis, R. J. (1977). A beta-logistic model for the analysis of sequential labor force participation by married women. *Journal of Political Economy, 85*(1).

Hoffman, E. P. (1982, Summer). Comparative labor supply of black and white women. *The Review of Black Political Economy, 11*(4).

Jackman, M. R., & Jackman, R. W. (1983). *Class awareness in the United States*. Berkeley, CA: University of California Press.

Johnson, N. E. & Lean, S. (1985). "Relative income, race, and fertility." *Population Studies, 39*.

Johnson, W. R., & Skinner, J. (1986, June). Labor supply and marital separation. *American Economic Review*.

Leuthold, J. H. (1984, October). Income splitting and women's labor force participation. *Industrial and Labor Relations Review, 38*(1).

———. (1985). Labor supply with and endogenous tax rate. *Public Finance, 40*(1).

Merton, R. K., & Rossi, A. K. (1968). Contributions to the theory of reference group behavior. In H. H. Hyman, & E. Singer (Eds.), *Readings in reference group theory and research*. New York: Free Press.

Messick, D. M., & Thorngate, W. B. (1967, January). Relative gain maximization in experimental games. *Journal of Experimental Social Psychology, 3*(1).

Mincer, J. (1962). Labor force participation of married women: A study of labor supply. In *Aspects of labor economics*. Princeton: Princeton University Press.

Mincer, J. & Ofek, H. (1982). Interrupted work careers: Depreciation and restoration of human capital. *Journal of Human Resources, 17*(1).

Molm, L. D. (1978, Autumn). Sex role attitudes and employment of married women: The direction of causality. *Sociological Quarterly, 19*.

Mroz, T. A. (1987, July). The sensitivity of an empirical model of married women's hours of work to economic and statistical assumptions. *Econometrica*, 55(4).

Nakamura, A. & Nakamura, M. (1985). *The second paycheck: A socioeconomic analysis of earnings*. New York: Academic Press.

Oppenheimer, V. K. (1976, September–December). The easterlin hypothesis: Another aspect of the echo to consider. *Population and Development Review, 2*.

Questor, A. O., & Greene, W. H. (1985). The labor market experience of black and white wives in the sixties and seventies. *Social Science Quarterly, 66*.

Rosen, H. S. (1976, May). Taxes in a labor supply model with joint wage-hours determination. *Econometrica*.

Runciman, W. G. (1968). Problems of research on relative deprivation. In H. H. Hyman, & E. Singer (Eds.), *Readings in reference group theory and research*. New York: Free Press.

Schultz, T. P. (1980). Estimating labor supply functions for married women. In J. P. Smith (Ed.), *Female labor supply: Theory and estimation*. Princeton, NJ: Princeton University Press.

Shapiro, D. & Shaw, L. B. (1982). Labor force attachment of married women age 30 to 34: An intercohort comparison. In *The Employment Revolution: Young American Women in the 1970s*. Cambridge, MA: MIT Press.

Smith, J. P., & Ward, M. P. (1985, January). Time-series growth in the female labor force. *Journal of Labor Economics, 3*(1, Pt. 2).

Smith, R. E. (Ed.). (1979). *The subtle revolution: women at work*. Washington, DC: The Urban Institute.

Stelcner, M. & Breslaw, J. (1985, April). Income taxes and the labor supply of married women in Quebec. *Southern Economic Journal, 51*(4).

Stolzenberg, R. M., & Waite, L. J. (1984, May). Local labor markets, children and labor force participation of wives. *Demography, 21*(2).

Strumpel, B. (1972). Economic life-styles, values, and subjective welfare: An empirical approach. In E. B. Sheldon (Ed.), *Family economic behavior, problems and prospects*. Philadelphia, PA: Lippincott.

Sweet, J. A. (1973). *Women in the labor force*. New York: Seminar Press.

United States Department of Commerce, Bureau of the Census. (1972, April). *Census of population and housing* (Public use samples of basic records from the 1970 Census, description and technical documentation). Washington, DC: U.S. Government Printing Office.

———. 1980. Census of population and housing. Washington, DC: U.S. Government Printing Office.

———. (1983). *Census of population and housing, 1980* (Public-use microdata samples, technical documentation). Washington, DC: U.S. Government Printing Office.

———. (1986). *Statistical abstract of the United States*. Washington, DC: U.S. Government Printing Office.

Welch, F. (1979). Effects of cohort size on earnings: The baby boom babies' financial bust. *Journal of Political Economy, 87*(5 Pt 2).

GENDER DIFFERENCES IN THE EFFECTS OF MENTAL HEALTH ON LABOR FORCE PARTICIPATION

John Mullahy and Jody Sindelar

I. INTRODUCTION AND RESEARCH DESIGN

Although female labor force participation decisions have received a tremendous amount of attention from economists (see, for example, Smith, 1980), mental health is a potentially important aspect of both female and male labor supply that has been largely overlooked. We propose that there exist important relationships among mental health, the quantity and quality of human capital, and labor supply decisions. These linkages have not been quantified in the past. Thus, the directions and magnitudes of the interconnections are not well understood. In this paper we analyze these relationships.

There are only a few economic studies of the effects of mental illness and labor market decisions (see, for example, Bartel & Taubman, 1979, 1986; Benham & Benham, 1982) and these produce some conflicting results. Lack of data has severely restricted empirical analysis of mental health and labor markets. However, a new survey both assesses the prevalence of psychiatric disorders in the

Research in Human Capital and Development, Vol. 6, pages 125–146.

ISBN: 1-55938-032-2

community and obtains data on labor force participation, allowing us to examine the effects of mental health, as well as other factors, on labor supply.

The Epidemiological Catchment Area (ECA) data set contains information from a large survey conducted in five sites, one of which is the New Haven, Connecticut metropolitan area (see Eaton & Kessler, 1985, for an overview). Information on socioeconomic, demographic, and mental health variables was gathered in the early 1980s. Mental health status is assessed through both professional as well as self-reported evaluations of mental disorders. Age of onset of symptoms and last symptom are recorded for those who ever are diagnosed as having a disorder. Thus, this data set provides a unique combination of data on both labor supply and a variety of measures of mental health. In addition, as it is a community-based survey, it avoids estimation problems introduced by sampling from only those who use mental health services, previously the typical source of individual-level mental health data.

II. FACTS ABOUT MENTAL HEALTH

In the past little was known about even the overall prevalence of specific mental health disorders, much less their prevalence cross-categorized by demographic characteristics. Statistics on prevalence were typically determined from clinical data and the populations surveyed were too small to assess prevalence in subpopulations. This lack of community-based data consequently limited our knowledge of the economic and demographic consequences of poor mental health.

The Epidemiological Catchment Area community surveys were conducted in five sites: Baltimore, Los Angeles, New Haven, the Piedmont area of North Carolina, and St. Louis. From these, researchers have been able to develop reasonably precise estimates of the prevalence of mental disorders in the United States by subpopulations. For example, Table 1 shows the percentage of the population having each of several disorders. We display the overall six-month prevalence of disorder, that is, the percentage of the population manifesting any symptoms of disorder during the six-month interval (as defined by the third edition of the *Diagnostic and Statistical Manual of Mental Disorders (DSM-III)*). For the nation, the six-month prevalence is estimated to be approximately 18.7%. Table 2 shows that lifetime prevalence rates are higher, estimated to be from 28.8% to 38%, depending on location. The two most common disorders are anxiety disorders, broadly defined, at approximately 8% of the population and substance abuse (which includes alcohol and drug abuse) at more than 6% of the population.

The ECA surveys have shown that prevalence rates vary considerably by gender and age. Females in all age categories are more likely than males to suffer from phobias. The second most prevalent disorder for females varies by age as follows: 18–24, substance abuse; 25–44, depression; 45–64, dysthymia; and

Table 1. Six-Month Prevalence of DIS/DSM-III Disorders for an Estimated Percent of U.S. Civilian Population, Based on 1980 U.S. Census and Three ECA Sites[1]

Disorder	*Estimated U.S. Population Aged 18 or Older (%)*
Any disorder	18.7
Any disorder except phobia	14.4
Any disorder except substance abuse	14.0
Substance abuse disorders	6.4
Alcohol abuse/dependence	5.0
Drug Abuse/dependence	2.0
Schizophrenic/Schizophreniform	1.0
Schizophrenia	0.9
Schizophreniform	0.1
Affective disorders	6.0
Manic episode	0.7
Major depressive episode	3.1
Dysthymia (Depressive neurosis)	3.2
Anxiety/somatoform disorders	8.3
Phobia	7.0
Panic	0.8
Obsessive compulsive	1.5
Somatization[2]	0.1
Antisocial personality	0.9
Cognitive impairment (severe)	1.0

Notes: 1. The three ECA sites were not chosen to be a representative sample of the United States, so the study results cannot be used to estimate precisely the number of Americans afflicted. However, by projecting the data and standardizing the rates to the 1980 Census on the basis of age, sex and race, an approach is provided for those who wish to make projections to the total population.

2. Somotoform disorders are characterized by complaints of physical symptoms suggesting a physical disorder and medical care is sought, but for which there is no demonstrable or known organic or physiological basis, typically has early onset, and is chronic but fluctuating (DSM-III). One percent of women are measured as being somatoform, but incidence among males is nil. (Some forms of somatization were previously called hysteria.)

Source: National Institute of Mental Health (1985).

65+, cognitive impairment. Males suffer most from alcohol abuse in all age categories except the elderly, for whom cognitive impairment is the most frequent mental problem. Phobias are the next most common disorder for men of all age categories except the youngest, in which drug abuse ranks second.

Despite the widespread prevalence of mental disorders, only a small percentage of those afflicted use medical care to treat the mental problem. Like the illnesses themselves, the use of medical care to treat psychiatric disorders also differs by gender. Women tend to seek professional care more frequently than

Table 2. Comparison of Total Prevalence of DIS/DSM-III Psychiatric Disorders by Time Period

Site	*Time Period and Rate (%)* 6-month	*Lifetime*
New Haven, CT	18.4	28.8
Baltimore, MD	23.4	38.0
St. Louis, MO	16.8	31.0

Source: National Institute of Mental Health (1985).

men in both the general medical sector (see Sindelar, 1982) and the mental health specialty sector (Leaf and Bruce, 1987). It is estimated that in 1980–1981, only 19.5% of those with a disorder visited a mental health care provider, including general medical care providers as well as mental health specialists. Only 12.4% of those diagnosed to have mental disorders visited mental health specialists.

The previous paucity of community data combined with the elusive nature of the etiology of the disorders leaves much uncertainty. The uncertainty surrounding mental disorders means that information that economists might like to use to model the causes and consequences of mental illness has been uncovered by neither social scientists nor clinicians. This clearly deters precise modeling of causes and effects, or structural modeling. Instead, empirical analysis at this stage is largely exploratory, suggesting that empirical analysis must be conducted through reduced form rather than structural estimation.

III. CONCEPTUAL FRAMEWORK

The role of mental health in labor supply and other decisions can be examined in a utility maximizing model, following Becker (1965) and Grossman (1972). The mental health of an individual may, depending on the disorder, affect all aspects of an individual's opportunity set, trade-offs, time preference, and therefore, choices. In a static environment, the model is one in which individuals maximize utility subject to a full income constraint by choosing quantities of goods and allocating time between market and household production. The mental health of an individual can affect full income in several ways. Mental disorders can reduce the total time available through time lost due to mental incapacity and also due to time taken in the treatment of disorders. Nonwage income may also be affected by mental health. The effect could occur in several different ways. Poor mental health in the past could have retarded earnings capacity and hence savings. Furthermore, poor mental health could reduce the ability to invest wisely. Poor mental health could furthermore affect marital status and/or labor force participation and the earning power of spouse and thus could affect the individual's nonwage income. On the other hand, to the extent that poor mental health generates governmental transfers, poor mental health could result in higher nonwage income, ceteris paribus.

Mental illness can also affect an individual's value of time both at home and in the market. Individuals in poor mental health may be less efficient in production and consumption. Although the value of time at home and in the market can be adversely affected by a disorder, it is likely that the effects may be felt differentially across market and nonmarket time (e.g., alcoholism is said to affect the family first, then the work place). The relative effect cannot be predicted a priori. It must be determined empirically. Even the reduced time available (due to days lost) can affect both the demand for "leisure" and the demand for goods and services. The net effect cannot be predicted on a priori grounds.

The relative effects on market versus nonmarket time are apt to vary by disorder; for example, mania can make an individual more productive at work during manic spells, while depression is likely to reduce market productivity. Furthermore, and of particular interest for our purposes, the labor market effects of mental health may vary by gender. Not only do men and women differ in the prevalence of disorders, as noted above, but they are also likely to differ in their response to disorder (e.g., females typically use more medical care than males), as well as to other factors (number of children, nonwage income, and so on).

In the context of a dynamic or lifetime maximizing model, the timing of the onset, as well as the persistence of the disorder relative to the timing of decisions becomes important. For example, early onset of a disorder could prevent educational achievement that might otherwise occur. The same holds true for marriage and fertility decisions. Even after recovery or treatment of symptoms, the early onset may have a lasting affect by reducing the stock of accumulated human and monetary capital as well as family stability. Alternatively, onset after education has been completed, occupation has been established, and a family has been developed may, in some circumstances, have less impact on the course of an individual's life.

The mental health of the individual could also affect life-cycle behavior through the actual, or at least perceived, rate of time preference. An extremely unstable individual, for example, may have a greater preference for current consumption than the average healthy individual. Thus, the dynamic aspects of the relationships between mental disorders and behavior are likely to be important. In particular the choices of goods and time allocation will depend on previous mental disorders as well as current mental health.

In a household utility maximizing model, the budget constraint can be extended to incorporate family members' time and nonwage assets. Mental disorders could affect how other family members allocate their time; for example, another member could work more hours in the labor force to compensate for lost wages or increased medical expenses and/or could spend more time providing care for the affected individual (see Parsons, 1977). Alternatively, time could be "lost" due to family conflict, resulting in fewer family resources to allocate and, consequently, a lower standard of family living, ceteris paribus. Moreover, family composition and household resources could be affected by either spouse having a mental disorder. For example, mental health disorder could result in divorce, fewer births, or children moving away from home early because of marital conflict.

IV. DATA

The data used in this analysis come from Wave I of the New Haven site of National Institute of Mental Health's Epidemiological Catchment Area survey of noninstitutionalized individuals. The survey was designed to assess the prevalence, incidence, and duration of mental disorders by demographic and socioeconomic variables. Individuals 18 years old and older are surveyed across three waves in New Haven. Interviews with 5,034 individuals were completed between 1980 and 1981 in Wave I, with a 77.6% completion rate. The New Haven SMSA was (approximately) the catchment area sampled. This area comprises 13 towns with a total adult population of 420,000. Two coordinate groups were sampled: (1) all adults (18+), and (2) individuals 65 and over. Households were randomly selected for interviews using electric utility billing address lists. One adult within each household was then selected randomly as the respondent. Then, all those 65 years old and older in the households were sampled, in addition to a supplementary sample of the elderly. Because this analysis focuses on current labor market behavior, the estimation samples are based on the 2,458 individuals who in Wave I were aged 18 to 64 years.

The ECA data set is a unique data source for analyzing labor supply issues in mental health. It is a large sample that combines information on labor market participation and income with medically sophisticated measures of mental health. This enables research of issues that previously could not be explored with either such a large sample or with reasonable assessment of the mental health states or both. Information was also gathered on socioeconomic and demographic variables, and self-rated physical and mental health, among other variables.

A major strength of this data set is that the sample is community based and assessment of mental health disorder is conducted by a professionally designed survey instrument, the Diagnostic Survey Instrument (DIS). This avoids both the self-reporting problem as well as the self-selection problem, in which only individuals who seek mental health care can be determined to have mental health disorders. Objective psychiatric-based assessment of disorders has not been previously available in data sets that are community based; mental health has typically been assessed only by self-reported means in large data sets.

V. ESTIMATION

Because the ECA data set, like most data sets, does not allow us to observe nonmarket value of time as well as market wages, we follow the long-standing tradition in such cases and specify a reduced-form model of the labor force participation. Our objective here is estimation of the decision whether to participate full time in the labor market. We use a binary indicator of whether the individual is employed in a full-time job ("WORKS") at the survey date as our indicator of labor force participation. This outcome is specified as a function of those socioeconomic and demographic variables (e.g., education, number of children) that affect value of time at home and at work. In addition, following the discussion in Section III, we specify the labor force participation equation as a function also of both current and previous mental health status.

Under the assumption that the binary "WORKS" responses are generated by independent latent normal variates, we estimate the following equation using the maximum likelihood probit estimation technique:

$$\text{WORKS}_{it} = a_o + X_{it}a_l + MH_{it}b_1 + MH_{it-N}b_2 + PH_{it}b_3 + e_{it}$$

where: X_{it} is a vector of exogenous socioeconomic characteristics described below, for individual i at time t;
MH_{it} and MH_{it-n} are, respectively, vectors of current and lagged mental health measures for individual i;
PH_{it} is a vector of physical health measures for individual i at time t;
the a and b are unknown coefficient vectors to be estimated;
and the e_{it} distributed $N(0,1)$, are the stochastic components that could include, among other things, unmeasured aspects of mental health, e.g., those who have a disorder that is not included in our set of disorders; those who have a mental health problem, but one which is not severe enough to be quantified; interactions among mental health disorders; and variations in severity. Obviously, the error term can also incorporate other unmeasured aspects of the decision to participate.

Dependent Variables

Our measure of current employment, WORKS, is a binary measure of current full-time employment that equals one if the individual gives a "working now" response to the question "When was the last time you worked full-time for pay?" and equals zero if this response is either "never worked full-time for pay" or "once worked full-time for pay" but did not do so at the time of the Wave-I interview. As we use the distinction of works/not works instead of the distinction "in the labor force" or not, we believe that we are more likely to find significant effects of disorder. This is because the definition of being in the labor force includes not only the currently working, but most of those searching for work but not currently employed. If disorders are likely to result in problems in securing and maintaining employment, then those with disorders in the labor force are likely to be in the unemployed category. Our "works" variable is synonymous with being employed. As it is employment that yields income and hence enhances well-being, we believe that this is the most appropriate definition for our purposes. Note that we eliminate full-time students from the sample even if they have a job, as working would not likely be their main activity.

Independent Variables

Mental Health

Self-reported. Self-reported mental health status is included as a set of control variables. Self-reported physical health status has been found in previous studies to be correlated with objective measures of health. We use measures of self-reported mental health with the expectation that they will correspond to the individual's assessment of his or her mental health. Individuals' perceptions of their mental health status may be a good indicator of how their health status affects their behavior. Controlling for psychiatric diagnoses, self-reported mental health status may indicate severity of disorder. It also may pick up some effects of other mental disorders that we do not control for. Accordingly, we use self-reported mental health status alone and in conjunction with psychiatric based measures.

Disorders. The ECA data set contains professionally-based measures of mental disorders. Diagnoses are made using the current state of the art in this area, the Diagnostic Interview Schedule (DIS). The DIS is a highly-structured interview designed to match the criteria defined by the American Psychiatric Association (APA, 1980) for mental disorders. Lay interviewers administer questionnaires designed on the basis of the DIS. The information that they elicit on signs and symptoms is used to generate diagnoses according to criteria specified in the APA's *DSM-III*. Furthermore, the questionnaire is designed to determine not only current disorders, but also age of onset of the symptoms associated with the disorders.

Signs and symptoms are classified into 12 specific disorders: somatization, panic disorders, phobias, depression, mania, schizophrenia, anorexia, alcohol dependence, drug abuse, obsessive behavior, compulsive behavior, and antisocial behavior. Of these, we select six representative and important disorders to examine in the present analysis. The six categories and their codes are:

1. Substance abuse (drug and alcohol) (ALCOHOL);
2. Depression (DEPRESS);
3. Manic-depressive behavior (MANIA);
4. Obsessive-compulsive behavior (OBSCOM);
5. Schizophrenia (SCHIZO); and
6. Anti-social personality (ANTISOC)

We create two sets of variables based on these categories. The first set contains binary variables on whether individuals who ever met the criteria for diagnosis of the disorder had symptoms from the illness during the 12 months preceding the survey. We use the observation of a disorder in the last year as an indication of a "current" disorder. The second includes measures of duration derived from the age of the first onset of symptoms, measured as the number of years since the onset of the first symptom associated with the disorders. The first set of variables is named according to the six codes described above, while for the second set we attach a prefix "Y" to the same codes to indicate that the variable is measured as years since the individual had the first symptom associated with this disorder. Note that as onset of symptoms is recorded for those that ever met the criteria for diagnoses of disorders, we do not know how many years they actually had a disorder. Furthermore, for the "recovered" or "in remission" individuals, we do not know exactly when they recovered, so our measure of "duration" introduces some ambiguity.

The first panel of Table 3 presents the sample frequency distribution of individuals' disorder counts, that is, the number of the six current-period disorders affecting each individual. Four is the maximum number of current disorders that affects any individual. The frequency distributions for women and men are remarkably similar although the disorder compositions differ considerably by sex. This is seen in greater detail in the second panel of Table 3. The matrix entries are the sample current-period disorder frequencies on the diagonals and the disorder cross-frequencies, or "comorbidities," on the off-diagonals. The male–female differences in both morbidity and comorbidity are compelling. Women's relatively high rate of depression is also seen to correspond with a relatively high rate of comorbidities with depression. For men, conversely, the key morbidities and comorbidities largely involve antisocial personality and alcohol abuse.

Table 4 presents by disorder what we term the sample remission or recovery rates, meaning, the numbers of individuals who have had a given disorder in the past but who do not currently manifest the disorder. The data in Table 4 are the counts of individuals in the sample showing remission or recovery and, in parentheses, the percentage of those ever having the disorder who do not currently show the disorder. Fairly similar tendencies are witnessed for men and women, with mania in both instances having the lowest remission rate.

In assessing the relationships between mental health and economic behavior,

Table 3. Sample Frequency Distribution of Mental Disorders

Count of Current Disorders

	Women			Men		
Number of Disorders	*(N = 985)*	*Percent*	*Percent with a Disorder*	*(N = 756)*	*Percent*	*Percent with a Disorder*
0	851	(86.4)		645	(85.3)	
1+	134	(13.6)		111	(14.6)	
1	105	(10.7)		86	(11.4)	
2	23	(2.3)	(17.2)	20	(2.6)	(18.0)
3	4	(0.4)	(3.0)	3	(0.4)	(2.7)
4	2	(0.2)	(1.5)	2	(0.3)	(1.8)

Morbidity and Comorbidity Frequencies: Current Disorders

	ANTISOC	*ALCOHOL*	*DEPRESS*	*MANIA*	*OBSCOM*	*SCHIZO*
Women						
ANTISOC	11	1	3	1	1	1
ALCOHOL	1	31	6	2	1	2
DEPRESS	3	6	76	9	7	6
MANIA	1	2	9	13	1	3
OBSCOM	1	1	7	1	21	3
SCHIZO	1	2	6	3	3	19
Men						
ANTISOC	26	12	2	2	2	2
ALCOHOL	12	73	6	0	1	0
DEPRESS	2	6	21	4	3	1
MANIA	2	0	4	8	2	2
OBSCOM	2	1	3	2	10	2
SCHIZO	2	0	1	2	2	5

the strengths of the ECA's measures of mental health disorders are many. As discussed previously, they are: (1) inclusion in the data set and diagnosis of disorder are not contingent on using medical care; (2) measurement of disorder is based on accepted current APA criteria, not simply self-reported; and (3) timing and duration measures are available for disorder.

However, some caveats should be considered. First, current disorder and age of onset are determined from self-reported responses to questions. An individual's response and recall may be biased, especially as related to disorder and perhaps to age. Second, severity is not measured. Severity can vary within each category of disorder (e.g., depression can vary in severity) and across disorders (e.g., schizophrenia is typically more severe than antisocial personality). Note, however, that self-reported mental health may control for severity given that a disorder has been diagnosed by the DIS. Furthermore, because we allow for

Table 4. Sample Remission or Recovery Counts and Rates by Disorder

	Females (N = 985)		*Males (N = 756)*	
Disorder	*Counts*[a]	*Rates*[b] *(%)*	*Counts*[a]	*Rates*[b] *(%)*
ANTISOC	9	(.450)	41	(.612)
ALCOHOL	31	(.508)	79	(.523)
DEPRESS	54	(.423)	21	(.513)
MANIA	5	(.293)	1	(.111)
OBSCOM	9	(.499)	5	(.501)
SCHIZO	10	(.357)	4	(.445)

Notes: [a] Counts refers to women (men) showing signs of remission/recovery.
[b] Rates refers to the percentage having the disorder who do not currently show the disorder.

separate coefficients by disorder, differences in severity across disorders can appear in estimation. Finally, for some disorders, preliminary analyses have shown relatively low correlation between disorders as measured by the DIS and psychiatrists' assessments of these disorders. (See Anthony, Folstein, & Romonosk, 1985). However, individual psychiatric assessment is not necessarily the benchmark against which to gauge the ability of a variable to measure the effect on labor market behavior; self-reported status, for example, may be related to behavior. Furthermore, some of the disorders measured in the ECA data, especially alcoholism, have a high correlation with psychiatrists' assessments.

Physical Health and Other Covariates

We also include self-reported measures (excellent, good, fair) of overall physical health status as control variables (poor health is the omitted category). In addition to the mental and physical health status measures, the other independent variables (i.e., the *X*) included in the various specifications are:

- an intercept;
- NONWAGE[1] (the greater of household income minus personal income [in $k] or zero);
- AGE (age in years);
- QAGE (AGE squared);
- ED (years of completed schooling);
- KIDS0005 (=1 if children aged 0–5 are at home; =0 else);
- KIDS0617 (=1 if children aged 6–17 are at home; =0 else);
- MARRIED (=1 if presently married; =0 else); and
- WHITE (=0 if nonwhite; =1 if white).

Descriptive Statics: Men versus Women

The means and standard deviations of the variables are presented in Table 5. The estimation sample consists of 1,741 observations on 985 women and 756 men. In our estimation sample, on average, women as compared to men: are less likely to be employed; have a higher nonwage income; are slightly less likely to be married; and are similar in mean education and race. Men are slightly more likely to rate themselves as being in excellent physical and mental health than are women, and are three times more likely to suffer from antisocial behavior and alcohol abuse. On the other hand, women are more apt to suffer from depression,

Table 5. Means of Variables for Women and Men

	Mean	
Variable	*Women*	*Men*
WORKS	.491	.857
NONWAGE	15.385	6.409
AGE	39.185	39.918
QAGE	1698.3	1767.6
ED	12.840	13.332
KIDS0005	.249	.192
KIDS0617	.390	.336
MARRIED	.547	.671
WHITE	.810	.862
EXCLMH	.376	.466
GOODMH	.479	.427
FAIRMH	.123	.090
ANTISOC	.011	.034
ALCOHOL	.031	.097
DEPRESS	.077	.028
MANIA	.013	.011
OBSCOM	.021	.013
SCHIZO	.019	.007
YANISOC	.437	1.197
YALCOHOL	.585	2.921
YDEPRESS	1.421	.646
YMANIA	.171	.188
YOBSCOM	.356	.159
YSCHIZO	.409	.120
EXCLPH	.455	.536
GOODPH	.399	.354
FAIRPH	.112	.082
OBSERVATIONS	985	756

obsessive–compulsive behavior, and schizophrenia. The sexes have similar prevalence rates for mania.

VI. RESULTS

For both women and men we estimate models of "WORKS" that are increasingly general in their specification of the health status covariate vectors. Because the models are nested, we are able to conduct straightforward likelihood ratio tests to determine whether incremental refinements of the health status measures contribute significant explanatory power to the models.

For these purposes, it is helpful to define four mutually exclusively subsets of explanatory variables.

1. Economic variables standardly used in labor force analyses: INTERCEPT, NONWAGE, AGE, QAGE, ED, KIDS0005, KIDS0617 MARRIED, WHITE.
2. Self-reported mental health variables: EXCLMH, GOODMH, FAIRMH.
3. Diagnosed mental health variables: ANTISOC, ALCOHOL, DEPRESS, MANIA, OBSCOM, SCHIZO, YANTISOC, YALCOHOL, YDEPRESS, YMANIA, YOBSCOM, YSCHIZO.
4. Self-reported physical health variables: EXCLPH, GOODPH, FAIRPH.

The first specification we estimate is a model of labor force participation that includes only the economic variables conventionally used. This specification is interesting in its own right and also because it enables us to compare results from the ECA data with estimates of similar labor force models obtained using other data sets. Moreover, we use the estimates from this specification as a guide to whether women's and men's labor force participation ought to be estimated separately. In results not reported here, we estimated the standard economic model using the pooled sample of women and men. We compared these pooled results to those reported in column 1 of Tables 6 and 7, which report the estimates of this specification based on separate samples of women and men, respectively. The likelihood ratio statistic for the test of the null hypothesis that the coefficient vectors are identical for women and men has an asymptotic chi-square distribution with nine degrees of freedom. The test statistic of 261.12 compared with a .01 critical value of 23.32, suggests compellingly that the structures of the WORKS models differ significantly by gender. This is consistent with previous analyses that have shown men and women to have significantly different responses to labor market variables. Based on other studies, we expect men and women to behave differently with regard to health variables as well (Sindelar, 1982). Accordingly, we estimate all further specifications on separate samples of women and men.

Table 6. Results for Women: Alternative Specifications
(t-statistics in parentheses)

Variables	*1*	*2*	*3*	*4*
INTERCEPT	−1.60874	−3.08029	−2.96813	−3.38204
	(−2.95300)	(−4.39500)	(−4.11200)	(−4.44900)
NONWAGE	−0.0116638	−0.0119184	−0.0119184	−0.012152
	(−3.94600)	(−4.01100)	(−3.99300)	(−4.04500)
AGE	0.0541637	0.0675669	0.0752387	0.0881988
	(1.98400)	(2.43700)	(2.65000)	(3.04600)
QAGE	−0.00085109	−0.00101302	−0.0011108	−0.0012404
	(−2.60100)	(−3.04800)	(−3.26300)	(−3.57700)
ED	0.128287	0.118975	0.119858	0.105048
	(7.12400)	(6.44700)	(6.35300)	(5.38500)
KIDS0005	−1.10581	−1.10529	−1.1223	−1.12619
	(−9.48100)	(−9.40900)	(−9.41300)	(−9.39200)
KIDS0617	−0.311778	−0.333923	−0.347193	−0.391738
	(−3.14000)	(−3.33400)	(−3.41500)	(−3.78500)
MARRIED	−0.255732	−0.283442	−0.307496	−0.362836
	(−2.45800)	(−2.66900)	(−2.83400)	(−3.28400)
WHITE	−0.0264284	−0.0388239	−0.0132054	−0.130372
	(−0.22300)	(−0.32300)	(−0.10800)	(−1.02400)
EXCLMH	—	1.41719	1.19048	0.809447
		(3.42900)	(2.70900)	(1.70300)
GOODMH	—	1.4328	1.20353	0.834914
		(3.48500)	(2.75800)	(1.76700)
FAIRMH	—	1.24781	1.07231	0.916088
		(2.94600)	(2.42500)	(1.92500)
ANTISOC	—	—	0.226005	0.328453
			(0.34200)	(0.48500)
ALCOHOL	—	—	−0.159784	−0.145066
			(−0.55700)	(−0.50100)
DEPRESS	—	—	0.09746	0.0382918
			(0.40800)	(0.15800)
MANIA	—	—	1.03848	0.949232
			(1.63300)	(1.50700)
OBSCOM	—	—	−0.77715	−0.831584
			(−1.90900)	(−1.99300)
SCHIZO	—	—	−0.431518	−0.587413
			(−0.99500)	(−1.32700)
YANTISOC	—	—	−0.00444117	−0.0049556
			(−0.21700)	(−0.23100)
YALCOHOL	—	—	−0.0100955	−0.0122064
			(−0.54600)	(−0.64600)
YDEPRESS	—	—	−0.0106291	−0.00924184
			(−0.86500)	(−0.73400)

Table 6. (*Continued*)

Variables	*1*	*2*	*3*	*4*
YMANIA	—	—	−0.0667554 (−1.70100)	−0.0645872 (−1.65100)
YOBSCOM	—	—	−0.00103669 (−0.07300)	−0.00160636 (−0.10800)
YSCHIZO	—	—	−0.011918 (−0.55900)	−0.00488754 (−0.22800)
EXCLPH	—	—	—	0.94805 (2.96100)
GOODPH	—	—	—	0.876912 (2.77100)
FAIRPH	—	—	—	0.18997 (0.56800)
Log-likelihood	−571.99	−563.32	−555.63	−542.27

We discuss the results of the basic model for men and women in order to create a base from which to compare alternative specifications. As can be seen in column 1 of Table 6, most of the standard economic variables are significant determinants of the probability of working full time for women and are consistent with existing studies. Nonwage income and the presence of children (in both age groups) are negatively and significantly related to the probability of working for women, ceteris paribus. Presence of children 0–5 years old has an effect over three times as large as that for children 6–17 years. Married women are, ceteris paribus, less likely to be working than unmarried women. Educational attainment increases the probability of being employed full time. The age profile is concave, with significant positive linear age effect and significant negative quadratic age effect. As no measure of labor force experience is included, the age variables are likely picking up both pure age effects as well as that part of the experience effect correlated with age. Race is the only one of this set of "standard economic" variables that does not have a significant effect for women.

The corresponding results for men, presented in column 1 of Table 7, reveal a different structure. The effects of nonwage income and children that were so important in the specification of the females WORKS model are not statistically important for men. Unlike women, married men are more likely to work full-time than unmarried men, ceteris paribus. Similar to the results for women, however, are the findings that: higher levels of educational attainment lead to higher probabilities of full-time work; age has a concave profile and both the linear and quadratic effects are significant; and race has no statistically significant effect.

The second specification adds the three self-reported mental health variables to

Table 7. Results for Men: Alternative Specifications
(*t*-statistics in parentheses)

Variables	*1*	*2*	*3*	*4*
INTERCEPT	−2.82632	−3.2269	−3.36466	−3.73647
	(−4.02900)	(−4.09000)	(−3.94300)	(−4.21700)
NONWAGE	−0.00634967	−0.00792967	−0.00585556	−0.00670842
	(−0.92900)	(−1.15300)	(−0.82000)	(−0.93600)
AGE	0.161131	0.158118	0.168829	0.168336
	(4.68700)	(4.56600)	(4.55500)	(4.50300)
QAGE	−0.00218995	−0.00215576	−0.00231152	−0.00224968
	(−5.45400)	(−5.33100)	(−5.38300)	(−5.18500)
ED	0.0698641	0.058304	0.0489942	0.0401912
	(3.114200)	(2.54600)	(2.06600)	(1.66000)
KIDS0005	−0.0770092	−0.0715445	−0.0167858	0.0233073
	(−0.35500)	(−0.32500)	(−0.07100)	(0.09700)
KIDS0617	−0.0864582	−0.100005	−0.0952705	−0.0763358
	(−0.57500)	(−0.65800)	(−0.60600)	(−0.47500)
MARRIED	0.629491	0.591443	0.594873	0.565757
	(4.09300)	(3.79100)	(3.67200)	(3.42600)
WHITE	0.30451	0.273662	0.328206	0.236249
	(1.77800)	(1.57700)	(1.83700)	(1.27700)
EXCLMH	—	0.824095	0.93555	0.469099
		(2.12900)	(2.31700)	(1.05400)
GOODMH	—	0.675069	0.786119	0.418452
		(1.77900)	(1.99100)	(0.97000)
FAIRMH	—	0.296515	0.426805	0.195092
		(0.72800)	(1.00700)	(0.43100)
ANTISOC	—	—	−0.572848	−0.547907
			(−1.67600)	(−1.60200)
ALCOHOL	—	—	0.074052	0.0409569
			(0.27600)	(0.15100)
DEPRESS	—	—	0.0378346	0.132095
			(0.08700)	(0.29200)
MANIA	—	—	−1.00236	−1.18785
			(−1.51100)	(−1.74700)
OBSCOM	—	—	−0.715207	−0.701348
			(−1.10900)	(−1.07400)
SCHIZO	—	—	6.4185	5.95828
			(0.40700)	(0.43400)
YANTISOC	—	—	−0.01197	−0.0097179
			(−1.22700)	(−0.98700)
YALCOHOL	—	—	0.00037403	0.00447141
			(0.03800)	(0.43600)
YDEPRESS	—	—	0.0190579	0.0172668
			(0.94800)	(0.87800)

Table 7. Results for Men: Alternative Specifications

Variables	*1*	*2*	*3*	*4*
YMANIA	—	—	0.0156726 (0.51300)	0.0126605 (0.40000)
YOBSCOM	—	—	0.00582363 (0.11300)	0.0104774 (0.19000)
YSCHIZO	—	—	−0.219417 (−1.30300)	−0.206326 (−1.19600)
EXCLPH	—	—	—	1.04335 (2.91700)
GOODPH	—	—	—	0.812518 (2.36600)
FAIRPH	—	—	—	0.471175 (1.29600)
Log-likelihood	−251.00	−246.33	−234.60	−229.07

the standard economic variables. Results are reported in column 2 of Tables 6 and 7. The omitted category in this set of dummies is poor mental health. For women, the results show that all three measures of self-reported mental health have positive and significant effects on the probability of full-time work. The point coefficient estimates of EXCLMH and GOODMH are of about the same magnitude, and are somewhat larger that the coefficient associated with FAIRMH. The likelihood ratio statistic for the test of the null hypothesis that the three self-reported mental health coefficients are jointly zero, which has a chi-square distribution with three degrees of freedom under the null, is 17.34, which is significant at better than the 99% level.

For men, a similar pattern emerges. The EXCLMH coefficient is positive and significant, and is larger than both the GOODMH and FAIRMH coefficients. Although neither GOODMH nor FAIRMH is significant at conventional levels, the likelihood ratio test of the joint significance of the three self-reported mental health coefficients is 9.34. This is significant at better than the 97% level, suggesting that for males as well as females the self-reported mental health variables are jointly important determinants of the probability of full-time work.

Next we add diagnosed mental health measures, both current and duration measures. These results are reported in column 3 of Tables 6 and 7. For women, with the addition of diagnoses, the self-reported mental health coefficients are all still positive and significant. None of the individual coefficient point estimates for the diagnosed mental illness is significant at conventional levels. Indeed, for women only 3 of the 12 coefficients have t statistics exceeding 1.6: MANIA, YMANIA, and OBSCOM. The likelihood ratio test of the joint significance of the 12 diagnosed mental health coefficients, given that the self-reported mental health variables are included, is not significant at even the 80% level.[2]

The corresponding results for men, presented in column 3 of Table 7, indicate a more important role of diagnosed disorders in labor force decisions. The inclusion of the 12 diagnosed mental illness variables increases the magnitudes and individual significance levels of the 3 self-reported mental health coefficients. Furthermore, the full set of disorders is found to be significant according to the likelihood ratio test of the null hypothesis that all 12 are jointly zero. This test statistic is 23.46, which exceeds the .025 critical level for a chi-square variate with 12 degrees of freedom. That none of the individual coefficients on the disorders is significant at conventional levels suggests that the likelihood ratio test derives its significance from "off-diagonal" effects, that is, comorbidities (see Table 3). The coefficients whose t values exceed unity for men are those associated with ANTISOC, YANTISOC, MANIA, OBSCOM, and YSCHIZO. Note that the MANIA coefficient, which has a positive point estimate for women, is negative for men; the OBSCOM point estimate is negative for both.

Column 4 of Table 6 reports the results for women of the estimates of the full model. This specification includes the standard economic variables, the self-reported and diagnosed mental health variables, and adds the three self-reported physical health variables. The inclusion of the self-reported physical health measures results in a reduction of the magnitude and individual significance of the self-reported mental health coefficients. This suggests some correlation between the two types of self-reported health status evaluations. The point estimates of both the EXCLPH and GOODPH coefficients are positive and significant at standard levels. Jointly, all three physical health measures are significant at better than the 99% level when compared to the model in column 3. Note also that as in column 3, the same three coefficients (MANIA, YMANIA, OBSCOM) have t statistics exceeding unity, while now the OBSCOM coefficient is significant at the 95% level. The coefficient of SCHIZO also now has a t statistic greater than unity.

A similar pattern emerges for men, as can be seen in column 4 of Table 7. Again, the inclusion of the self-reported physical health variables reduces the magnitudes and individual significance levels of the self-reported mental health coefficients, and again the physical health coefficients are jointly significant (this time at slightly less than the 99% level) and each has a positive point estimate. With the exception of YANTISOC, the individual point estimates of the diagnosed mental health coefficients whose t values exceeded unity in column 3 again do so in column 4. The point estimate of the MANIA coefficient is now somewhat more significant and larger in absolute value.

VII. DISCUSSION

The results using only the "standard economic" variables, as discussed above, are similar to findings of other studies. With a few very important exceptions, which we emphasize below, these results are stable across specifications. Thus, we feel that these results portray a meaningful description of the structure of labor force participation.

The addition of health variables was shown to enhance the explanatory power of the equations and adds a new dimension to our understanding of labor market participation. We find that mental and physical health are significant determinants of participation outcomes. Although mental and physical health are important for both men and women, the effects vary by gender. Self-reported mental health is of greater significance and magnitude for women than for men. Conversely, measures of disorders add significant explanatory power for men but not for women. Physical health variables have similar coefficients for women and men. However, as we are estimating probit equations, the coefficients alone do not indicate responsiveness of decisions to variables. To indicate responsiveness, the coefficients must be adjusted by the probability density function associated with the population's participation. As men have a higher participation rate, the adjustment to the coefficient is smaller for men than women (approximately .4 for women and .2 for men, using sample population means). Thus, although the coefficients are similar, women are on average more responsive to perceived physical health than are men.

The addition of health variables has several interesting effects on marital status and education, both of which are important because they are endogenous variables when viewed in a lifetime framework. It is seen that as richer arrays of health status measures are included as explanatory variables, the EDUC coefficient becomes less positive for both women and men. The MARRIED coefficients shrink in absolute value for both sexes, becoming less negative for women and less positive for men. The finding of such changes suggests the presence of nontrivial correlation between education and marital status and the set of health status measures. The change in the EDUC coefficient, for example, suggests that when the health status variables are omitted, education is absorbing some of the effects of health status on labor force participation. Because the education coefficient shrinks toward zero as the health status covariates are included, the exclusion of health variables gives an overestimate of the effects of education on participation. As most of the information on the effects of education on participation comes from empirical studies that exclude health variables, the measured effect of education on labor market outcomes is likely to overestimate the true effect.[3]

The extent and even direction of the bias could vary by gender as the correlation of health and other determinants of labor force participation can vary by gender. Men and women differ in the structure of the relationships that characterize participation decisions, in the prevalence of disorders, and in responsiveness to disorders. For example, our results show that education loses much of its significance for men when health controls are included in the specification. For women, on the other hand, education retains its significance. The percentage change in the responsiveness is greater for men than for women, suggesting that the bias due to the omission of health is greater for men.

We believe that such relationships indicate that despite the plethora of analyses of labor force participation, a key element has been missing. Omission of health variables biases the coefficients of those variables correlated with health. There are reasons to believe that many of the standard economic variables may have such non-zero correlations. One of the challenging research issues is to disentangle the effects of these variates on labor market outcomes. For example, to the extent that disorders having onset in childhood or young adulthood are correlated positively with adults' disorder propensities, it is possible that the correlation between measured educational attainment and current disorders is due at least in part to the correlation between disorders having early onset and ultimate educational attainment. This would imply that adults' measured educational attainment depends structurally on the past history of disorders, and to the extent that these past disorders are imperfectly controlled in statistical analyses, the "pure" relationship between education and outcomes of interest (e.g., labor force participation) will not be identified.[4]

VII. CONCLUSIONS

We have shown that mental health, both self-rated and diagnosed, and physical health have significant effects on labor force participation and these effects vary considerably by gender. Although these measures of health have important impacts on the labor supply decision, such measures are often excluded from models of labor market behavior. Thus we know less about the role of health and labor markets than we should and than we would with increased focus on health and productivity. Our results suggest that the omission of health measures could lead to potentially serious biases resulting, for example, in overestimates of the importance of education. As disorder prevalence and the correlation between health variables and other determinants differ by gender, so will the extent of the bias. Furthermore, based on these findings, we suggest that future analyses of labor market behavior should not only incorporate current health status, but should also trace the structural endogeneity of the effects of mental health status on other determinants of labor market behavior.

NOTES

1. The variable that we call NONWAGE is composed of household income from all sources minus the amount of income "brought in" from all sources by the individual under observation. The category "brought in" by an individual could include a variety of payments in addition to pure earnings, such as unemployment compensation, welfare, alimony, disability payments, return on one's own capital (not family's), and so on. The residual, our NONWAGE, is a proxy for the true nonwage. It excludes some elements of nonwage (e.g., return on own personal capital). As is typical

in such definitions, NONWAGE includes spouse's earnings. While the inclusion of spouse's earnings is the standard way to measure nonwage income from an individual's perspective, it is worth knowing that in the broader family context spouse's labor supply is endogenous to the family decision-making process.

2. In results not reported here, we estimated specifications for women and men that included the standard economic variables, the self-reported mental health variables, and the six diagnosed mental health variables describing current disorder manifestations (ANTISOC, ALCOHOL, DEPRESS, MANIA, OBSCOM, SCHIZO). For women, the addition of these six variables to the specification reported in column 2 of Table 6 did not add significant explanatory power to the model as judged by a likelihood ratio test; moreover, when this specification is compared with the specification reported in column 3, in which all 12 diagnosed mental health measures are included, it is also the case that a likelihood ratio test reveals no statistically significant basis for including the duration measures.

For men, however, a quite different story emerges. The addition of the six current period disorders to the specification in column 2 of Table 7 is significant at better than the 95% level by a likelihood ratio test. In addition, comparing the specification in column 3 with this interim specification, a likelihood ratio test also informs us that the addition of the duration measures to the current period measures is also statistically significant at better than the 95% level.

3. For illustrative purposes, the situation can be viewed as an omitted variable problem in the context of a simple linear model in which disorders are omitted variables. Let e_i be a scalar measure of education, X_i be a *1xk* vector of all other nondisorder covariates, and D_i be a *1xd* vector of disorders. Then with

$$\text{WORKS}_i = ae_i + X_ib + D_ig + E_i$$

and supposing

$$E(E_i) = E(e_iX_i) = 0$$

and that all variables are measured as differences from sample means, then OLS gives

$$E(\hat{a}) = a + \text{cov}(e,D)/\text{var}(e)$$

Since $\text{var}(e) > 0$ and assuming $a > 0$, then the sign of the omitted variable bias depends on the sign of $\text{cov}(e,D_j)$. If all the $\text{cov}(e,D)$ have the same signs as the corresponding g_j, then the bias of â is positive.

4. In recent research we have attempted to parcel out the effects of the endogenous decisions on educational achievement as effected by health by using the ECA data. A set of simultaneous equations with education and marital status as a function of early onset of disorder helps to disentangle the effects of health versus education on participation (Mullahy & Sindelar, 1990).

REFERENCES

American Psychiatric Association. (1980). *Diagnostic and statistical manual of mental disorders* (3rd ed.). Washington, DC: Author.

Anthony, J., Folstein, & Romanosk, A. (1985). Comparisons of lag DIS and a standardized psychiatric diagnosis. *Archives of General Psychiatry, 42*, 667–675.

Bartel, A., & Taubman, P. (1979). Health and labor market success: The role of various diseases. *Review of Economics and Statistics, 61*(1), 1–8.

———. (1986). Some economic and demographic consequences of mental illness. *Journal of Labor Economics, 4*(21), 243–256.

Becker, G. S. (1965). A theory of the allocation of time. *Economic Journal*, *75*, 493–517.

Benham, L., & Benham, A. (1982). Employment, earnings, and psychiatric diagnosis. In V. Fuchs (Ed.), *Economic aspects of health.* Chicago: University of Chicago Press.

Eaton, W., & Kessler, L. (1985). *Epidemiologic methods in psychiatry, the NIMH epidemiologic catchment area program.* New York: Academic Press.

Grossman, M. (1972). *The demand for health: A theoretical and empirical investigation.* New York: Columbia University Press.

Leaf, P. J. & Bruce, M. L. (1987). Gender differences in the use of mental health-related services: A re-examination. *Journal of Health and Social Behavior*, *28*, 171–183.

Mincer, J. (1974). *Schooling, experience, and earnings.* New York: NBER.

Mullahy, J. & Sindelar, J. L. (1990). An ounce of prevention: Productive remedies for alcoholism. *Journal of Policy Analysis and Management*, *9*, 249–253.

National Institute of Mental Health. (1985). *Mental Health, United States, 1985* (DHHS Publication No. ADM 85–1378). Washington, DC: U.S. Government Printing Office.

Parsons, D. O. (1977, September). Health, family structure and labor supply. *American Economic Review, 67*(4).

Sindelar, J. L. (1982). Differential use of medical care by sex. *Journal of Political Economy*, *90*, 1003–1019.

Smith, J. P. (Ed.). (1980) *Female labor supply: Theory and estimation.* Princeton, NJ: Princeton University Press.

CHILD HEALTH AND OTHER DETERMINANTS OF SINGLE MOTHERS' LABOR SUPPLY AND EARNINGS

David S. Salkever

I. INTRODUCTION

With the rise in maternal labor force activity over the past several decades, studies of maternal labor supply have become a staple of the empirical literature in economics and sociology. The great bulk of this research has focused on married women with children, because these women represent a large segment of the population with rapidly increasing labor force participation rates; in contrast, analyses of the labor market experience of nonmarried mothers are much less common.

Recent demographic trends point to the need to adjust this imbalance in the current literature. While the number of women with children under 18 increased by 7.5 percent from 1975 to 1987 (Table 1), the number of these women who were married with their spouse present in the household actually declined by

Research in Human Capital and Development, Vol. 6, pages 147–181.

ISBN: 1-55938-032-2

Table 1. Estimated Population and Labor-Force Participation Rates For Women with Children under 18

	Population (millions)			*Labor-Force Participation Rate*	
	1975	*1987*	*Change (%)*	*1975*	*1987*
All Women	30.8	33.1	7.5	47.4	64.7
With children under 6	14.6	15.8	8.2	39.0	56.7
With children 6 to 17	16.2	17.3	6.8	54.9	72.0
Married Women, Spouse Present	25.7	25.0	−2.7	44.9	63.8
With children under 6	12.3	12.2	−0.8	36.7	56.8
With children 6 to 17	13.4	12.8	−4.5	52.2	70.6
Widowed, Divorced & Separated Women	4.5	5.5	22.2	61.7	73.7
With children under 6	1.8	1.8	0	54.0	62.2
With children 6 to 17	2.7	3.8	40.7	67.9	78.5
Single Women	0.7	2.6	271.4	42.2	54.1
With children under 6	0.6	1.8	200.0	37.0	49.9
With children 6 to 17	0.2	0.8	300.0	61.1	64.1

Note: Population figures shown here were derived by dividing labor force estimates by participation rates. Labor force and population estimates for widowed, divorced, and separated women were computed as the difference in estimates for all married women and married women with spouse present.

Source: U.S. Bureau of Labor Statistics (1988, Tables C–13, C–14).

about 2.7 percent. In contrast, the number of widowed, divorced, and separated women with children under 18 increased by more than 20 percent over this period, while the corresponding number of single women almost quadrupled. Labor force participation rates also rose over this period for all women with children, but the increase tended to be slightly larger for married women with spouses present than for other groups. Additional data for the period 1981 to 1987 reported by the Bureau of Labor Statistics (1988, Table C–15) show a large increase in the number of families maintained by women with children under 18, from 5.9 million to 6.7 million, but only a very small increase in their labor force participation rate from 67.9 to 69.1.

In short, mothers with no spouses present contributed substantially to labor force growth over the last decade and experienced slower growth in labor force participation rates than did mothers with spouses present. Descriptive data and previous research (discussed below) also indicate important differences between these groups in the determinants of labor force activity. Thus, findings from the voluminous literature on the labor supply of married mothers with spouses present may not carry over to their spouse-less counterparts, and a better understanding of the latter's behavior requires that data on their own experiences be studied in detail.

This paper reports on a study of single mothers' labor supply and earnings using data from the Survey of Income and Education (U.S. Department of Commerce, 1978).[1] A particular focus of the analysis is the effects of children's health problems. Statistics from the Health Interview Survey, a national household survey carried out annually by the U.S. Department of Health and Human Services, show that prevalence rates for children's disabilities due to chronic health problems increased sharply during the 1970s and early 1980s (Table 2). Although these overall rates leveled off during the mid-1980s, rates for lower-income groups (into which single mothers would most likely fall) continued to increase. This trend, in conjunction with the increases in numbers of single (i.e., spouse-less) mothers and in maternal labor force participation rates, suggests that the magnitude of the economic impact of child health problems on labor supply for these mothers has grown substantially.[2] Recent studies of married mothers have shown fairly strong negative effects of these problems on maternal work status, hours, and earnings, particularly for mothers in white families (Salkever, 1982a, 1982b). More limited research on single mothers has shown only weak evidence of negative effects on work status, but these findings may have been at

Table 2. Percent of Children Reporting Activity Limitation Due to Chronic Conditions

	Year	*Activity Limitation*	*Limitation in Major Activity*
Age 0 to 16	1967	2.1	1.1
	1981	3.8	2.0
Age 0 to 17	1983	5.1	3.5
	1987	5.0	3.5
Family Income	1983	6.7	5.2
Under $10,000	1987	7.8	5.9
Family Income	1983	5.6	4.0
$10,000–$19,999	1987	5.7	4.3
Family Income	1983	4.5	2.9
$20,000–$34,999	1987	5.0	3.4
Family Income	1983	4.3	2.5
$35,000+	1987	3.7	2.3

Sources: U.S. Department of Health and Human Services (Various years).

least partly due to limited sample sizes. The study described in this paper attempted to verify these findings by examining a much larger and richer data base.

Our discussion begins with a brief review of the literature on single mothers' labor force activity, which serves to point up the major differences between research findings for married and single mothers. In addition, previous results regarding child health effects are reviewed in detail. Subsequent sections of the paper describe the data, methods, and results of our new empirical analyses.

II. PREVIOUS RESEARCH

Some information on the labor supply of single mothers can be found in several types of previous econometric studies, including labor supply studies for female household heads in general, and studies of low-income mothers who are recipients or potential recipients of welfare payments. Generalizations from such studies are hazardous, however, because many female household heads have no children under 18 living with them and because the range of variation of many relevant variables will be truncated in studies restricted to low-income single mothers. One study by Garfinkel and Masters (date) does report regression results based strictly on data for female household heads with children. In this study, significant wage and other income effects (positive and negative, respectively) are reported, which the authors argue are quite similar to findings for married mothers. Note, however, that the regression models from which these results were extracted contained only a limited number of independent variables. In particular, factors such as marital history were not included even though descriptive statistics suggest that mothers who are divorced or separated are much more likely to work than are mothers who are widowed or never married.

Results from several more recent studies indicate that single mothers' labor supply responses to variations in wages and in other income are smaller than those of mothers in two-parent households, but larger than those of male household heads. Robins, West and Stieger (1983) use data from the Seattle and Denver Income Maintenance Experiments to estimate the reduction in labor supply due to the implementation of a negative income tax. Their estimated percentage reduction for husbands ranges from 8.8 to 21.4. For wives and single female household heads the corresponding figures are 22.4 to 29.5 percent and 14.4 to 32.9 percent, respectively. Hausman (1981), using data from the Panel Study on Income Dynamics, reports estimated wage elasticities of labor supply of approximately 0, 0.5 and 1.0 for husbands, female heads with children, and wives, respectively. Other income effects were similar for wives and female heads, while own health effects were smaller but more significant for female heads than for wives. In a study using Current Population Survey data for 1968 and for 1975, Mitchell (1979) estimates labor force participation and hours regressions separately for married women and three categories of single women—never married, divorced, and separated. She does not find consistent differences in wage effects on hours and participation but does report that other income tends to have a larger effect on nonmarried women. Note, however, that she did not restrict her sample to women with children; in fact, many of the nonmarried women in her study had no children under 18 so the applicability of her findings to labor supply behavior of single mothers in particular may be somewhat limited. Lehrer and Nerlove (1982) used data from the 1973 National Survey of Family Growth to study factors affecting the employment status of previously married mothers and of single mothers. Analyses were done separately for the periods preceding the birth of the first child, for the period when at least one child was under age 6, and for the period when all children were age 6 or older. Their results point up a number of differences between mothers with and without spouses present. In particular, they find that the race differential in employment for married mothers generally is not observed in their data; they also note that the increase in maternal employment as the youngest child reaches school age is more pronounced for mothers with spouses present than for other mothers.

Three recent studies have examined child health effects on labor supply of single mothers, although the data bases used in all three studies were not satisfactory in all important respects. In the first of these, Salkever (1980) used data from the 1972 wave of the Panel Study of Income Dynamics to examine maternal work hours and employment status. His results for single mothers indicated that the presence of a disabled child significantly reduces the probability that the child's mother works but has little effect on hours worked for working mothers; however, he cautioned that these findings be viewed as preliminary because his study sample was only 285 mothers, including only 19 with disabled children. In a subsequent study using 1972 data from the U.S. National Health Interview Survey, Salkever (1982b) failed to detect any significant negative effect of children's disabilities on the probability that a mother had worked in the preceding two weeks or the probability that she was "usually working" in the previous year. The effect for white single mothers for the latter probability was much more negative than for nonwhites, but it was not significant at conventional levels. While the sample sizes for this analysis were fairly large, it is nevertheless true that only 60 white and 37 nonwhite mothers with disabled children were included in the data. Moreover, the data base did not contain information on hours or earnings so these aspects of labor market activity could not be examined in the study.

The most recent of the three previous studies, by Breslau, Salkever and Staruch (1982), used data on 186 single mothers (including 91 with a disabled child) from the Cleveland area in 1978 and 1979. In this study there was only weak evidence of a negative child disability effect on the probability that a mother worked; the corresponding effect on hours of work for working mothers was negative with a *t*-value of 1.18. When a severity measure was used instead of a dummy for the presence of a disabled child, only the hours effect becomes slightly stronger (but still not significant). As in the earlier studies, the small numbers of single mothers with disabled children in the data base suggests that the results be treated cautiously.

III. DATA AND MODEL SPECIFICATION

The data base for this study was the Survey of Income and Education (SIE) (see U.S. Department of Commerce, 1978, for information) conducted by the U.S. Bureau of the Census in early 1976. The SIE was administered to a stratified random sample of 151,170 households throughout the United States and included detailed questions about labor market activity, income, sociodemographic characteristics, housing, health insurance, and disabilities of household members. For children age 3 to 4, disability was reported if it limited participation in play activities. For children age 5 to 17 disabilities that limited either participation in play activities or the child's ability to do regular school work were reported. In addition, for children with schoolwork limitations, inability to attend school and the occurrence of frequent absences due to the disability were also coded. For all disabled children age 5 to 17, questions were also asked about the frequency with which the child needed assistance in looking after "personal needs such as eating, dressing, undressing, or personal hygiene," and in going outdoors or getting around outside the house. No disability information was recorded for children under age 3. For adults age 18 to 64, reported disabilities included health problems that limited the kind or amount of market work or work around the house a person was able to do. In addition, limitations on ability to do school work were reported for adults age 18 to 25 who were enrolled in school or "interested in attending school." In all cases, interviewers were instructed to record only limitations due to long-term health problems, rather than acute or temporary conditions (e.g., broken bones).

Our study samples included female-headed households with a single family, at least one child age 17 or less, and no other relatives besides the mother and children. Because of the very large number of households participating in the SIE, only a sample of these households was used for our analyses. More specifically, we drew a 10 percent random sample of households with no disabled children; all households with disabled children were included since these households only comprised a small fraction of all SIE respondents. The resulting study sample for our analyses contained 848 households with disabled children and 546 households with no disabled children. Preliminary tabulations on these households revealed that a high percentage (29.6) of mothers of disabled children were themselves disabled. Because health limitations have a powerful effect on labor force activity, and because only 16.3 percent of mothers with no disabled children reported health limitations, most of the analyses reported below were restricted to the 597 mothers of disabled children and the 457 mothers of nondisabled children who were not disabled themselves.

The dependent and independent variables used in the study are defined in Table 3. Four different measures of labor market activity serve as the dependent variables in the study: a dichotomous indicator of whether or not each mother worked at all in the past year (DHDWORK); hours of work in the past year (HOURS); the logarithm of earnings in the past year (LEARN); and the logarithm of earnings per hour in the past year (LWAGE). Independent variables include indicators of the presence and severity of children's disabilities, numbers of disabled and nondisabled children in various age groups in the household, personal characteristics of the mother that are presumed to affect either her tastes for market work or her wage opportunities, two measures of area labor-market conditions (HDUNEMRT and LOGHAW), and a series of location-specific dummy variables that are included to capture effects of other omitted measures of labor-market conditions, availability of income through transfer-payment programs (e.g., AFDC), and the availability of child care resources. HDUNEMRT and LOGHAW were calculated from data on all adult female SIE respondents. In most instances these variables were defined for the metropolitan area of residence (when this was specifically identified) or for metropolitan and nonmetropolitan regions of each state.[3]

Regressions on employment status (DHDWORK) are estimated with data for all households, and for all households where the mother reports no health limitations. Both OLS and probit techniques are employed. Regressions on HOURS, LEARN, and LWAGE are only estimated for mothers with no health limitations who worked in the past year. These OLS regressions include a selectivity variable ($X1$, $X2$, or $X3$), which was calculated from a probit employment status regression and which corrects for the bias introduced by excluding nonworking mothers from the regressions.[4]

Characteristics of the two study samples are described in Table 4. For most of the independent variables, differences between disabled and nondisabled families are quite small. An obvious exception is HEALTHLM; as we have already noted, maternal disabilities were much more common among mothers of disabled children. The fact that the disabled sample could not include families only having children under the age of 3 also produced some demographic differences between the samples, such as the smaller mean value for KID0T2 and the higher mean value for HEADAGE in the disabled sample. Because the probability of having a disabled child in the family increases with the number of children, and with the age of the children, the much higher mean values for KID5T9, KID10T13, and KID14T17 in the disabled sample were also to be expected. The statistical association between the presence of a disabled child and the family size may also explain the lower education level for mothers in the disabled sample, because education and fertility are negatively related.

Average characteristics of disabled children age 5 to 17 can be computed by

Table 3. Variable Names and Definitions

Name	*Definition*
DUMDIS	= 1, if family has a child with a health problem.
WORK[a]	Number of children limited in schoolwork (but no attendance) by health problems.
CANTABS[a]	Number of children limited in schoolwork and unable to attend regular school or frequently absent because of health problems.
PLAY[a]	Number of children with health problems but not limited in schoolwork or attendance.
USMOB[a]	Number of children usually or occasionally needing assistance in getting around outside the home.
USHELP[a]	Number of children usually or occasionally needing assistance in daily activities.
DIS3T4	Number of children aged 3 to 4 with health problems.
DIS5T9	Number of children aged 5 to 9 with health problems.
DIS10T13	Number of children aged 10 to 13 with health problems.
DIS14T17	Number of children aged 14 to 17 with health problems.
DIS5T17	Number of children aged 5 to 17 with health problems.
NE	= 1, if in New England.
MA	= 1, if in Mid-Atlantic region.
ENC	= 1, if in East North Central region.
WNC	= 1, if in West North Central region.
SA	= 1, if in South Atlantic region.
ESC	= 1, if in East South Central region.
WSC	= 1, if in West South Central region.
M	= 1, if in Mountain region.
BIGSMSA	= 1, if residence is in one of the 20 largest SMSA's.
MEDSMSA	= 1, if residence is in one of the 78 next largest SMSA's.
OTHMETRO	= 1, if identified in SIE as in other SMSA's.
OTHNONM	= 1, if identified in SIE as not in an SMSA
DFARMINC	= 1, if family has income or losses from farming.
CASHDUM	= 1, if family assets in savings accounts, savings bonds, checking accounts, and cash total more than $5000.
DUMSPAN	= 1, if head is of Spanish origin.
DUMALIEN	= 1, if head immigrated to United States since 1970.
HEALTHLM	= 1, if head has any reported health problem.
KID0T2	Number of children 0–2 years.
KID3T4	Number of children 3–4 years.
KID5T9	Number of children 5–9 years.
KID14T17	Number of children 14–17 years.
KID10T13	Number of children 10–13 years.
OWNHOME	= 1, if home is owned or being bought.
HDBLACK	= 1, if head is black.
HDOTHER	= 1, if head is other nonwhite radce.
DIVORCE	= 1, if head is divorced.
SEP	= 1, if head is separated.
NEVER	= 1, if head is never married.
LOGHAW	Logarithm of race-education-area specific wage rate for women.HDUNEMRT Race-area specific unemployment rate for women.
HEADAGE	Head's age (years).

(*continued*)

Table 3. (Continued)

Name	*Definition*
HDAGESQR	Head's age squared.
HDED	Head's years of education.
$X1$	Selectivity variable based on probit work probability regression with DUMDIS
$X2$	Selectivity variable based on probit work probability regression with WORK, CANTABS, USMOB, USHELP, DIS3T4, and DIS5T17.
$X3$	Selectivity variable based on probit work probability regression with CANTABS, USMOB, USHELP, and DIS5T17.
DHDWORK	= 1, if head worked in past year.
HOURS	Head's hours of work in past year.
LWAGE	Logarithm of head's wage, salary, self-employment and farm income per hour in past year.
LEARN	Logarithm of head's wage, self-employment and farm income in past year.

Note: [a]This variable is based on data for disabled children aged 5–17.

dividing the mean values for WORK, CANTABS, PLAY, USMOB and USHELP by the mean value for DIS5T17. These calculations reveal that roughly 60 percent of such children had limitations in their ability to do schoolwork, an additional 6 or 7 percent had health problems that caused frequent absences or prevented attendance at regular schools, and the remaining third of these children had limitations in play activities but not schoolwork or attendance. Less than 4 percent needed frequent assistance in getting around, but roughly 7 percent needed frequent assistance with daily activities or attending to personal needs. Based on the mean values for DIS3T4 and DIS5T17, we calculate that only 6.3 percent of the disabled children were age 3 to 4. The distribution among the other age categories (5 to 9, 10 to 13, and 14 to 17) was fairly even.

Comparisons of mean values for our dependent variables show several differences. First, the fraction of mothers working at all (i.e., DHDWORK = 1) is roughly 0.10 lower for those with disabled children. Second, the difference in means for LWAGE indicated that average hourly earnings are 8 percent lower for mothers of disabled children; however, the corresponding differential for earnings (LEARN) is only 5 percent and the mean hours worked for the two subsamples are almost identical.

IV. EMPIRICAL RESULTS: MATERNAL WORK STATUS

OLS regressions on the work-status dummy (DHDWORK) for the full samples and for the subsample of mothers with no health limitations are reported in Tables 5 and 6, respectively. In both sets of regressions, results for the regional dummies indicated considerable geographic variability in work status, with residents of the New England, Middle Atlantic, and East North Central regions having

Table 4. Mean Values of Variables

	Mothers of Disabled Children		*Mothers with No Disabled Children*	
	All (n = 848)	*With no Health Limitations (n = 597)*	*All (n = 546)*	*With no Health Limitations (n = 457)*
NE	0.154	0.157	0.150	0.151
MA	0.100	0.102	0.095	0.101
ENC	0.144	0.142	0.134	0.127
WNC	0.083	0.074	0.115	0.107
SA	0.120	0.112	0.119	0.123
ESC	0.040	0.044	0.049	0.055
WSC	0.081	0.077	0.070	0.070
M	0.167	0.178	0.145	0.151
BIGSMSA	0.255	0.258	0.233	0.239
MEDSMSA	0.235	0.246	0.231	0.232
OTHMETRO	0.113	0.114	0.093	0.088
OTHNONM	0.177	0.179	0.192	0.188
DFARMINC	0.002	0.002	0.002	0.002
CASHDUM	0.060	0.070	0.066	0.068
DUMSPAN	0.061	0.060	0.055	0.057
DUMALIEN	0.008	0.010	0.011	0.011
HEALTHLM	0.296	—	0.163	—
KID0T2	0.137	0.147	0.245	0.256
KID3T4	0.205	0.224	0.212	0.230
KID5T9	0.850	0.905	0.584	0.586
KID10T13	0.817	0.807	0.449	0.457
KID14T17	0.638	0.618	0.399	0.370
OWNHOME	0.279	0.305	0.317	0.319
HDBLACK	0.248	0.236	0.225	0.245
HDOTHER	0.033	0.035	0.031	0.022
DIVORCE	0.507	0.509	0.469	0.473
SEP	0.261	0.268	0.244	0.234
NEVER	0.098	0.094	0.134	0.144
LOGHAW	1.174	1.184	1.213	1.224
HDUNEMRT	0.091	0.089	0.087	0.088
HEADAGE	35.153	34.188	32.718	32.013
HDAGESQR	1302.1	1222.1	1153.2	1101.5
HDED	11.261	11.521	11.874	12.055
HDEDSQR	134.0	139.2	147.2	150.5
WORK	0.644	0.626	—	—
CANTABS	0.068	0.059	—	—
PLAY	0.367	0.360	—	—
USMOB	0.040	0.039	—	—
USHELP	0.072	0.074	—	—
DIS3T4	0.072	0.077	—	—
DIS5T9	0.375	0.392	—	—
DIS10T13	0.355	0.340	—	—
DIS14T17	0.072	0.077	—	—

(*continued*)

Table 4. (Continued)

	Mothers of Disabled Children		Mothers with No Disabled Children	
	All (n = 848)	With no Health Limitations (n = 597)	All (n = 546)	With no Health Limitations (n = 457)
DIS5T17	1.079	1.045	—	—
DHDWORK	0.577	0.645	0.687	0.733
HOURS	—	1549.9*	—	1545.0**
LWAGE	—	1.067*	—	1.148**
LEARN	—	8.195*	—	8.245**

Notes: *Based on data for the 385 mothers who work%$ during the year.
**Based on data for the 335 mothers who worked during the year.

significantly lower probabilities of working.[5] Among the other location-related variables, only the nonmetropolitan residence dummy (OTHNONM) is significant with a negative coefficient in the full sample regressions (Table 5), although a number of these variables often have negative coefficients with F-statistics greater than 1. Another highly significant variable, with the expected negative sign for its coefficient, is HEALTHLM in the full sample regressions. The results for the marital history variables confirm the finding noted elsewhere (McEaddy, 1976; Mitchell, 1979) that divorced women are more likely to be in the labor force and working. The coefficients for SEP are also strongly positive, particularly in the regressions for mothers with no health limitations. Never-married women and widows (the reference category) have the lowest probabilities of working. With regard to ethnic background, we observe no significant difference in work probabilities between blacks and whites, but significantly lower probabilities for other racial groups and for mothers of Spanish origin.

Results relating to the number and ages of children show the expected pattern. The probability of working is significantly reduced as the number of children under age 14 increases and the effect diminishes steadily with the age of the children. The number of children over 14 has no significant effect. Work probability also is positively related to both maternal age and education. In the latter case, the square of years of schooling has an insignificant negative coefficient, and its deletion from the regressions greatly increases the significance of the years-of-schooling coefficient. The negative coefficients on HDAGESQR imply that the wage effect eventually diminishes to zero and then becomes negative. The age at which this occurs varies considerably in the full sample regressions, ranging from about 40 (equation 1) to more than 70 (equation 6). In the regressions for mothers with no health limitations, this age is consistently around 60 or 70 years, obviously at the upper end of the distribution of observed ages in our sample. The F-statistics for both age coefficients in these regressions range from

Table 5. OLS Probability of Working Regressions, Full Sample (*F*-Statistics in parentheses)

Variables	*(1)*	*(2)*	*(3)*	*(4)*	*(5)*	*(6)*
NE	−0.180	−0.188	−0.180	−0.177	−0.186	−0.177
	(15.13)	(32.41)	(15.24)	(14.55)	(31.59)	(14.59)
MA	−0.095	−0.104	−0.154	−0.089	−0.100	−0.147
	(3.30)	(5.95)	(8.82)	(2.89)	(5.44)	(8.02)
ENC	−0.069	−0.075	−0.070	−0.071	−0.078	−0.072
	(2.22)	(4.44)	(2.24)	(2.34)	(4.82)	(2.35)
WNC	−0.041		−0.043	−0.039		−0.041
	(0.62)		(0.64)	(0.56)		(0.57)
SA	0.003		−0.008	0.009		−0.003
	(0.003)		(0.02)	(0.030)		(0.004)
ESC	0.003		0.033	0.002		0.033
	(0.002)		(0.23)	(0.001)		(0.24)
WSC	−0.062	−0.049	−0.083	−0.062	−0.052	−0.085
	(1.09)	(1.25)	(1.96)	(1.11)	(1.40)	(2.01)
M	0.021		0.024	0.019		0.023
	(0.19)		(0.27)	(0.17)		(0.25)
OTHMETRO	−0.040	−0.045	−0.013	−0.046	−0.050	−0.017
	(0.082)	(1.12)	(0.12)	(1.06)	(1.36)	(0.21)
DIVORCE	0.162	0.148		0.162	0.147	
	−18.83)	(26.17)		(19.03)	(25.82)	
SE	0.064	0.049		0.064	0.049	
	(2.41)	(2.31)		(2.45)	(2.26)	
NEVER	0.027			0.029		
	(0.27)			(0.32)		
OWNHOME	0.096	0.091		0.095	0.090	
	(11.81)	(11.23)		(11.63)	(10.94)	
CASHDUM	−0.013			−0.014		
	(0.07)			(0.08)		
DUMALIEN	0.182	0.196		0.191	0.196	
	(2.19)	(2.45)		(2.40)	(2.60)	
DUMSPAN	−0.232	−0.222		−0.236	−0.227	
	(17.87)	(18.63)		(18.33)	(19.26)	
BIGSMSA	−0.049	−0.059		−0.050	−0.058	
	(1.41)	(2.64)		(1.49)	(2.55)	
MEDSMSA	−0.039	−0.038		−0.040	−0.037	
	(1.19)	(1.26)		(1.24)	(1.22)	
OTHNONM	−0.064	−0.066		−0.069	−0.070	
	(3.09)	(3.44)		(3.51)	(3.86)	
DFARMINC	0.132			0.120		
	(0.30)			(0.24)		
KID0T2	−0.186	−0.184	−0.202	−0.183	−0.182	−0.200
	(41.25)	(41.09)	(47.53)	(40.05)	(39.74)	(46.38)

(*continued*)

Table 5. (Continued)

Variables	*(1)*	*(2)*	*(3)*	*(4)*	*(5)*	*(6)*
KID3T4	−0.112	−0.110	−0.113	−0.113	−0.113	−0.114
	(16.01)	(15.75)	(15.75)	(13.86)	(13.95)	(13.77)
KID5T9	−0.074	−0.072	−0.079	−0.070	−0.069	−0.076
	(24.40)	(26.49)	(27.81)	(20.90)	(23.47)	(24.52)
KID10T13	−0.025	−0.025	−0.029	−0.023	−0.023	−0.028
	(2.74)	(2.76)	(3.56)	(2.33)	(2.36)	(3.21)
KID145T17	−0.004		−0.011	−0.0003		−0.007
	(0.06)		(0.39)	(0.000)		(0.17)
HDBLACK	0.032		0.008	0.033		0.011
	(0.49)		(0.03)	(0.054)		(0.07)
HDOTHER	−0.170	−0.188	−0.179	−0.178	−0.197	−0.184
	(6.12)	(8.29)	(6.82)	(6.74)	(9.11)	(7.21)
HDUNEMRT	−0.569	−0.266	−0.572	−0.565	−0.246	−0.576
	(1.99)	(0.90)	(2.00)	(1.95)	(0.77)	(2.02)
HEALTHUM	−0.209	−0.211	−0.207	−0.208	−0.210	−0.207
	(58.58)	(60.44)	(56.43)	(57.42)	(59.17)	(55.38)
LOGHAW	−0.038		−0.066	−0.032		−0.061
	(0.24)		(0.84)	(0.18)		(0.71)
HEADAGE	0.008	0.006	0.023	0.006	0.006	0.220
	(0.51)	(0.36)	(4.88)	(0.36)	(0.31)	(4.31)
HDAGESQR	−0.0002	−0.0001	−0.0004	−0.0002	−0.0001	−0.0003
	(1.57)	(1.35)	(7.23)	(1.25)	(1.18)	(6.43)
HDED	0.016	0.035	0.040	0.015	0.035	0.039
	(0.069)	(51.53)	(4.68)	(0.63)	(50.68)	(4.51)
HDEDSQR	0.001		0.0004	0.001		−0.0004
	(1.22)		(0.22)	(1.25)		(0.25)
PLAY				−0.041	−0.039	−0.039
				(2.14)	(2.03)	(1.93)
WORK				−0.016	−0.016	−0.013
				(0.51)	(0.48)	(0.33)
CANTABS				−0.087	−0.091	−0.074
				(2.37)	(2.66)	(1.67)
USMOB				0.07	0.010	−0.038
				(0.007)	(0.01)	(0.17)
USHELP				−0.120	−0.116	−0.099
				(3.12)	(2.94)	(2.07)
DIS3T4				−0.018	−0.013	−0.017
				(0.09)	(0.05)	(0.07)
DUMDIS	−0.043	−0.041	−0.042			
	(2.96)	(2.83)	(2.83)			
Constant	0.528	0.429	0.167	0.538	0.429	0.178
R^2	0.288	0.285	0.253	0.291	0.289	0.256

Table 6. OLS Probability of Working Regressions, Mothers with No Health Limitations (*F*-Statistics in parentheses)

Variables	*(1)*	*(2)*	*(3)*	*(4)*	*(5)*	*(6)*	*(7)*
NE	−0.158	−0.171	−0.179	−0.155	−0.168	−0.176	−0.079
	(9.39)	(17.60)	(23.00)	(9.01)	(16.99)	(22.26)	(4.54)
MA	−0.129	−0.139	−0.164	−0.117	−0.134	−0.153	
	(4.85)	(7.09)	(12.43)	(4.00)	(6.99)	(10.78)	
ENC	−0.092	−0.103	−0.127	−0.094	−0.110	−0.128	
	(3.13)	(5.27)	(10.49)	(3.26)	(6.45)	(10.72)	
WNC	−0.066	−0.076	−0.080	−0.063	−0.075	−0.079	
	(1.21)	(2.35)	(2.93)	(1.12)	(2.30)	(2.86)	
SA	0.023	0.017		0.026	0.018		
	(0.16)	(0.14)		(0.21)	(0.17)		
ESC	0.050	0.041		0.050	0.041		
	(0.48)	(0.42)		(0.47)	(0.42)		
WSC	−0.055	−0.063	−0.069	−0.058	−0.070	−0.069	
	(0.67)	(1.29)	(1.93)	(0.77)	(1.64)	(1.93)	
M	0.019			0.018			0.055
	(0.14)			(0.12)			(2.25)
OTHMETRO	−0.041	−0.044		−0.048	−0.041	−0.033	
	(0.66)	(0.80)		(0.92)	(0.89)	(0.60)	
DIVORCE	0.161	0.161	0.160	0.165	0.167	0.162	0.148
	(15.04)	(15.83)	(15.79)	(15.83)	(16.98)	(16.33)	(19.54)
SEP	0.093	0.094	0.091	0.095	0.097	0.093	0.062
	(3.97)	(4.23)	(4.03)	(4.19)	(4.51)	(4.14)	(2.81)
NEVER	0.070	0.075	0.069	0.076	0.835	0.075	
	(1.48)	(1.77)	(1.53)	(1.75)	(2.19)	(1.82)	

OWNHOME	0.092	0.091	0.093	0.090	0.089	0.089	0.096
	(9.00)	(8.89)	(9.43)	(8.54)	(8.61)	(8.74)	(9.95)
CASHDUM	−0.017			−0.021			
	(0.10)			(0.16)			
DUMALIEN	0.059			0.071	0.714		
	(0.20)			(0.29)	(0.30)		
DUMSPAN	−0.242	−0.121	−0.254	−0.242	−0.245	−0.252	
	(15.29)	(16.96)	(19.99)	(15.17)	(17.25)	(19.60)	
BIGSMSA	−0.021	−0.023		−0.019			−0.007
	(0.22)	(0.27)		(0.18)			(0.04)
MEDSMSA	−0.053	−0.053	−0.035	−0.054	−0.043	−0.041	
	(1.77)	(1.73)	(1.27)	(1.85)	(1.85)	(1.67)	
OTHNONM	−0.049	−0.053	−0.033	−0.055	−0.049	−0.044	
	(1.42)	(1.93)	(0.92)	(1.76)	(1.88)	(1.60)	
DFARMINC	−0.160	−0.158		−0.175	−0.165		−0.237
	(0.31)	(0.030)		(0.37)	(0.33)		(0.66)
KID0T2	−0.201	−0.200	−0.196	−0.201	−0.199	−0.196	−0.203
	(41.82)	(41.65)	(40.63)	(41.40)	(41.16)	(40.27)	(42.34)
KID3T4	−0.115	−0.114	−0.113	−0.121	−0.120	−0.119	−0.118
	(14.34)	(14.25)	(13.97)	(13.86)	(13.67)	(13.62)	(14.96)
KID5T9	−0.074	−0.073	−0.072	−0.069	−0.068	−0.066	−0.063
	(19.92)	(20.15)	(19.33)	(16.35)	(16.16)	(15.81)	(12.35)
KID10T13	−0.044	−0.043	−0.043	−0.040	−0.038	−0.038	−0.053
	(6.32)	(6.06)	(6.23)	(5.08)	(4.84)	(4.82)	(6.94)
KID14T17	−0.020	−0.020	−0.018	−0.016	−0.151	−0.014	
	(1.03)	(1.04)	(0.85)	(0.64)	(0.57)	(0.48)	
HDBLACK	0.018			0.022			0.107
	(0.14)			(0.20)			(6.19)

(continued)

Table 6. (Continued)

Variables	*(1)*	*(2)*	*(3)*	*(4)*	*(5)*	*(6)*	*(7)*
HDOTHER	−0.236	−0.242	−0.251	−0.246	−0.257	−0.264	
	(8.93)	(10.12)	(11.26)	(9.82)	(11.31)	(12.47)	
HDUNEMRT	−0.605	−0.507	−0.462	−0.639	−0.523	−0.465	−1.141
	(1.76)	(2.29)	(1.98)	(1.96)	(2.46)	(2.00)	(7.80)
LOGHAW	−0.052	−0.058		−0.050	−0.068		−0.103
	(0.37)	(0.51)		(0.35)	(0.78)		(1.94)
HEADAGE	0.014	0.014	0.014	0.013	0.012	0.012	0.013
	(1.30)	(1.24)	(1.21)	(1.05)	(1.00)	(0.94)	(1.11)
HDAGESQR	−0.0002	−0.0002	−0.0002	−0.0002	−0.0002	−0.0002	−0.0002
	(1.84)	(1.82)	(1.805)	(1.42)	(1.39)	(1.34)	(1.86)
HDED	0.034	0.034	0.030	0.031	0.344	0.030	0.045
	(1.82)	(20.93)	(27.51)	(1.57)	(21.52)	(26.38)	(40.22)
HDEDSQR	0.00004			0.0001			
	(0.001)			(0.01)			
PLAY				−0.054	−0.055		
				(2.86)	(2.98)		
WORK				−0.033	−0.033	0.022	
				(1.41)	(1.50)	(0.42)	
CANTABS				−0.130	−0.132	−0.080	
				(3.44)	(3.59)	(1.20)	
USMOB				−0.119	−0.121	−0.114	
				(1.27)	(1.32)	(1.19)	
USHELP				−0.117	−0.114	−0.113	
				(2.34)	(2.24)	(2.24)	
DIS3T4				−0.0003	−0.003	0.0006	
				(0.000)	(0.002)	(0.000)	

DUMDIS	−0.051	−0.051	−0.053				
	(3.46)	(3.52)	(3.85)				
DIS5T17						−0.056	
						(3.10)	
DIS5T9							−0.084
							(6.03)
DIS10T13							−0.040
							(1.19)
DIS14T17							−0.046
							(1.64)
Constant	0.331	0.352	0.328	0.359	0.362	0.355	0.256
R^2	0.274	0.274	0.272	0.283	0.283	0.281	0.243

0.94 to 1.86; however, it seems reasonable to guess that deletion of HDAGESQR would increase the significance of HEADAGE's positive coefficient. In the full sample regressions, the *F*-Statistics are lower (particularly for HEADAGE) except when a number of other significant independent variables are not included (Equations 3 and 6).

Results for the labor-market variables tend to confirm the belief that the labor-supply of single women is not strongly related to market opportunities. While the HDUNEMRT coefficients always have the expected negative signs, their *F*-statistics are not highly significant except in one instance (Table 6, Equation 7). The market wage variable (LOGHAW) has consistently negative and insignificant coefficients.

Turning to the results for the child disability variables, we observe that the overall average effect of the presence of disabled children, as indicated by the coefficient of DUMDIS, is consistently negative and significant. When a more detailed specification of the severity of disabilities is used in the full sample regressions (Table 5, Equations 4–6), however, results are less consistent. Although we might expect PLAY to have the weakest negative effect, in fact we observe that WORK and USMOB have the smallest and least significant coefficients. The results for DIS3T4 indicate that the presence of children under the age of 5 with disabilities does not impact negatively on maternal work status.

The same general pattern of results is observed in Table 6 but the DUMDIS coefficients (Equations 1–3) suggest a slightly larger and even more significant negative effect. Equations 6 and 7 indicate that the presence of children over the age of 5 with disabilities, and particularly those in the age range 5 to 9, significantly reduces the probability that a single mother will work.

Probit employment status regressions for mothers with no health limitations are presented in Table 7. In addition to the child disability variables, other independent variables were those having *F*-statistics of approximately 1.0 or greater in the OLS regressions in Table 5. Qualitative aspects of the results for the probit and OLS regressions are, as expected, virtually identical. The most inclusive child disability variables, DUMDIS, and DIS5T17, have significantly negative coefficients; variables relating to severity and to the 3–4 age group do not. The three regressions reported here were used to construct the selectivity variables $X2$, $X1$ and $X3$ (respectively) used in the hours and earnings regressions reported in the next section.

V. EMPIRICAL RESULTS: MATERNAL HOURS AND EARNINGS

Regressions on annual work hours, the logarithm of annual earnings, and the logarithm of annual earnings per hour were estimated on data for the 720 mothers with no health limitations who reported any work during the previous year. Results of the work hours regressions are presented in Table 8. Results for the

Table 7. Probit Probability or Working Regressions, Mothers with No Health Limitations (*t*-Statistics in parentheses)

Variables	*Coefficients*	*Coefficients*	*Coefficients*
KID0T2	−0.6437 (5.55)	−0.6408 (5.59)	−0.6381 (5.53)
KID3T4	−0.33905 (3.41)	−0.3774 (3.51)	−0.3960 (3.68)
KID5T9	−0.2109 (3.63)	−0.2410 (4.08)	−0.2088 (3.60)
KID10T13	−0.1364 (2.13)	−0.1522 (2.40)	−0.1358 (2.12)
KID14T17		−0.0676 (.93)	
HDOTHER	−0.9832 (3.50)	−0.9190 (3.28)	−0.9817 (3.49)
HDUNEMRT	−1.3374 (1.13)	−1.2165 (1.03)	−1.2898 (1.09)
HEADAGE	0.0388 (0.89)	0.0530 (1.18)	0.0392 (0.89)
HDAGESQR	−0.0006 (1.01)	−0.0008 (1.33)	−0.0006 (1.02)
HDED	0.1094 (4.74)	0.1109 (4.84)	0.1087 (4.73)
NE	−0.6324 (4.69)	0.6277 (4.71)	−0.6219 (4.64)
MA	−0.5474 (3.31)	−0.5728 (3.50)	−0.5421 (3.28)
ENC	−0.4811 (3.34)	0.4608 (3.21)	−0.4727 (3.29)
WNC	−0.3332 (1.97)	−0.3382 (2.01)	−0.3282 (1.94)
WSC	−0.2667 (1.41)	−0.2402 (1.27)	−0.2641 (1.40)
DIVORCE	0.6670 (4.50)	0.6486 (4.41)	0.6704 (4.53)
SEP	0.3915 (2.39)	0.3818 (2.34)	0.3890 (2.38)
NEVER	0.3585 (1.80)	0.3289 (1.67)	0.3501 (1.76)
OWNHOME	0.3746 (3.16)	0.3856 (3.26)	0.3724 (3.15)
DUMSPAN	−0.9121 (4.14)	−0.8724 (4.01)	−0.9049 (4.11)

(*continued*)

Table 7. (Continued)

Variables	*Coefficients*	*Coefficients*	*Coefficients*
MEDSMSA	−0.0671 (5.78)	−0.0684 (5.94)	−0.0700 (6.04)
OTHNONM	−0.1156 (0.93)	−0.0944 (7.61)	−0.1163 (0.94)
DUMDIS		−0.1992 (1.96)	
WORK	0.1081 (0.88)		
CANTABS	−0.2650 (1.03)		−0.3287 (1.32)
USMOB	−0.3762 (0.97)		−0.3586 (0.93)
USHELP	−0.3638 (1.31)		−0.3382 (1.23)
DIS3T4	−0.0355 (0.15)		
DIS5T17	−0.2344 (2.03)		−0.1685 (1.90)
Constant	−0.7868 (0.95)	−1.0130 (1.20)	−0.7946 (0.96)

location variables SA, ESC, WSC, M and OTHNOMN indicate that working mothers in less urbanized regions of the country and nonmetropolitan locations tend to work longer hours. On the other hand, mothers who received any (positive or negative) farm income worked much shorter hours. The magnitude of the coefficient DFARMINC suggests that these mothers tend to report only seasonal or occasional work for pay. Coefficients for KID0T2, KID3T4, KID5T9, KID10T13 and KID14T17 indicate the same pattern as in the work status regressions. Mothers with more children and with younger children work significantly fewer hours. The significant linear and quadratic terms for both age and education indicate an inverted U-shaped relationship of those variables to work hours; for age, the peak of this inverted U occurs in the 40–45 years range, while for education the peak occurs at about 12 years. Neither of the two labor-market variables, HDUNEMRT and LOGHAW, are highly significant, although the latter's coefficients have the expected positive sign and often exceed their standard errors. The marital history variables once again have significantly positive coefficients, as does the recent immigrant variable (DUMALIEN).

In general, the child disability variables fail to show any strong effect on hours of work (Table 8). The only exception is the significantly negative coefficient of WORK in Equation 9. Other coefficients for WORK, and for DIS5T17 when

Table 8. Maternal Annual Work Hours Regressions, Mothers with No Health Limitations (*F*-Statistics in parentheses)

Variables	*(1)*	*(2)*	*(3)*	*(4)*	*(5)*	*(6)*	*(7)*	*(8)*	*(9)*	*(10)*
NE	−83.903			−100.726		−95.734				
	(0.31)			(0.47)		(0.44)				
MA	−15.721			−37.818						
	(0.01)			(0.05)						
ENC	−50.697			−70.617		−62.098				
	(0.160)			(0.31)		(0.24)				
WNC	−50.992			−68.157		−62.581				
	(0.14)			(0.26)		(0.22)				
SA	316.553	341.603	359.773	313.054	338.05	315.727	344.295	363.704	357.250	353.953
	(7.52)	(13.77)	(16.73)	(7.32)	(13.39)	(7.45)	(14.00)	(17.08)	(16.85)	(18.44)
ESC	243.838	275.969	291.818	241.003	272.27	241.255	275.842	287.123	290.451	283.256
	(2.83)	(4.83)	(5.51)	(2.75)	(4.66)	(2.76)	(4.79)	(5.33)	(5.50)	(5.45)
WSC	143.813	205.382	212.475	132.211	205.03	137.191	208.75	219.160	211.119	212.064
	(1.03)	(3.38)	(3.64)	(0.87)	(3.33)	(0.94)	(3.49)	(3.87)	(3.61)	(3.69)
M	220.906	245.814	239.161	226.053	249.282	223.650	249.716	241.961	243.931	236.255
	(4.31)	(10.30)	(9.81)	(4.49)	(10.60)	(4.40)	(10.64)	(10.08)	(10.46)	(10.72)
OTHMETRO	78.242			81.617		83.302				
	(0.52)			(0.56)		(0.59)				
DIVORCE	431.206	376.493	369.671	468.590	387.40	451.548	382.016	380.191	380.228	364.047
	(9.53)	(14.81)	(14.36)	(11.44)	(15.46)	(10.63)	(14.95)	(15.13)	(15.90)	(16.82)
SEP	220.75	176.638	180.186	243.692	184.554	233.046	180.805	191.564	186.413	181.219
	(3.34)	(3.03)	(3.19)	(4.10)	(3.28)	(3.77)	(3.15)	(3.58)	(3.44)	(3.26)
KID14T17	−46.787	−38.534		−42.466	−38.323	−37.553	−33.529			
	(1.13)	(0.84)		(0.99)	(0.84)	(0.77)	(0.64)			

(continued)

Table 8. (Continued)

Variables	*(1)*	*(2)*	*(3)*	*(4)*	*(5)*	*(6)*	*(7)*	*(8)*	*(9)*	*(10)*
HDBLACK	115.482	70.253		113.138	68.035	115.423	68.485			
	(1.23)	(0.85)		(1.17)	(0.79)	(1.23)	(0.81)			
HDOTHER	2.119			−77.235		−37.506				
	(0.000)			(0.08)		(0.02)				
HDUNEMRT	−812.953			−884.793		−875.082				
	(0.60)			(0.70)		(0.69)				
LOGHAW	179.614	217.340	217.158	168.182	206.406	176.167	217.248	219.128	204.010	215.590
	(0.97)	(1.80)	(1.82)	(0.84)	(1.60)	(0.92)	(1.78)	(1.85)	(1.61)	(1.78)
HEADAGE	69.589	65.119	56.244	72.033	68.101	70.296	66.842	61.892	58.776	58.171
	(5.04)	(4.79)	(3.96)	(5.54)	(5.24)	(5.28)	(5.05)	(4.66)	(4.43)	(4.25)
HDAGESQR	−0.819	−0.747	−0.650	−0.854	−0.785	−0.;827	−0.768	−0.712	−6.638	−0.670
	(4.03)	(3.71)	(3.03)	(4.55)	(4.11)	(4.27)	(3.93)	(3.57)	(4.66)	(3.25)
HDED	174.93	162.95	166.266	185.01	165.71	181.827	167.041	167.08	167.661	163.826
	(3.79)	(4.08)	(4.27)	(4.43)	(4.24)	(4.27)	(4.29)	(4.29)	(4.52)	(4.59)
HDEDSQR	−6.690	−6.559	−6.681	−6.853	−6.594	−6.867	−6.705	−6.700	−6.638	−6.655
	(4.09)	(4.43)	(4.61)	(4.35)	(4.45)	(4.36)	(4.60)	(4.61)	(4.66)	(4.75)
*X*1	208.151	46.938	32.588					58.288		
	(0.26)	(0.06)	(0.031)					(0.10)		
*X*2				342.440	83.207				73.425	
				(0.74)	(0.19)				(0.19)	
*X*3						275.194	64.384			
						(0.48)	(0.11)			
NEVER	297.073	261.929	289.569	308.182	260.458	307.033	265.027	293.983	284.649	291.539
	(4.46)	(3.96)	(5.13)	(4.73)	(3.90)	(4.73)	(4.04)	(5.27)	(4.98)	(5.19)
OWNHOME	58.962			77.312						
	(0.53)			(0.97)						

CASHDUM	39.66			29.430		38.588				
	(0.15)			(0.08)		(0.14)				
DUMALIEN	887.80	919.993	972.156	828.419	897.181	888.722	944.033		915.818	1008.17
	(2.34)	(2.63)	(2.96)	(1.95)	(2.40)	(2.26)	(2.67)		(2.61)	(3.08)
DUMSPAN	29.706			−37.057						
	(2.34)			(0.02)						
BIGSMSA	29.863			36.122						
	(0.097)			(0.141)						
MEDSMSA	1.053			−3.025						
	(0.000)			(0.001)						
OTHNONM	130.153	123.032	113.899	122.198	121.52	125.409	120.61	113.536	112.417	111.873
	(2.21)	(3.05)	(2.67)	(1.91)	(2.96)	(2.03)	(2.92)	(2.65)	(2.62)	(2.57)
DFARMINC	−1674.72	−1649.43	−1614.575	−1703.167	−1664.18	−1692.46	−1663.80	−1645.899	−1628.310	−1633.75
	(5.49)	(5.45)	(5.24)	(5.68)	(5.53)	(5.60)	(5.53)	(5.44)	(5.35)	(5.36)
KID0T2	−486.397	−444.177	−444.852	−525.880	−452.578	−506.361	−449.136	−447.737	455.715	−433.986
	(9.36)	(17.70)	(18.08)	(11.49)	(18.23)	(10.79)	(18.01)	(18.64)	(20.04)	(24.23)
KID3T4	−243.054	−216.432	−202.502	−290.716	−244.007	−264.398	−226.909	−217.892	−231.709	−206.235
	(5.29)	(7.32)	(6.62)	(7.01)	(8.10)	(6.34)	(7.95)	(7.45)	(7.83)	(8.21)
KID5T9	−113.512	−93.367	−79.056	−115.73	−88.769	−110.755	−88.669	−91.548	−76.190	−70.042
	(3.51)	(4.32)	(3.51)	(4.30)	(4.03)	(4.00)	(4.02)	(4.01)	(3.45)	(3.65)
KID10T13	−120.089	−107.075	−97.861	−121.860	−104.147	−117.895	−103.372	−91.286	−95.093	−91.432
	(6.30)	(6.94)	(6.02)	(7.07)	(6.59)	(6.61)	(6.47)	(4.14)	(5.75)	(5.73)
WORK				−92.442	−106.713				−100.569	
				(1.42)	(2.05)				(3.48)	
CANTABS				−103.383	−68.95	−37.975	5.329			2.72
				(0.25)	(0.13)	(0.04)	(0.001)			(0.000)
USMOB				−25.748	41.282	−43.902	15.163			20.256
				(0.01)	(0.02)	(0.02)	(0.003)			(0.005)

(*continued*)

Table 8. (Continued)

Variables	*(1)*	*(2)*	*(3)*	*(4)*	*(5)*	*(6)*	*(7)*	*(8)*	*(9)*	*(10)*
USHELP				−44.285	−3.282	−50.779	−22.148			−9.378
				(0.04)	(0.000)	(0.06)	(0.01)			(0.002)
DIS3T4				69.040	70.755				68.825	
				(0.20)	(0.21)				(0.20)	
DUMDIS	−47.591	−31.684	−38.567							
	(0.51)	(0.3)	(0.45)							
DIS5T17				−19.105	10.159	−72.976	−56.043			−59.026
				(0.06)	(0.021)	(1.56)	(1.19)			(1.41)
DIS5T9								−11.225		
								(0.02)		
DIS10T13								−73.435		
								(0.90)		
DIS14T17								−99.407		
								(1.80)		
Constant	−1355.57	−1200.65	−1053.20	−1517.06	−1279.64	−1437.98	−1263.36	−1178.26	−1116.68	−1047.15
R^2	0.159	0.156	0.154	0.164	0.160	0.160	0.157	0.156	0.158	0.155

Table 9. Maternal Earnings Regressions, Mothers with No Health Limitations (*F*-Statistics in parentheses)

Variables	*(1)*	*(2)*	*(3)*	*(4)*	*(5)*	*(6)*	*(7)*	*(8)*	*(9)*	*(10)*
NE	−0.139			−0.118		−0.124				
	(0.45)			(0.34)		(0.39				
MA	−0.031			−0.023		−0.023				
	(0.02)			(0.01)		(0.01)				
ENC	−0.003			−0.004		−0.0003				
	(0.000)			(0.001)		(0.000)				
WNC	−0.136			−0.140		−0.139				
	(0.53)			(0.58)		(0.58)				
SA	0.331	0.318	0.321	0.322	0.305	0.325	0.311	0.321	0.317	0.288
	(4.32)	(6.90)	(7.03)	(4.07)	(6.33)	(4.13)	(6.59)	(7.06)	(6.98)	(6.03)
ESC	0.166			0.159		0.159				
	(0.69)			(0.63)		(0.63)				
WSC	0.198	0.223	0.214	0.184	0.208	0.191	0.214	0.224	0.203	0.208
	(1.03)	(2.22)	(2.07)	(0.88)	(1.89)	(0.96)	(2.03)	(2.26)	(1.86)	(1.93)
M	0.089			0.098		0.094				
	(0.37)			(0.45)		(0.41)				
OTHMETRO	0.094			0.107		0.103				
	(0.40)			(0.50)		(0.47)				
DIVORCE	0.597	0.560	0.551	0.591	0.559	0.583	0.554	0.552	0.562	0.485
	(9.53)	(15.36)	(14.94)	(9.52)	(15.19)	(9.29)	(4.70)	(15.04)	(16.72)	(15.12)
SEP	0.351	0.318	0.309	0.350	0.323	0.345	0.318	0.318	0.319	0.279
	(4.44)	(4.70)	(4.47)	(4.43)	(4.84)	(4.33)	(4.70)	(4.72)	(4.87)	(3.86)
NEVER	0.350	0.324	0.318	0.347	0.327	0.348	0.328	0.312	0.322	0.306
	(3.25)	(3.10)	(2.99)	(3.15)	(3.15)	(3.19)	(3.18)	(2.89)	(3.17)	(2.80)

(continued)

Table 9. (Continued)

Variables	*(1)*	*(2)*	*(3)*	*(4)*	*(5)*	*(6)*	*(7)*	*(8)*	*(9)*	*(10)*
OWNHOME	0.189	0.161	0.165	0.189	0.166	0.182	0.160	0.163	0.173	0.127
	(2.82)	(2.90)	(3.07)	(3.04)	(3.15)	(2.85)	(2.93)	(3.00)	(3.55)	(2.35)
CASHDUM	−0.151	−0.141	−0.138	−0.165	−0.155	−0.155	−0.146	−0.141	−0.147	−0.135
	(1.12)	(1.00)	(0.97)	(1.35)	(1.21)	(1.19)	(1.07)	(1.00)	(1.10)	(0.92)
DUMALIEN	0.709			0.544		0.007				
	(0.78)			(0.44)		(0.55)				
DUMSPAN	0.188			0.174		0.187				
	(0.27)			(0.23)		(0.27)				
BIGSMSA	0.117			0.124		0.119				
	(0.78)			(0.87)		(0.81)				
MEDSMSA	0.072			0.081		0.082				
	(0.39)			(0.49)		(0.50)				
OTHNONM	0.137	0.075		0.136	0.071	0.134	0.069			
	(1.28)	(0.59)		(1.25)	(0.52)	(1.22)	(0.49)			
DFARMINC	−0.897	−0.840		−0.924	−0.872	−0.916	−0.866			
	(0.83)	(0.74)		(0.88)	(0.80)	(0.86)	(0.78)			
KID0T2	−0.645	−0.587	−0.590	−0.649	−0.596	−0.638	−0.590	−0.588	−0.605	−0.524
	(8.63)	(16.26)	(16.44)	(9.17)	(16.69)	(8.98)	(16.35)	(16.61)	(18.74)	(18.64)
KID3T4	−0.424	−0.387	−0.388	−0.430	−0.398	−0.426	−0.391	−0.397	−0.403	−0.351
	(8.44)	(12.21)	(12.31)	(8.05)	(11.18)	(8.61)	(12.35)	(12.64)	(14.05)	(12.27)
KID5T9	−0.275	−0.247	−0.247	−0.262	−0.241	−0.261	−0.241	−0.260	−0.240	−0.214
	(10.76)	(15.21)	(15.26)	(11.52)	(15.02)	(11.62)	(15.06)	(15.52)	(15.87)	(16.01)
KID10T13	−0.201	−0.186	−0.184	−0.190	−0.178	−0.188	−0.177	−0.146	−0.179	−0.158
	(9.26)	(10.62)	(10.38)	(8.99)	(9.77)	(8.85)	(9.65)	(5.32)	(10.14)	(8.72)
KID14T17	−0.115	−0.109	−0.107	−0.111	−0.111	−0.105	−0.105	−0.106	−0.103	−0.096
	(3.58)	(3.49)	(3.33)	(3.51)	(3.62)	(3.17)	(3.25)	(2.71)	(3.26)	(2.78)

HDBLACK	0.412 (8.22)	0.460 (11.83)	0.449 (11.40)	0.408 (7.99)	0.453 (11.33)	0.414 (8.27)	0.459 (11.69)	0.443 (11.04)	0.444 (11.23)	0.434 (10.74)
HDOTHER	−0.119 (0.104)			−0.142 (0.14)		−0.119 (0.10)				
HDUNEMRT	−3.352 (5.38)	−3.382 (6.68)	−3.396 (6.75)	−3.364 (5.32)	−3.383 (6.55)	−3.416 (5.54)	−3.450 (6.87)	−3.389 (6.72)	−3.381 (6.90)	−3.142 (6.22)
LOGHAW	0.791 (9.83)	0.889 (17.00)	0.869 (16.70)	0.758 (8.92)	0.852 (15.41)	0.772 (9.29)	0.866 (15.96)	0.886 (17.38)	0.845 (15.86)	0.868 (16.73)
HEADAGE	0.128 (8.88)	0.120 (8.49)	0.119 (8.30)	0.129 (9.28)	0.124 (9.09)	0.128 (9.16)	0.123 (8.94)	0.119 (8.36)	0.121 (8.86)	0.116 (8.17)
HDAGESQR	−0.002 (7.94)	−0.001 (7.47)	−0.001 (7.35)	−0.002 (8.41)	−0.002 (8.12)	−0.002 (8.26)	−0.002 (7.94)	−0.001 (7.37)	−0.001 (7.92)	−0.001 (7.20)
HDED	0.096 (0.60)	0.047 (2.94)	0.049 (3.27)	0.086 (0.51)	0.049 (3.24)	0.098 (0.52)	0.047 (3.01)	0.048 (3.15)	0.052 (3.97)	0.037 (2.63)
HDEDSQR	−0.001 (0.08)			−0.009 (0.04)		−0.0009 (0.05)				
*X*1	0.417 (0.54)		0.253 (0.81)					0.261 (0.89)		
*X*2				0.405 (0.54)	0.244 (0.76)				0.288 (1.38)	
*X*3						0.380 (0.48)	0.228 (0.65)			
WORK				−0.119 (1.22)	−0.133 (1.66)				−0.134 (3.24)	
CANTABS				0.120 (0.18)	0.147 (0.30)	0.190 (0.45)	0.226 (0.74)			0.270 (1.11)
USMOB				0.153 (0.14)	0.240 (0.36)	0.116 (0.08)	0.198 (0.25)			

(*continued*)

Table 9. (Continued)

Variables	*(1)*	*(2)*	*(3)*	*(4)*	*(5)*	*(6)*	*(7)*	*(8)*	*(9)*	*(10)*
USHELP				−0.173	−0.183	−0.189	−0.207			−0.177
				(0.35)	(0.44)	(0.43)	(0.56)			(0.42)
DIS3T4				0.004	0.020					
				(0.000)	(0.01)					
DUMDIS	−0.070	−0.047	−0.047							
	(0.57)	(0.35)	(0.36)							
DIS5T17				−0.029	0.003	−0.100	−0.079			−0.067
				(0.07)	(0.001)	(1.53)	(1.23)			(0.93)
DIS5T9								0.020		
								(0.04)		
DIS10T13								−0.055		
								(0.24)		
DIS14T17										
Constant	3.811	4.309	4.358	3.891	4.272	3.908	4.305	4.332	4.305	4.637
R^2	0.239	0.230	0.229	0.243	0.235	0.241	0.232	0.231	0.232	0.230

Table 10. Maternal Average Hourly Earnings Regressions, Mothers with No Health Limitations (*F*-Statistics in parentheses)

Variables	*(1)*	*(2)*	*(3)*	*(4)*	*(5)*	*(6)*	*(7)*	*(8)*
NE	−0.099	−0.098	−0.055	−0.087	−0.057	−0.087	−0.098	−0.091
	(0.65)	(1.78)	(0.209)	(1.43)	(0.23)	(1.43)	(1.81)	(1.60)
MA	−0.064		−0.031		−0.033			
	(0.22)		(0.06)		(0.06)			
ENC	0.021		0.048		0.047			
	(0.04)		(0.21)		(0.20)			
WNC	0.061		0.077		0.076			
	(0.31)		(0.49)		(0.48)			
SA	0.015		0.012		0.012			
	(0.23)		(0.02)		(0.02)			
ESC	−0.108		−0.110		−0.110			
	(0.82)		(0.848)		(0.85)			
WSC	−0.050		−0.038		−0.039			
	(0.18)		(0.11)		(0.11)			
M	−0.142	−0.126	−0.138	−0.123	−0.138	−0.123	−0.125	−0.124
	(2.61)	(4.34)	(2.47)	(4.16)	(2.47)	(4.14)	(4.28)	(4.18)
OTHMETRO	0.021		0.024		0.025			
	(0.06)		(0.07)		(0.08)			
DIVORCE	0.183	0.172	0.130	0.156	0.133	0.158	0.169	0.167
	(2.52)	(5.83)	(1.30)	(4.72)	(1.35)	(4.80)	(6.02)	(5.90)
SEP	0.115	0.088	0.087	0.083	0.088	0.084	0.093	0.088
	(1.35)	(1.54)	(0.77)	(1.35)	(0.79)	(1.37)	(1.72)	(1.55)
NEVER	0.062		0.042		0.043			
	(0.29)		(0.13)		(0.14)			

(*continued*)

Table 10. (Continued)

Variables	*(1)*	*(2)*	*(3)*	*(4)*	*(5)*	*(6)*	*(7)*	*(8)*
OWNHOME	0.155	0.151	0.134	0.144	0.135	0.145	0.148	0.148
	(5.37)	(7.56)	(4.27)	(7.02)	(4.41)	(7.11)	(7.55)	(7.63)
CASHDUM	−0.016		0.015		−0.015			
	(0.04)		(0.03)		(0.03)			
DUMALIEN	−0.205		−0.251		−0.251			
	(0.18)		(0.26)		(0.27)			
DUMSPAN	0.093		0.170		0.166			
	(0.19)		(0.63)		(0.61)			
BIGSMSA	0.090	0.071	0.091	0.068	0.091	0.068	0.072	0.071
	(1.30)	(1.41)	(1.31)	(1.27)	(1.33)	(1.28)	(1.48)	(1.44)
MEDSMSA	0.051		0.063		0.063			
	(0.55)		(0.85)		(0.85)			
OTHNONM	−0.032		−0.024		−0.023			
	(0.20)		(0.10)		(0.11)			
DFARMINC	0.940	0.953	0.952	0.936	0.951	0.936	0.929	0.939
	(2.55)	(2.68)	(2.61)	(2.57)	(2.61)	(2.58)	(2.55)	(2.60)
KID0T2	−0.180	−0.184	−0.123	−0.168	−0.126	−0.170	0.178	−0.177
	(1.89)	(4.38)	(0.93)	(3.61)	(0.99)	(3.69)	(4.34)	(4.31)
KID3T4	−0.120	−0.131	−0.094	−0.133	−0.095	−0.132	−0.138	−0.139
	(1.89)	(3.97)	(1.08)	(3.45)	(1.20)	(3.92)	(4.50)	(4.55)
KID5T9	−0.110	−0.106	−0.085	−0.095	−0.086	−0.095	−0.108	−0.098
	(4.87)	(8.76)	(3.42)	(6.96)	(3.55)	(7.04)	(8.28)	(8.07)
KID10T13	−0.055	−0.056	−0.039	−0.049	−0.040	−0.049	−0.037	−0.051
	(1.94)	(2.82)	(1.08)	(2.13)	(1.11)	(2.16)	(0.99)	(2.40)
KID14T17	−0.031		−0.023		−0.023			
	(0.73)		(0.42)		(0.43)			

HDBLACK	0.227	0.241	0.226	0.241	0.226	0.241	0.2380	0.242
	(7.02)	(10.000)	(6.91)	(9.78)	(6.95)	(9.83)	(9.71)	(10.11)
HDOTHER	−0.102		−0.037		−0.040			
	(0.22)		(0.03)		(0.03)			
HDUNEMRT	−2.056	−2.209	−1.954	−2.162	−1.955	−2.154	−2.173	−2.182
	(5.69)	(8.46)	(5.03)	(7.90)	(5.10)	(7.95)	(8.32)	(8.41)
LOGHAW	0.583	0.685	0.576	0.685	0.576	0.684	0.689	0.685
	(15.03)	(27.81)	(14.47)	(27.56)	(14.55)	(27.58)	(28.12)	(27.91)
HEADAGE	0.034	0.021	0.032	0.023	0.032	0.023	0.023	0.023
	f (1.74)	(0.84)	(1.59)	(0.97)	(1.60)	(0.97)	(0.92)	(0.96)
HDAGESQR	−0.047	−0.0003	−0.0004	−0.0003	−0.0004	−0.0003	−0.0003	−0.0003
	(1.94)	(0.08)	(1.74)	(1.16)	(1.76)	(1.17)	(1.12)	(1.17)
HDED	−0.045	0.049	−0.067	0.046	−0.066	0.046	0.048	0.048
	(0.37)	(9.63)	(0.85)	(8.38)	(0.83)	(8.49)	(9.69)	(9.71)
HDEDSQR	0.004		0.005		0.005			
	(2.11)		(2.79)		(0.23)			
*X*1	0.272	0.297						
	(064)	(3.04)						
*X*2			0.090	0.243			0.288	0.280
			(0.08)	(1.98)			(3.41)	(3.25)
*X*3					0.099	0.249		
					(0.09)	(2.05)		
WORK			0.005	0.017				
			(0.01)	(0.07)				
CANTABS			0.189	0.131	0.184	0.121		
			(1.25)	(0.68)	(1.20)	(0.60)		
USMOB			0.044	0.033	0.044			
			(0.03)	(0.02)	(0.03)			

(continued)

Table 10. (Continued)

Variables	*(1)*	*(2)*	*(3)*	*(4)*	*(5)*	*(6)*	*(7)*	*(8)*
USHELP			0.038	0.009	0.038	0.012		
			(0.05)	(0.003)	(0.05)	(0.01)		
DIS3T4			0.006	0.008				
			(0.002)	(0.004)				
DUMDIS	−0.062	−0.064						
	(1.26)	(1.80)						
DIS5T17			−0.071	−0.090	−0.069	−0.081		−0.075
			(1.19)	(2.48)	(2.05)	(3.64)		(3.26)
DIS5T9							−0.033	
							(0.27)	
DIS10T13							−0.121	
							(3.42)	
DIS14T17							−0.076	
							(1.55)	
Constant	−0.216	−0.631	0.045	−0.610	0.033	−0.613	−0.649	−0.640
R^2	0.208	0.198	0.211	0.200	0.211	0.200	0.201	0.200

WORK is excluded, are negative and greater in absolute value than their standard errors, but they are not significant at conventional levels. The same is true for the coefficient of DIS14T17 in Equation 8.

Results from the earnings regressions (Table 9) parallel those from the work hours regressions. Once again the child disability variables are not significant except for WORK in Equation 9. Other coefficients for WORK are weaker but consistently negative with F-values greater than 1.0. A different pattern of child disability effects is observed, however, on maternal earnings per hour (Table 10). The overall average effect of children's disabilities, as indicated by the results for DUMDIS, is more strongly negative. Moreover, this negative effect is insignificant in several regressions for DIS5T17 and DIS10T13. On the whole, the results suggest that the negative effect on earnings per hour increases with the age of the disabled child. This parallels our earlier finding for mothers in white two-parent families (Salkever, 1982b) and again may reflect a cumulative negative effect of children's disabilities on maternal human capital formation.

VI. CONCLUSIONS

In contrast to earlier studies based on small samples of single mothers with children (which contained very small numbers of mothers with disabled children), the present study used a much larger data base and found stronger evidence that the presence of a disabled child reduces the probability of maternal employment. Evidence of child disability effects on hours, wages, and earnings for working mothers was much weaker. This pattern of results differs from earlier results obtained from this same data set for mothers with spouses present; the earlier results showed stronger negative child disability effects on hours, earnings, and wages than on employment probability (Salkever 1982b). A possible rationale for the finding reported here is that the fixed cost of working for single mothers is increased substantially when a child is disabled. For example, if the mother is to work at all, some nonparental source of child care and/or an appropriate school placement must be found. Because the availability of such care for disabled children is much more limited than for nondisabled children, the effect of a child's disability will primarily be to keep the mother from working at all. Our results suggest that further examination of lack of day care or other factors that may keep single mothers of disabled children out of the labor force be undertaken.

ACKNOWLEDGMENTS

This research was supported by Grant from the Maternal and Child Health Service of the U.S. Department of Health and Human Service. The assistance and programming support of Alison Jones is gratefully acknowledged.

NOTES

1. Note that the term "single" will be used here to denote women with no spouse present whether or not they have ever been married. This differs from the Bureau of Labor Statistics terminology in which only never-married women are labeled as "single."

2. It as been suggested that the increased prevalence of children's disabilities is due to more complete case-finding and diagnostic activities and "shifting perceptions on the part of parents, educators, and physicians" rather than to change in the true prevalence of the chronic conditions themselves (Newacheck, Budetti, & Halfon, 1986). Even in this event, however, parental time allocations (and hence labor-force behavior) are presumably affected by these shifting perceptions and more parental time is spent in managing their children's problems than would be spent if they were unaware of the exact nature of the problems or of the services and treatments needed to manage them.

3. In a small number of cases, the entire state or larger geographical aggregates had to be used because more specific areas were not identified on the SIE tapes or because numbers of adult female respondents in particular race-education groups were small.

4. For a description of the method of computing the selectivity variable and its use in labor-supply regressions, see J. Heckman (1980).

5. Because welfare payments tend to be higher in these regions, our results are consistent with the Lehrer and Nerlove's (1982) findings for their AFDC payment level variable, which was defined on a regional basis.

REFERENCES

Breslau, N., Salkever, D., and Staruch, K. S. (1982, June). Women's labor force activity and responsibilities for disabled dependents: A study of families with disabled children. *Journal of Health and Social Behavior, 23,* 169–183.

Garfinkel, I., & Masters, S. (1974). *The effect of income and wage rates on the labor supply of prime Age women* (Discussion paper No. 203–74). Madison, WI: University of Wisconsin-Madison.

Hausman, J. A. (1981). Labor supply. In H. J. Aaron & J. A. Pechman (Eds.), *How taxes affect economic behavior.* Washington, DC: Brookings Institute.

Heckman, J. J. (1980). Sample selection bias as a specification error with an application to the estimation of labor supply functions. In J. P. Smith (Ed.), *Female labor supply: Theory and estimation.* Princeton, NJ: Princeton University Press.

Lehrer, E., & Nerlove, M. (1982). An econometric analysis of the fertility and labor supply of unmarried women. In T. P. Schultz (Ed.), *Research in Population Economics* (Vol. 4, pp. 217–235). Greenwich, CT: JAI Press.

McEaddy, B. J. (1976, June). Women who head families: A socioeconomic analysis. *Monthly Labor Review.*

Mitchell, O. S. (1979, November). *The labor supply of nonmarried women.* Unpublished manuscript, Department of Labor Economics, New York State of Industrial and Labor Relations, Cornell University.

Newacheck, P. W., Budetti, P., & Halfon, N. (1986, February). Trends in activity-limiting chronic conditions among children. American *Journal of Public Health, 76,* 178–184.

Robins, P. K., West, R. W., & Stieger, G. (1983). Labor supply responses to a negative income tax. In R. Zeckhauser & D. Leelaert (Eds.), *What role for government?* Durham, NC: Duke University Press.

Salkever, D. S. (1980, July). Effects of children's health on maternal hours of work: A preliminary analysis. *Southern Economic Journal, 47,* 156–166.

———. (1982a). Children's health problems: Implications for parental labor supply and earnings. In V. R. Fuchs (Ed.), *Economic aspects of health.* Chicago: University of Chicago Press.

———. (1982b, Winter). Children's health problems and maternal work status. *Journal of Human Resources, 17,* 94–109.

U.S. Bureau of Labor Statistics. (1988, August). *Labor force statistics derived from the current population survey, 1948-1987* (Bulletin No. 2307. Washington, DC: U.S. Government Printing Office.

U.S. Department of Commerce, Bureau of the Census. (1978). *Microdata from the survey of income and education* (Data Access Description No. 42). Washington, DC: U.S. Government Printing Office.

U.S. Department of Health and Human Services. National Center for Health Statistics. (Various years). *Current estimates from the national health interview survey, vital and health statistics: Data from the national health survey* (Series 10, Nos. 52, 85, 130, 154, 166). Washington, DC: U.S. Government Printing Office.

SUMMARY AND DISCUSSION

Richard G. Frank and Catherine A. Jackson

The dramatic growth in female labor force participation in developed societies since World War II has provided formidable challenges to economists and sociologists interested in labor markets. The majority of research examining labor force participation has focused on married women's labor supply, modeling participation as a function of wages, demographics, and human capital formation of both wife and husband. The three papers in this section represent an attempt to extend this prior research by looking at other influences that may affect women's labor force participation. The focus of each of these papers is on factors which precipitate dynamic effects on labor force participation.

Each of the papers in this section presents observed patterns in female labor force participation that seem underexplained within the traditional paradigm of female labor supply. Elster and Kamlet are concerned with the role of income aspirations in labor supply decisions of married women. Mullahy and Sindelar argue that little attention has been given to the influence of mental health on the labor supply decisions of either men or women. They posit that mental health can affect the acquisition of human capital, and thus have dynamic effects on labor force participation. Finally, Salkever focuses on the effect child illness can have on labor force participation decisions of single mothers.

The paper by Elster and Kamlet builds on previous work in the economic and demographic literature. Following the work of Easterlin and others, which re-

Research in Human Capital and Development, Vol. 6, pages 183–185.

ISBN: 1-55938-032-2

vealed the importance of relative income and expected standards of living on behavior, Elster and Kamlet examine the importance of income aspirations and social class on married women's labor force decisions. Their analysis provides a social–psychological twist to the traditional economic analysis of female labor force participation. Using social psychology as a foundation, the authors carefully make the case for how commonly used notions of aspirations develop relative to some reference group. The role of income aspirations (or unfulfilled aspirations) is introduced as a factor that, in addition to absolute household income, may influence the labor force participation decisions of married women.

Using census data from 1970 and 1980 for the Pittsburgh area, Elster and Kamlet analyze the role of income aspirations in labor supply decisions of married women. Data from 1970 are used to construct a reference group measure of anticipated income based on husband's characteristics. The 1980 data are then used to create an index of aspiration fulfillment defined as the difference between actual and aspired income. The empirical analysis offers strong support for the importance of aspirations in determining the labor supply of married women. The authors extend this approach by also examining the importance of social class. Their results suggest that social class, as defined by husband's occupation, affects the impact of traditional variables on labor force participation. Moreover, the role of attitudes and social norms in determining female labor force participation varies by social class. This work takes a dynamic view of the process of aspiration formation and social class in a manner that parallels that of human capital formation.

The work by Mullahy and Sindelar examines the effect of mental disorders on human capital formation and labor supply decisions by gender. Roughly 18 percent of all adults suffer from a mental disorder at any point in time. The types of mental disorders that are prevalent vary significantly by gender; the predominant mental disorder for women is depression, while for men it is substance abuse, particularly alcohol. Given these differences, it is likely to be informative to carefully assess the labor market effects of mental disorders by gender.

Mullahy and Sindelar use a standard human capital approach to assess both the shortrun and longrun impacts of mental disorders on labor force participation. The data set used for the analysis derives from an epidemiological survey of mental disorders as well as information on individual demographics and labor force participation.

The results suggest that self-reported mental distress significantly reduces the labor force participation of women. Objective measures of mental disorders do not significantly affect labor force participation. Physical health status contributes significantly to labor supply. Thus, this analysis shows that this relatively rich characterization of health status, for both physical and mental health, reveals important determinants of labor supply. Inclusion of health status variables in supply models also reduces the estimated impacts of educational attainment and marital status. The implication is that mental health has a dynamic effect on labor supply that works through other forms of human capital formation, such as education.

The final paper by Salkever explores labor force participation of single women with children. Between 1970 and 1985 there was tremendous growth in the number of female-headed households. The growth has been particularly great in the black population, where the portion of black households headed by females grew from 28 to 44 percent. A number of previous studies have examined the interaction of labor supply, human capital formation, and child care decisions. The work by Salkever builds on this tradition and takes up the special set of circumstances that influences the interaction. The health status of children in a single mother's household is argued to have a different sort of effect on the single mother's labor supply compared to the case of married mothers.

Salkever uses a data set that is considerably larger than those used in previous studies of single mother's labor force participation (several of them by Salkever). The results show a significant reduction in maternal labor force participation when a child is disabled and between the ages of 5 and 9 years old. The estimated effect of a disabled child on hours of work, however, was not significantly different from zero. There was a significant relation between child disability and hourly earnings. Moreover, the size of the effect grew with the age of the child. The inference drawn by Salkever from this finding reflects the dynamic effects of disruptions in human capital formation stemming from the presence of a disabled child.

The three papers in this section are concerned with issues reflecting dynamic effects on labor supply decisions. Elster and Kamlet examined the impact of income aspirations and social class on married women's labor supply decisions; Mullahy and Sindelar examined the differential impact of mental health disorders on men's and women's labor force participation, where marital status was used as an independent variable; and Salkever examined the impact of the presence of a disabled child on single mothers' labor supply decisions. These three papers both fill various gaps in the literature and extend our knowledge base of labor force participation behavior.

PART III

FEMALE LABOR FORCE PARTICIPATION IN DEVELOPING COUNTRIES

THE LABOR FORCE PARTICIPATION OF AMERICAN INDIAN WOMEN

C. Matthew Snipp and Isik A. Aytac

I. INTRODUCTION

Despite the fact that American Indians represent one of the most poverty stricken segments of American society, very little is known about the ways in which this group participates in the labor market. What is known is that American Indians typically experience high levels of unemployment and overall low rates of labor force participation. American Indians neither seek nor hold jobs in large numbers. Beyond these simple facts, social scientists know little about Indian labor force behavior.

This paper deals with labor force participation of a subset of the American Indian population: American Indian women. By virtue of their race and gender, American Indian women are doubly disadvantaged in the labor market. The experiences of these women reflect the depths of economic hardship among one of the most disadvantaged groups in American society. If this fact alone is not enough to attract attention, there are other reasons why the labor force participation of American Indian women should interest an audience beyond those with specific ties to the Indian population.

Research in Human Capital and Development, Vol. 6, pages 189–211.

ISBN: 1-55938-032-2

American Indian women, and American Indians in general, occupy a unique position in the American social landscape. By dint of history, legal precedents, and public policy, American Indians have a relationship with the federal government unlike that of any other minority group in American society. To risk oversimplifying an extremely complex arrangement, the federal government has a formally established, legal obligation to oversee the affairs of American Indians in such a way as to preserve or enhance their social and economic well-being—hence, the Bureau of Indian Affairs and "Indian Law" as a legal specialty area. Whether this trust responsibility has been carried out faithfully can be debated. Yet, the fact that such a responsibility exists makes information about American Indians important for public policy purposes.

In reference to American Indian women, especially single women with children, the burgeoning numbers of women on the poverty roles include a sizable number of American Indian women. Compared to black women, American Indian women are somewhat more likely to reside in homes with intact families (Sandefur & Sakamoto, 1988). Yet, sizable numbers of Indian women, single and married, have incomes below official poverty levels. For example, in 1979, 27.6 percent[1] of all American Indian women over the age of 16 had incomes below official poverty levels (U.S. Bureau of the Census, 1983). American Indian men had 21.5 percent of their number in poverty in 1979. Among white individuals, the official poverty rate was 9.4 percent in 1980. Furthermore, nearly 24 percent of all American Indian families had incomes below poverty and of this number, over 44 percent were headed by single females (U.S. Bureau of the Census, 1983).

The labor force participation of American Indian women is also interesting because they are relative newcomers in the labor market. Historically, American Indians, men and women alike, have been isolated from the economic mainstream of American society; and they have not participated in large numbers in the labor market (Jacobsen, 1984). The recent experiences of American Indian women in the labor market reflect the kinds of opportunities that are available in the economy, especially for traditionally disadvantaged groups with relatively little background in the work force.

Finally, American Indians in general and American Indian women in particular can be seen as a kind of "miner's canary" for the rest of American society. American Indians have traditionally occupied the lowest rung of the American socioeconomic ladder. American Indians are one of the poorest, least educated, most unemployed, least healthy, and most economically disadvantaged groups in American society. As such, the economic experiences of American Indians speak to the overall well-being of American society. The wealth of a society cannot be fully assessed without knowing the full measure of its poverty. In this regard, American Indians represent the baseline for judging the socioeconomic well-being in American society.

This paper presents a number of different perspectives on the labor force participation of American Indian women. Among the issues addressed below, the first set of questions concerns the correlates of American Indian female labor force participation. In particular, these questions focus on ways in which American Indian women are different or similar to other women, and especially how the labor force participation of American Indian women is conditioned by supply-side factors known to influence the labor market experiences of other women—namely, factors such as age, education, fertility, and child care responsibilities. On the demand side, the kind of work done by American Indian women provides insights into the types of opportunities these women have available to them in the labor market. A third set of related issues concerns how the characteristics of the husbands of married American Indian women condition the labor force participation of their wives.

II. DISTRIBUTION OF THE AMERICAN INDIAN POPULATION

As an introduction, it will probably help many readers if they have some idea where the American Indian population resides, and the places where it is most concentrated. To begin, American Indians are predominantly a rural population, with about 51 percent residing in nonmetropolitan areas and about 49 percent living in metropolitan places. In contrast, about 81 percent of blacks and 73 percent of whites reside in metropolitan localities.

The urban American Indian population is concentrated within a relatively small number of cities. About one-half of urban American Indians reside in 1 of 17 cities. These 17 cities (shown in Table 1) each have 10,000 or more American Indian residents. The largest urban Indian population is located in southern California and numbered over 91,000 in 1980. Except for New York, large urban Indian populations are found only in cities of the western U.S., with Chicago and Detroit being the most eastern of these localities. One reason, among many, why these cities have large American Indian populations is that they are the former sites of relocation programs in which American Indians were encouraged to move from their reservations into predesignated "relocation centers." Between 1952 and 1972, 8 of 17 cities shown in Table 1 served as relocation centers for programs in which over 100,000 American Indians participated (Fixico, 1986; Sorkin, 1978).[2]

It may come as a surprise to some readers, but the number of American Indians residing on reservations is considerably smaller than the number of American Indians living in cities.[3] In 1980, approximately 340,000 American Indians were living on reservations and another 30,000 occupied special tribal trust lands. Figure 1 shows the distribution of the American Indian population for different types of areas. Most notable is that about one-quarter of the total Indian population resides on reservation lands and an additional 15 percent live near a reservation.

Finally, the data in Table 2 show the number of American Indians residing on

Table 1. Standard Metropolitan Statistical Areas (SMSAs) with 10,000 or more American Indians (1980)

SMSA	*Population*
Los Angeles, Long Beach, CA	47,234
Tulsa, OK	38,463
Phoenix, AZ	27,788
Oklahoma City, OK	24,695
Albuquerque, NM	20,721
San Francisco, Oakland, CA	17,546
Riverside, San Bernardino, Ontario, CA	17,107
Minneapolis, St. Paul, MN	15,831
Seattle, Everette, WA	15,162
Tucson, AZ	14,880
San Diego, CA	14,355
New York, NY	13,440
Anaheim, Santa Ana, Garden Grove, CA	12,782
Detroit, MI	12,372
Dallas, Ft. Worth, TX	11,076
Sacramento, CA	10,944
Chicago, IL	10,415
Total in SMSAs	324,811
Percent of Total U.S. Indian Population	23.8

Source: U.S. Bureau of the Census (1983a).

the 16 largest reservations. Although there are 278 Federal and State reservations located throughout the United States, 192 in the west, these 16 reservations represent 57 percent of the reservation Indian population. The Navajo reservation overlapping the Four Corners region of northeastern Arizona is clearly the largest, in numbers as well as in size. Over 100,000 Navajo occupy an arid territory approximately the size of West Virginia. Trailing far behind but second in size is the Pine Ridge reservation in South Dakota. All of these reservations, except the Navajo, involve relatively small numbers of people, especially compared to urban locations. Few of these reservations exceed 5,000 and the vast majority of reservations nationwide are much smaller.

III. SUPPLY SIDE CHARACTERISTICS

Race

Although race has little bearing on the productivity of workers, or the value of their labor, it is well known that racial and ethnic minorities participate less in the labor force than members of the white majority. In part, this can be explained by

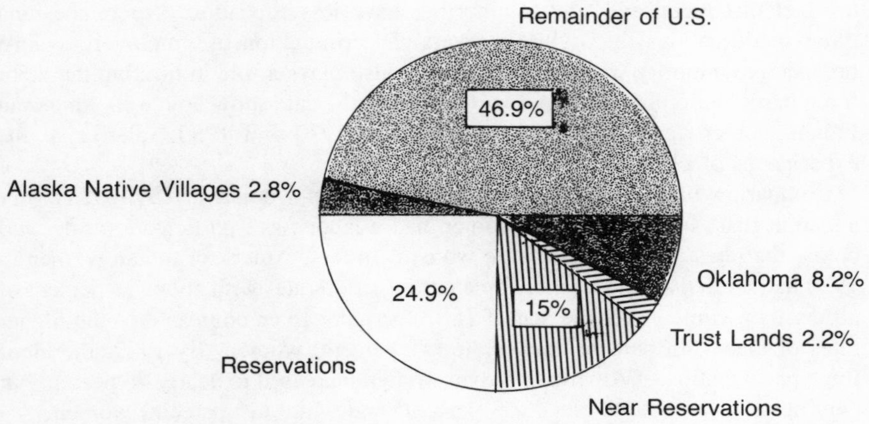

Source: U.S. Bureau of the Census (1983a).

Figure 1. Percent distribution of American Indians and Alaska Natives residing on native lands, 1980.

Table 2. Population Sizes of the Sixteen Largest American Indian Reservations in 1989

Reservation	*1980 Population*
Navajo (AZ, NM, UT)	104,968
Pine Ridge (SD)	11,882
Gila River (AZ)	7,067
Papago (AZ)	6,959
Fort Apache (AZ)	6,880
Hopi (AZ)	6,601
Zuni Pueblo (NM)	5,988
San Carlos (AZ)	5,872
Rosebud (SD)	5,688
Blackfeet (MT)	5,080
Yakima (WA)	4,983
Eastern Cherokee (NC)	4,844
Standing Rock (ND, SD)	4,800
Osage (OK)	4,749
Fort Peck (MT)	4,273
Wind River (WY)	4,150
Total of 16 Reservations	194,784
Percent of U.S. Indian Population	14.3

Source: U.S. Bureau of the Census (1983a).

the fact that racial and ethnic minorities have less education, experience, and other qualifications than white workers. Discrimination by employers against prospective minority workers undoubtedly also plays a role in limiting the labor force participation of these groups. In Table 3, the data show how well American Indian women fared in the labor market in 1970 and 1980, relative to the experiences of black and white women.

Comparing black, white, and American Indian women in 1970, it is very apparent that American Indian women had a labor force participation rate well below the rates of black and white women. In fact, American Indian women in 1970 had a relatively low labor force participation rate, with about 35 percent of all civilian women over the age of 16 in the labor force compared to the higher rates of black (48 percent) and white (41 percent) women. By 1980, the labor force participation of American Indian women increased to nearly 48 percent but continued to lag behind black (53 percent) and white (49 percent) women.

Another way of viewing these changes over time is in terms of how increases in labor force participation is distributed between employment and unemployment. From this perspective American Indian women gained more than black women between 1970 and 1980, but not as much as white women. For example, between 1970 and 1980 the labor force participation of American Indian women increased 12.6 percentage points. About 17 percent of this gain (2.1 percentage points) was manifest in higher unemployment. For white women, their labor force participation increased by 8.8 percentage points between 1970 and 1980. Yet, only 10 percent of this gain (0.9 percentage points) appeared as higher unemployment. Black women fared worst, as 41 percent of their 5.6 percentage point increase in labor force participation was in the form of higher unemployment. In sum, higher rates of labor force participation meant more unemployment for American Indian women than for white women, but not nearly so much as for black women.

Table 3. Distribution of Labor Force Participation by Black, White, and American Indian Women Age 16 and Over, 1970 and 1980 (In Percent)

	Blacks		*Whites*		*American Indians*	
	1970	*1980*	*1970*	*1980*	*1970*	*1980*
Employed	43.8	47.1	38.6	46.5	31.7	42.2
Unemployed	3.7	6.0	1.9	2.8	3.6	5.7
Not in Labor Force	52.5	46.9	59.5	50.7	64.7	52.1
Total	100.0	100.0	100.0	100.0	100.0	100.0
Unemployment Rate[a]	7.8	11.3	4.7	5.7	10.2	11.9

Note: [a]Percent of civilian labor force unemployed.
Source: U.S. Bureau of the Census (1983a).

This conclusion is further reinforced by the changes in unemployment rates between 1970 and 1980.[4] Joblessness in 1970 was much more widespread among Indian women than among either white or black women. However, among black women unemployment increased from 8 to 11 percent, while it grew from 10 to 12 percent among American Indian women. For white women, the increase in unemployment was smaller, 5 to 6 percent. In other words, due to worsening conditions among blacks the unemployment gap between American Indian and black women narrowed between 1970 and 1980. However, in the same period, the gap between these women and white women widened.

Age

Age plays a role in the working lives of American Indian women in two ways. First, age can be seen as a proxy for work experience. Older women are more likely to have spent more time in the work force, and therefore are likely to be more productive workers than younger women. Needless to say, the relationship between age and experience is no more than approximate. In view of recent trends toward greater female labor force participation, it is true that some, if not many, older American Indian women have never worked or worked very little. Compared with younger women active in the work force, these older women have very little experience. Nevertheless, there is at least an approximate connection between age and experience.

Age also reflects stages in the life cycle that are, or are not, conducive to labor force participation. When Indian women are relatively young, they are less likely to have child care responsibilities and more likely to be in the labor force. As these women enter their childbearing years, family obligations make them more likely to leave the labor force. Finally, as their children become older and more self-sufficient, these women may find it economically worthwhile to reenter the work force.

Table 4 shows the distribution of labor force participation and unemployment across five-year cohorts of American Indian women age 16 and over in 1980. The data in this table follow a predictable pattern and demonstrate, at the very least, that American Indian women are not particularly unique with respect to the relationship between age and labor force participation. Teenage females are the most likely to be out of the labor force but their labor force participation sharply increases as they complete their schooling. For example, 31 percent of American Indian women under age 21 were employed, compared to nearly 49 percent of women age 21 to 25. Interestingly, American Indian women in the peak childbearing years do not have labor force participation rates significantly lower than those for women of other ages. In fact, Indian women in their thirties are most likely to be employed (about 55 percent), followed by women in their twenties, and with employment decreasingly less common in successive cohorts of older women.

The unemployment rates in Table 4 more or less mirror age-specific labor

Table 4. Distribution of Labor Force Participation and Age of American Indian Women, 1980 (In Percent)

Age	*Employed*	*Unemployed*	*Not in Labor Force*	*Total*	*Unemployment Rate*[a]
16 to 20	31.0	8.5	60.5	100.0	21.5
21 to 25	48.6	8.2	43.3	100.0	14.4
26 to 30	52.8	7.4	39.8	100.0	12.3
31 to 35	55.1	5.5	39.4	100.0	9.1
36 to 40	55.0	5.0	40.0	100.0	8.3
41 to 45	52.6	5.0	42.4	100.0	8.7
46 to 50	45.0	4.0	51.0	100.0	8.2
51 to 55	42.6	3.7	53.6	100.0	8.0
56 to 60	33.3	2.8	63.9	100.0	7.8
61 to 65	22.7	1.5	75.8	100.0	6.2
66 to 70	11.5	1.1	87.4	100.0	8.7
Over 70	4.4	0.5	95.1	100.0	10.2

Note: [a]Percent of civilian labor force unemployed.
Source: U.S. Bureau of the Census (1983a).

force participation but they also reveal why these figures can be misleading in the absence of other information about labor force participation. As a percentage of the total civilian labor force, which never exceeds 61 percent of the female population over 16, the unemployment rate is very high for teenagers (22 percent) and declines for subsequent cohorts. Unemployment rates are lowest among the oldest cohorts of women, where, incidentally, labor force participation rates are also lowest. Not surprisingly, among women over age 60, only 25 percent or less are in the labor force; low rates of labor force participation and low unemployment rates illustrate a pattern of behavior observed for women of other races. Namely that women, especially older women, when confronted with the choice of engaging in a possibly prolonged job search that would keep them in the labor force as unemployed, frequently choose instead to drop-out of the workforce altogether (Haber, Lamas, & Green, 1983).

Education

An extensive literature in sociology and economics documents the unparalleled importance of education in the work lives of men and women alike. Educational attainment in the form of years of schooling completed is associated with higher productivity and higher earnings (Becker, 1964; Mincer, 1974; Sewell & Hauser, 1975). Educational credentials are also believed important as signals to employers and for gaining access to special economic advantages (Berg, 1970; Collins, 1979).

For American Indians, the role of education in determining socioeconomic

Table 5. Distribution of Civilian Labor Force Participation and Education of American Indian Women Age 16 and Over in 1980
(In Percent)

Years of Education	*Employed*	*Unemployed*	*Not in Labor Force*	*Total*	*Unemployment Rate*
Under 9	19.7	3.1	77.2	100.0	13.6
9 to 11	30.8	6.5	62.7	100.0	17.4
12	50.3	6.6	43.1	100.0	11.6
13 to 15	58.4	6.2	35.4	100.0	9.6
16 and over	66.4	3.7	29.9	100.0	5.3

Source: U.S. Bureau of the Census (1983a).

outcomes has not been extensively studied. However, the levels of educational attainment have been associated with the limited success of American Indians in the labor market (Levitan & Johnston, 1975; Sorkin 1971, 1978). Sandefur and Scott (1983) found that the earnings derived from years of education were somewhat more than received by black workers but below those received by whites. Snipp and Sandefur (1986) found that gender and education both had important impacts on the labor force participation of American Indians. Other studies have found similar results (Gwartney & Long, 1978; Trosper, 1980).

Table 5 shows the relationship between schooling and employment for American Indian women age 16 and over in 1980. Not surprisingly, labor force participation is highest among those American Indian women with the most education, and it is lowest for the most poorly educated American Indian women. Among Indian women with less than a ninth grade education, barely 20 percent are employed and 77 percent are not in the labor force.

Unemployment is also closely related to educational attainments. Not surprisingly, Indian female high school dropouts have the highest unemployment (17 percent). In comparison college graduates are least unemployed. One noteworthy observation is that all American Indians with less than a college education have unemployment rates markedly higher than the white population (cf. Table 3). Only American Indian college graduates have unemployment rates comparable to the white population as a whole.

Childbearing and Child Care

Fertility

The inverse relationship between fertility and labor force participation is well known but poorly understood. At issue is whether women curtail their fertility to take advantage of opportunities in the labor market, or whether childbearing necessarily limits the ability of women to be active in the workforce (Bianchi & Spain, 1986). As Bianchi and Spain point out, the conumdrum is unlikely to be resolved soon.

Nevertheless, the negative relationship between fertility and education can be clearly seen in Table 6. This table shows the educational achievements and average number of children ever born to cohorts of women ages 15 to 54 in 1980. Net of age, these data indicate that employed American Indian women have substantially fewer children ever born than women not in the labor force, 2.6 and 3.4, respectively. However, the most significant distinction is between women who are and are not in the work force. Overall, women in the labor force, employed and unemployed, have noticeably fewer children ever born than women who are not active in the workforce.

Child Care

It hardly needs stating that greater child care responsibilities are an inevitable result of childbearing. And equally apparent, these responsibilities have an important bearing on the labor force participation of American Indian women. Following up the data in Table 6, the figures in Table 7 show how the presence and age of children combine to impact the labor force participation of Indian women. Several observations can be made about this table, and most apparent is that for Indian women, child care responsibilities pose a major obstacle to labor force participation. This is significant because it suggests that the extensive kin networks prevalent in many American Indian communities do not function to enhance female labor force participation. Complex family networks are common in many American Indian communities, especially reservations, but such networks do not appear to have a decisive role in freeing Indian women from the responsibilities of child care. Predictably, Indian women with no children are most likely to be in the labor force and employed, while those with the largest child care responsibilities (children at all ages under 18) are least likely to be

Table 6. Civilian Labor Force Participation and Mean Number of Children Ever Born to Ever Married American Indian and Alaska Native Women Ages 15 to 54, in 1980

Age	*Employed*	*Unemployed*	*Not in Labor Force*
15 to 24	0.99	1.24	1.44
25 to 34	1.98	2.24	2.63
35 to 44	3.32	3.90	3.97
45 to 54	3.92	4.77	4.54
Total	2.58	2.65	3.43

Source: U.S. Bureau of the Census (1983a).

Table 7. Distribution of Labor Force Participation and Age of Children at Home for American Indian Women Age 16 and Over in 1980
(In Percent)

Age of Children	*Employed*	*Unemployed*	*Labor Force*	*Total*	*Unemployment Rate*
Under 18	39.4	7.4	53.2	100.0	15.8
6 to 17	59.9	7.7	32.4	100.0	11.5
Under 6	51.5	5.8	42.6	100.0	10.1
No Children	63.;2	5.8	31.0	100.0	8.4

Source: U.S. Bureau of the Census (1983a).

employed and most likely to be out of the labor force. Another interesting detail in Table 7 is that American Indian women tend to be employed, or out of the labor force, but less inclined to be engaged in a job search as implied by the status of "unemployed"—again, this pattern is consistent with the labor force behavior of other groups of women (Haber, et al., 1983) and the data in Table 4.

IV. DEMAND SIDE CHARACTERISTICS

Residence

To illustrate how market demand impacts the labor force participation of American Indians, the next series of tables focus on the kinds of labor into which Indian women are drawn. As an introduction, the next table, Table 8, shows the distribution of labor force participation for American Indian men and women in metropolitan and nonmetropolitan localities. The implications of these numbers should be readily apparent. Metropolitan labor markets, for men and for women,

Table 8. Distribution of Labor Force Participation and Place of Residence for American Indian Men and Women, 1980
(In Percent)

	Metropolitan		*Nonmetropolitan*	
	Men	*Women*	*Men*	*Women*
Employed	63.6	45.6	51.7	37.1
Unemployed	9.4	5.8	10.4	5.7
Not in Labor Force	27.0	48.6	37.9	57.2
Total	100.0	100.0	100.0	100.0
Unemployment Rate	12.9	11.3	16.7	13.3

Source: U.S. Bureau of the Census (1983a).

offer a greater variety of opportunities for employment, especially in the secondary and tertiary sectors of the economy. Nonmetropolitan labor markets are not only more sluggish than metropolitan markets, on average, but nonmetropolitan labor markets typically have fewer of the jobs traditionally open to women, such as clerical or service jobs. It is also worth noting that most reservations are located in nonmetropolitan areas and by tradition have seriously depressed local economies.

The results in Table 8 are hardly surprising, and they are consistent with the experiences of women in other racial and ethnic groups. First, American Indian women are less likely to be in the labor force than men. American Indian men out-number Indian women among the ranks of the employed and the unemployed. Similarly, the unemployment rates for Indian men are higher than the unemployment rates for Indian women. These conditions exist in metropolitan and nonmetropolitan areas alike. Although the labor force participation of Indian women in urban areas is lower than the labor force participation of Indian men in urban *or* rural places, urban Indian women are nonetheless more likely to be actively employed than their nonmetropolitan counterparts. Interestingly, joblessness is about the same in both types of areas suggesting again, that Indian women participate in the labor force as active workers or drop out in the absence of employment. Finally, the relative gap between men and women is nearly identical in metropolitan and nonmetropolitan areas. In metropolitan areas, employment is 39.5 percent higher for Indian men than for Indian women and in nonmetropolitan places, the gap is 39.4 percent.

Occupational Class

The concept of occupational class describes the kinds of employers who purchase the labor of workers, American Indian and otherwise. In general, employers can be subdivided into three major groups: private sector, public sector, and self-employment. Private sector employers and self-employment entails self-explanatory classes of employers. However, the meaning of public sector employment in relation to American Indians is unique because of the special political status of American Indians.

By virtue of an extremely complex set of political arrangements, American Indians have access to two types of public sector employment typically not available to other groups. Tribal governments are a form of local government that often hire significant numbers of American Indians. Tribal governments are usually restricted to reservations and locations in Oklahoma. The Bureau of Indian Affairs (BIA) and other agencies of the federal government with mandates to serve the Indian population also hire significant numbers of American Indians. In fact, the BIA routinely applies an "Indian Preference" criterion in the selection of job applicants.

The data in Table 9 show the extent to which American Indian women (and

Table 9. Distribution of Occupational Class for Black, White, and American Indian Women Age 16 and Over in 1980 (In Percent)

Occupational Class	*Blacks*	*Whites*	*American Indians*
Private Wage and Salary	67.2	76.0	62.8
Federal Government	7.6	3.0	12.4
State Government	8.5	5.3	7.5
Local Government	15.3	10.9	13.8
Self-Employed	1.2	4.0	3.0
Unpaid Family Worker	0.2	0.8	0.5
Total	100.0	100.0	100.0

Source: U.S. Bureau of the Census (1983a).

American Indians generally) depend on federal and local government employment. Compared with black and white women. American Indian women are much more concentrated in federal government jobs. About 12 percent of employed Indian women and 3 percent of white women have such employment. Similarly, American Indian women and black women are both heavily dependent on local government jobs, 15 and 14 percent, respectively; about 11 percent of white women are employed by local government. Not surprisingly, American Indian women are least likely to have private sector employment. Compared to 76 percent of white women in the private sector, about 63 percent of Indian women have private sector jobs.

Industry and Occupation

Yet another way of viewing the demand for the labor of American Indian women is in terms of the industries and occupations in which they are employed. Table 10 shows the distribution of American Indian men and women across broad classes of industry. Table 11 displays the kinds of employment that make up the occupational structure for American Indian workers.

Industry

In Table 10 there are two noteworthy characteristics of American Indian female labor force participation. Perhaps most obvious is the extent of industrial segregation between American Indian male and female workers. The demand for American Indian female labor is heavily concentrated in the tertiary, nongoods producing sectors of the economy. Over 40 percent of working Indian women are employed alone in service industries. Overall, over three-fourths of the Indian female labor force is employed in tertiary industries. This pattern does vary

Table 10. Distribution of Residence and Industry of American Indians and Alaska Natives, 1980 (In Percent)

	Metropolitan		*Nonmetropolitan*	
Industry	*Men*	*Women*	*Men*	*Women*
Agriculture, Forestry, and Fisheries	2.9	0.9	8.2	2.2
Mining	1.7	0.5	14.9	1.2
Construction	13.0	1.5	14.9	1.2
Manufacturing	25.2	16.0	18.0	14.7
Transportation, Communications, and Other Public Utilities	10.3	4.7	8.3	2.5
Wholesale Trade	4.7	2.2	2.2	1.0
Retail Trade	12.2	17.3	8.3	13.8
Finance, Insurance, and Real Estate	2.9	6.7	1.3	2.2
Services	19.1	41.3	17.5	44.0
Public Administration	8.0	8.9	15.4	17.6
Total	100.0	100.0	100.0	100.0

Source: U.S. Bureau of the Census (1983a).

greatly by residence. In fact, American Indian women are *more* likely to be in tertiary industries if they reside in rural areas than if they are living in an urban labor market. A related, second observation is that gender segregation across industries is greater in nonmetropolitan than in metropolitan areas. The index of dissimilarity, a commonly used measure of segregation, is 6.4 for metropolitan based industries and 7.0 for nonmetropolitan areas.

Given that service industries are a primary source of employment for American Indian women, then what kinds of work does this entail? In general, most of these women are not employed in low wage, low skill personal and household services; nor are they in the ranks of high prestige business services. In fact, most (75.6 percent) of the 93,693 Indian women in service industries are employed in "Professional and Related Services" (U.S. Bureau of the Census, 1983). Among these services, 41 percent are school related, another 41 percent are in health care, and third largest are jobs in social service organizations, 13 percent. In other words, for Indian women employed in service industries, a large number are involved in jobs such as teachers, teachers' aides, clerical, nurses, physicians' assistants, medical technicians, and social service workers.

Occupation

The information about the occupations of American Indian women in Table 11 is generally consistent with the image of Indian female workers found in the data

Table 11. Distribution of Place of Residence and Occupations of American Indians, 1980 (In Percent)

	Metropolitan		*Nonmetropolitan*	
Occupation	*Men*	*Women*	*Men*	*Women*
Managerial and Professional	13.7	14.6	10.9	14.0
Technical, Sales and Administrative Support	12.9	38.7	7.9	30.3
Service	13.2	26.1	14.9	30.9
Farming, Forestry and Fishing	5.3	1.7	11.4	3.4
Precision Production, Craft, and Repair	23.5	3.4	22.2	3.3
Operators, Fabricators, and Laborers	31.4	15.5	32.7	18.1
Total	100.0	100.0	100.0	100.0

Source: U.S. Bureau of the Census (1983a).

for industries. American Indian women rely heavily on lower level white collar occupations for employment, and this is true in metropolitan and nonmetropolitan areas alike. Nearly two-thirds (65 percent) of urban Indian women work in "service" or "technical, sales, and administrative support" occupations, and the percentage of rural Indian women who work in these occupations is only slightly smaller (61.2 percent). In contrast, American Indian men are concentrated in blue collar, manual occupations.

It is worth noting that service occupations and service industries entail very different activities. Although American Indian women in service industries are concentrated in health, education, and welfare organizations, the largest number of Indian women in service occupations are employed in food service occupations. Specifically, about 35 percent of American Indian women in service occupations have jobs such as cooks or waitresses. In "technical, sales, and administrative support" occupations, the largest number of Indian women (24 percent) are clerical workers followed by Indian women in sales work (21 percent).

V. The Role of Husbands

For many, if not most married American Indian women, participation in the labor force transcends the relatively simple economic calculations that determine whether single women enter the work force. As any married person knows, marriage entails shared household responsibilities, decisions about the apportionment of labor inside and outside the home, and mutual economic obligations. In deciding to enter the job market, married American Indian women (or women of any race) typically make their decisions in the framework of being part of a larger economic unit—their families. As a consequence, the labor market situation of their husbands represents a major contingency in the labor force participation of married Indian women. The impact of spousal characteristics on the labor market behavior of American Indian women can be viewed from two different perspectives.

One way of thinking about the role of husbands in the labor force participation of American Indian women is from the standpoint of economic utility. An *economic utility* perspective might predict, for example, an inverse relationship between the labor force participation of wives and those characteristics that govern the labor force participation of husbands. If husbands are active in the labor force, then the economic importance of wives' participation is reduced. Conversely, wives may also be economically compelled to enter the labor market as a way of compensating for the marginal position of husbands who have sporadic or nonexistent labor force participation.

Aside from economic utility, another way of thinking about the impact of husbands on the labor market behavior of Indian women is in terms of *status homogamy*. A well known fact in family sociology is that marriage partners tend to be status equals. High-status men tend not to marry low-status women and vice versa. Or well-educated women tend not to marry poorly educated men. This perspective advocates a positive relationship between husbands' characteristics and the labor force participation of their wives. Concretely, this means that if husbands are well-qualified and active in the labor force, then the principle of status homogamy predicts that wives will be equally well-qualified and more likely to be active in the labor force. By the same logic, husbands with marginal positions in the labor market are likely to have wives who are equally marginal.

Age and Education

There is insufficient space to examine at length the ways in which husbands' characteristics affect the labor force participation of wives. Yet in the remaining pages, the last series of tables offer some provisional insights into this matter. The relationship between the age of husbands, their education and the labor force participation of their wives is shown in Tables 12 and 13, respectively.

Age

For men and women alike, and for obvious reasons, age is an important determinant of labor force participation. As discussed earlier, labor force participation is lowest for young workers without experience and for older workers nearing retirement. The economic utility perspective would predict that as husbands enter their peak working ages, the labor force participation of their wives would diminish. Conversely, wives would be more likely to be in the labor force if they have particularly young or old husbands. In contrast, the status homo-

Table 12. Distribution of the Labor Force Participation of Married American Indian Women and the Age of Their Husbands, 1980 (In Percent)

Husbands' Age	*Employed*	*Unemployed*	*Labor Force*	*Total*	*Unemployment Rate*
Under 21	36.7	10.2	53.1	100.0	21.7
21 to 30	47.4	6.8	45.8	100.0	12.5
31 to 40	51.9	4.8	43.3	100.0	8.5
41 to 50	51.6	3.5	44.9	100.0	6.4
51 to 60	40.5	2.9	56.6	100.0	6.7
61 to 70	27.7	1.2	71.1	100.0	4.2
70 and Over	11.3	1.2	87.5	100.0	9.6

Source: U.S. Bureau of the Census (1983a).

gamy perspective would predict that women with particularly old or young husbands would themselves be relatively young or old, and therefore would be no more advantaged in the labor market than their husbands.

The data addressing these expectations are shown in Table 12. These figures suggest that American Indian women do not, or cannot, enter the labor force to compensate for their husband's age. American Indian women also do not seem to be more inclined to leave the labor market if they have husbands in their peak working ages. Among Indian women with husbands under age 21, a relatively large percentage are in the labor force, almost 47 percent. However, much of this participation is in the form of job-seeking activities instead of actual employment. Unemployment for this group is an exceedingly high 22 percent. American Indian women with husbands in their prime working years have substantially less unemployment. This is a result of greater employment and not because these women have dropped out of the labor force. The American Indian

Table 13. Distribution of the Labor Force Participation of Married American Indian Women and the Educational Attainments of Their Husbands, 1980 (In Percent)

Husbands' Education	*Employed*	*Unemployed*	*Labor Force*	*Total*	*Unemployment Rate*
Under 9	29.5	3.5	67.0	100.0	10.6
9 to 11	41.5	5.0	53.5	100.0	10.8
12	47.9	5.1	47.0	100.0	9.6
13 to 15	52.8	4.7	42.5	100.0	8.2
16 and Over	56.6	2.8	40.6	100.0	4.7

Source: U.S. Bureau of the Census (1983a).

women least attached to the labor force are those with older husbands, especially Indian women with husbands age 51 and older.

With regard to husband's age, status homogamy appears to be a major consideration affecting the labor force participation of Indian women. This is hardly surprising, as young men tend to marry young women and both share the disadvantage of their age in the labor market. More interesting is that Indian women with older husbands in their prime working years do not elect to drop-out of the labor force in noticeable numbers.

Education

Social norms regarding mate selection have a sanctioning role in maintaining the age homogamy of marriage partners. However, it is not clear whether education homogamy is as binding as age homogamy. Nor is it clear how the education of husbands affects the labor force participation of their wives. Again, status homogamy would predict that the wives of poorly educated men would themselves be poorly educated and more likely to be out of the labor force. However, an economic utility view would anticipate compensatory labor force participation on the part of Indian women with poorly educated husbands.

The percentages in Table 13 suggest that, like age, educational homogamy appears to have an overriding effect on the labor force participation of Indian women. Among women with husbands who never reached high school, 67 percent are not in the labor force. Of the 33 percent who are in the labor force, nearly 11 percent are unemployed. In sharp contrast are those women with husbands who have the equivalent of a college education. Nearly 57 percent of these women are employed, under 5 percent are unemployed, and only 41 percent are not in the labor force.

The fact that better-educated husbands tend to have better-educated wives is one obvious explanation for the results in Table 13, but there may be other factors that are operant. For instance, well-educated couples are more likely to have fewer children and this facilitates female labor force participation. Furthermore, better-educated husbands may be less traditional and more supportive of a working wife. In short, status homogamy entails a host of complexly related conditions that facilitate or impede labor force participation.

Employment and Income

Employment

Although the age and education of a husband has an important bearing on a wife's decision to work, the income and labor force participation of the husband may have an even more important role in the wife's labor force participation. A husband may be young and well-educated, but if he is not employed, the economic utility perspective would suggest that his wife would seek to augment the family's resources through employment. However, as the data in Table 14 indicate, employed husbands tend to have employed wives. Similarly, if a husband is not in the labor force, it is highly likely that his wife also is not in the labor force.

The figures in Table 14 show that among employed husbands, about one-half have employed wives. However, among unemployed husbands, only 41 percent of their wives are employed and nearly one-half are not in the labor force. The wives of unemployed husbands also have an exceedingly high rate of unemployment, nearly 21 percent. High unemployment among these women reflects, at least in part, the unsuccessful job seeking of persons who might otherwise be out of the labor force if their husbands were employed. From this perspective, the concept of economic utility explains why women with unemployed husbands are seeking work while status homogamy accounts for their lack of success in the labor market—namely, that the wives of unemployed men are themselves disadvantaged in the labor market. Finally, among men not in the labor force, 71 percent have wives who are also not in the labor force. This is most likely a reflection of women withdrawing from the labor force in response to their own or their husbands' retirement.

Income

The income received by husbands, or lack thereof, is another obvious inducement for American Indian women to enter the labor force. Given that American Indian men tend not to have high paying jobs, the opportunity to work would present Indian women with a means of augmenting family incomes. However, as the percentages in Table 15 indicate, and consistent with the preceding tables, there is little evidence that wives find employment to compensate for the low incomes received by their husbands.

In terms of employment, there is a positive relationship between the income of husbands and whether their wives have jobs. Among men with $20,000 or more personal income, 58 percent have employed wives. In contrast, only 30 percent

Table 14. Distribution of Labor Force Participation of Married American Indian Women by the Labor Force Participation of Their Husbands, 1980 (In Percent)

Husbands' Labor Force Participation	*Employed*	*Unemployed*	*Labor Force*	*Total*	*Unemployment Rate*
Employed	50.4	4.2	45.4	100.0	7.7
Unemployed	40.5	10.5	49.0	100.0	20.6
Not in Labor Force	26.8	2.4	70.8	100.0	8.2

Source: U.S. Bureau of the Census (1983a).

Table 15. Distribution of the Labor Force Participation of American Indian Women and the Incomes of Their Husbands, 1980
(In Percent)

Husbands' Income ($)	*Employed*	*Unemployed*	*Labor Force*	*Total*	*Unemployment Rate*
Under 5,000	29.9	5.4	64.7	100.0	15.3
5,001 to 10,000	26.1	5.7	68.2	100.0	17.9
10,001 to 15,000	39.0	5.5	55.5	100.0	17.3
15,001 to 20,000	47.4	4.2	48.4	100.0	8.1
Over 20,000	58.4	3.4	38.2	100.0	5.5

Source: U.S. Bureau of the Census (1983a).

of the wives of the poorest men have employment. Likewise, nearly 65 percent of the wives of the poorest men are not in the labor force, whereas only about 38 percent of the wives of high income men are not active in the labor market.

Despite the fact that the low income of husbands does not translate into greater numbers of employed women, the relationship between husbands' income and wives' labor force participation parallels the relationship between husbands' and wives' labor market behavior. This is most apparent in unemployment rates. The wives of low-income men have relatively high rates of unemployment compared with the wives of higher income men. As before, these high rates of unemployment suggest that the wives of low income men participate in the labor market, perhaps to augment their husbands' income, by seeking employment but they are not particularly successful in finding work—hence their high rates of unemployment. Similarly, the lack of success these women have in the job market suggests that they very likely share in common with their husbands many of the same disadvantages responsible for their husbands' low income.

VI. SUMMARY AND CONCLUSIONS

This discussion of the labor market experience of American Indian women has tried to describe, in relatively simple terms, how and why American Indian women participate in the U.S. labor force, specifically in terms of participation, nonparticipation, and unemployment. Although American Indian women are culturally and socially unique in many respects, they are nonetheless subject to many of the same constraints and market forces affecting other American women. Consequently, the labor force participation of American Indian women can be described in relation to the economic position of their family, especially their husbands' characteristics.

Supply Factors: In connection with supply-side characteristics, race, age, education, and family obligations each has an effect on the labor force participation of American Indian women. Compared to either black or white women, American Indian women have a more tenuous attachment to the labor market—they are employed less and out of the labor force more than other women. Age and education have a predictable impact on employment. American Indian women in their peak working years, and/or those who are better educated, are more likely to be actively employed than other Indian women. Although American Indian women are most likely to be active workers in their peak working ages, these years are also the childbearing years. As a result, age-related labor force participation is dampened by child care responsibilities. Fertility and the presence of young children are both inversely related to the labor force participation of American Indian women. However, there is some evidence that women with school age children are somewhat more active in the labor force than women with young children.

Demand Factors: In the context of this discussion, demand factors are reflected in the residence and the kinds of works performed by employed American Indian women—namely, sector, occupation, and industry. Not surprisingly, American Indian women residing in rural areas have fewer employment opportunities than women in urban labor markets, and this is reflected in the lower employment and higher unemployment rates for rural American Indian women. In large part due to their unique political status, American Indian women are unique in their dependence on public sector employment. For these women, organizations such as the Bureau of Indian Affairs and tribal governments are an important source of employment. Public administration is a key industry of employment, but American Indian women are most heavily concentrated in service industries. Most likely, these women are employed in occupations such as "Technical, Sales, and Administrative Support" or in jobs classed as "Service."

The Role of Husbands: In principle, wives with economically marginal husbands might join the labor force to augment the economic well-being of their family, unless, of course, these women have the same kinds of disadvantages that prevent their husbands from working. There is some evidence that this describes the situation confronting many married American Indian women. American Indian women with husbands who are weakly attached to the labor force appear to be drawn into the labor force, but this does not automatically translate into higher levels of female employment. Many of these women have the same limitations as their husbands, and the result of their entry into the work force is higher unemployment. At the same time, there is equally compelling evidence indicating that married men who are not in the labor force have wives who also are not in the work force. Conversely, men who are well-qualified not only are in the work force but they also have American Indian wives who are similarly qualified and actively employed.

Conclusions

The discussion has focused on the descriptive characteristics of American Indian female labor force participation, and as such it fills an important gap in what is known about this topic. Yet in many respects this work touches only the surface details of the labor market behavior of American Indian women. Certainly, this is not enough information upon which to make policy recommendations and none are offered here. To make such recommendations will require considerably more information than presented in this paper, or than is available in the extant literature. Specifically, in-depth multivariate modeling of labor force participation would be the next logical step beyond this discussion.

What can be said is that American Indian women are a profoundly disadvantaged group. To become a larger part of the labor force than they are today, they must overcome numerous barriers. American Indian women are handicapped by their lack of education, their residence, and their parental responsibilities, to mention only a few of these barriers. American Indian women most likely have been aware of these barriers for a very long time and the foregoing statistics only verify their suspicions. Yet, in the absence of positive steps to remove these barriers, and in the absence of well-informed public policy, the hindrances to the labor force participation of American Indian women are unlikely to disappear in the foreseeable future.

NOTES

1. The Public-Use Microdata Sample (PUMS) A File distributed by the U.S. Bureau of the Census, is the source for most of the statistics reported in this chapter. Ideally, it would be desirable to report more up-to-date information about American Indians. Unfortunately, the 1980 Census of Housing and Population represents the only available source of detailed social and economic characteristics for the total U.S. population of American Indians and Alaska Natives. Throughout this chapter, the term "American Indians" is substituted for the more cumberson "American Indians and Alaska Natives," strictly as a matter of editorial convenience. Very little data are available separately for American Indians and Alaska Natives.

2. The initial sites of BIA relocation programs were Chicago, Cleveland, Dallas, Denver, Los Angeles, Oakland, San Francisco, and San Jose, California. In 1968, offices were opened in Tulsa, Oklahoma and Oklahoma City (see Sorkin, 1971, P. 105).

3. It is also true that some reservations are located within the boundaries of large metropolitan areas. The Osage reservation is part of the Tulsa, Oklahoma SMSA, the Puyallap reservation is within the Tacoma, Washington SMSA, and a number of small rancherias are in the San Bernardino, California SMSA.

4. The "unemployment rate" in this and all other tables in this discussion is the percent of the civilian labor force unemployed. The other figure for unemployment is the percent of *all* adults age 16 years and over without work, regardless of whether they are in the labor force.

REFERENCES

American Indian Policy Review Commission. (1976). *Report on reservation and resource development and protection* (Task Force Seven, Reservation and Resource Development and Protection, Final Report to the Commission, Committee Print). Washington, DC: U.S. Government Printing Office.

Becker, G. (1964). *Human capital.* New York: National Bureau of Economic Research.

Berg, I. (1970). *Education and jobs: The great training robbery.* New York: Praeger.

Bianchi, S., & Spain, D. (1986). *American women in transition.* New York: Russell Sage.

Collins, R. (1979). *The credential society: An historical sociology of education and stratification.* New York: Academic Press.

Fixico, D. L. (1986). *Termination and relocation: Federal Indian policy, 1945–1960.* Albuquerque, NM: University of New Mexico Press.

Gwartney, J. D., & Long, J. E. (1978). The relative earnings of blacks and other minorities. *Industrial and Labor Relations Review, 31,* 336–346.

Haber, S. E., Lamas, E. J., & Green, G. (1983). A new method for estimating job separation by sex and race. *Monthly Labor Review, 106,* 20–27.

Jacobsen, C. K. (1984). Internal colonialism and Native Americans: Indian labor in the United States from 1871 to World War II. *Social Science Quarterly, 65,* 158–171.

Levitan, S. A., & Johnston, W. B. (1975). *Indian giving: Federal programs for Native Americans.* Baltimore, MD: The Johns Hopkins University Press.

Mincer, J. (1974). *Schooling, experience and earnings.* New York: National Bureau of Economic Research.

Sandefur, G. D., & Sakamoto, A. (1988). American Indian household structure and income. *Demography, 25,* 71–80.

Sandefur, G. D., & Scott, W. F. (1983). Minority group status and the wages of Indian and black males. *Social Science Research 12,* 44–68.

Sewell, W. H., & Hauser, R. M. (1975). *Education, occupation and earnings: Achievements in the early career.* New York: Academic Press.

Snipp, C. M., & Sandefur, G. D. (1988). Earnings of American Indians and Alaska natives: The effects of residence and migration. *Social Forces, 66,* 994–1008.

Sorkin, A. L. (1971). *American Indians and federal aid.* Washington, DC: The Brookings Institute.

———. (1978). *The urban American Indian.* Toronto: Lexington Books.

Trosper, R. L. (1980). *Earnings and labor supply: A microeconomic comparison of American Indians and Alaskan natives to American whites and blacks.* Boston: Boston College, Social Welfare Research Institute.

U.S. Bureau of the Census. (1983a). *General social and economic characteristics, 1980, United States Summary* (Part 1). Washington, DC: U.S. Government Printing Office.

———. (1983b). *Public-use microdata sample A file.* Washington, DC: Author.

Vinje, D. (1977). Income and labor force participation on Indian reservations. *Growth and Change, 8,* 38–41.

FEMALE WORK ROLES IN A TRADITIONAL, OIL ECONOMY: KUWAIT

Nasra M. Shah and Sulayman S. Al-Qudsi

I. INTRODUCTION

Among the many transitions that the Kuwaiti society is undergoing, the one related with the female role and status is certainly noteworthy. Perhaps the most significant social transformation that has occurred as a result of the sudden oil wealth is the rapid spread of female education in Kuwait. Both the nationals and expatriates got a chance to gain from the free education provided by the government. Over the last two decades, 1965–1985, the percentage of literate females aged 10+ increased from 28 to 63 among the Kuwaiti nationals. The corresponding percentages among the non-Kuwaitis went up from 58 to 81 percent. A very important demographic effect of the increased educational level is the rise in women's age at marriage. Among Kuwaiti women, the singulate mean age at marriage (SMAM) increased from 18.9 years in 1965 to 22.4 years in 1985; the corresponding increase among non-Kuwaiti women was from 18.9 years to 23.4

Research in Human Capital and Development, Vol. 6, pages 213–246.

ISBN: 1-55938-032-2

years. These sociodemographic changes have had a notable impact on the economic roles of women in recent years.

The measured labor force participation rate of Kuwaiti women increased from 2 percent in 1965 to almost 14 percent in 1985 (Table 1). The participation rate of non-Kuwaiti women, which was about 19 percent in 1965, more than doubled to 43 percent in 1985. The big jumps in the participation rates are indicative of significant socioeconomic and cultural changes in Kuwaiti society. A comprehensive discussion of the factors that facilitate or discourage female economic activity in Kuwait is the basic objective of the present paper. The likely impacts of increased economic activity on sociodemographic factors such as age at marriage and fertility are also discussed.

Our study is organized as follows. Section II gives a descriptive analysis of the nature of female work, presented in terms of: (a) the trends in activity rates and unemployment; (b) structure of the labor force with regard to occupational concentration and segregation; and (c) sociodemographic characteristics of the workers. This discussion is guided by an analytical framework, shown in Figure 1. The major concern here is to highlight the sociocultural and demographic determinants of work participation. Section III focuses on selected aspects of the dualism of the labor market as reflected in wages, both in terms of sex and nationality of workers. An attempt is made to estimate the extent of wage discrimination that exists in Kuwait's labor market in terms of sex and ethnic background, using multivariate regression analysis. Section IV concentrates on the sociodemographic impacts of female work participation. The final section contains a discussion of the government policy regarding female work, and the likely future growth of such work in view of the current labor force structure and motivation for work.

It is clear from the outset that any discussion of social change in Kuwait must be formulated with reference to two distinct groups, the citizens and the expatriates. The Kuwaiti nationals comprise 40 percent of the population, while the non-Kuwaitis, consisting mainly of Palestinians/Jordanians, Egyptians, Iraqis, Indians and Pakistanis, constitute the remaining 60 percent. The percentage of expatriates in the labor force is even higher; about 81 percent of the labor force in 1985 was non-Kuwaiti. Worker migration in Kuwait is selective of adult males, resulting in an imbalanced sex ratio among non-Kuwaitis (161 males per 100 females) compared to Kuwaitis (99).

A substantial percentage of the migrant population, especially Arabs, have resided in Kuwait for a fairly long time. For example, 57 percent of the Arabs aged 30 and over had lived in Kuwait for 10 or more years in 1985. Also, about 41 percent of all Arabs were born in Kuwait according to the 1985 Census. The above pattern indicates that a sizeable percentage of non-Kuwaitis are fairly stable members of the population as well as of the labor force. A thorough appreciation of the trends and structure of migration is therefore essential for an understanding of the growth and development of the labor force. Ethnic back-

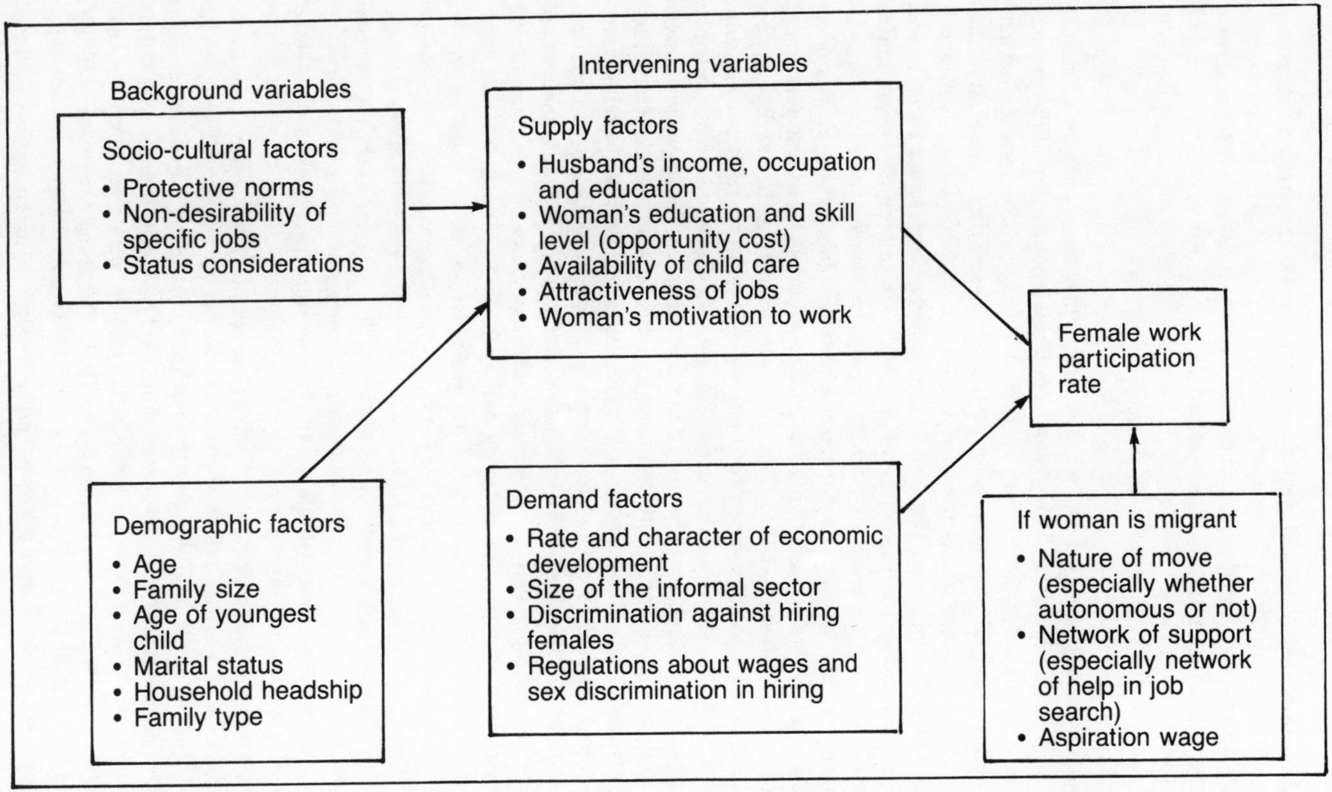

Source: Shah and Smith (1984).

Figure 1. Framework for Analyzing Influences on Female Labor Force Participation

ground represents one distinct dimension along which the labor force is segmented. The analysis in this paper, therefore, differentiates between groups of nationals and expatriates. Before proceeding with the analysis, however, a word about the data sources and quality is in order.

Data

Two main sources provided data for this paper. First, the Population Censuses, the first of which was held in 1957, prior to independence in 1961. Our analysis, however, is restricted to the 1965–1985 period, during which quinquennial censuses were conducted. In addition to published census data, the authors had access to a 25 percent sample tape of the 1980 and 1985 Censuses, which was used for part of the analysis. The second source is the 1983 Labor Force Survey based on a nationally representative sample of 5,374 households, representing about 3 percent of all households, conducted by the Ministry of Planning.

As in surveys and censuses in other Arab and Gulf countries, the measurement of female work is likely to contain some conceptual errors in Kuwait (Azzam & Moujabber, 1985; Zurayk, 1985). The undercount of economic activity may be substantial in the case of women who are not regular wage earners, are self-employed, and work in the private sector. The 1985 Census shows that a majority (97 percent) of the Kuwaiti women work in the public sector in return for regular wages. It is possible that Kuwaiti women engaged in part-time work in activities such as making and selling crafts (e.g., sadu cushions or wall hangings) are underreported. The extent of such underreporting is, however, likely to be small in view of the fact that a majority of low-income families in which the women may have needed previously to supplement the income are now assisted by the government welfare program, including cash payments.

Among the non-Kuwaiti women (74 percent of whom are engaged in private sector employment) several factors may encourage the misreporting of economic activity. One example is that of a woman who does part-time work at home (e.g., sewing or embroidering) but does not have a visa allowing her to engage in such activity. It is highly likely that the work of this woman will be underreported to the Census authorities who ask about whether an individual worked for pay or profit during a specified time period.

On the contrary, the work participation of certain other women may be overreported in case they are on a domestic service visa but are not actually employed as such. Kuwait has a law whereby the husband must earn a minimum wage (KD. 400 per month if employed in the public and KD. 650 if employed in the private sector) in order to bring his wife and children with him. Until the new immigration law was implemented in November 1987 some expatriates earning lower wages brought their wives to Kuwait on the visa of a *Khadima* (domestic servant) that they bought from a Kuwaiti *kafeel* (sponsor). In the above situation, the nonworking wife may have been reported to the census authorities as a member of the labor force. Since November 1987, the government allows the issuance of domestic servant visa only for women who are genuinely employed as khadimas. Fairly heavy penalties are imposed in case of a fraudulent visa on both the kafeel and worker. Apart from the above instances, the enumeration of work participation of most other non-Kuwaiti women is likely to be fairly valid and reliable.

II. THE EVOLUTION AND STRUCTURE OF FEMALE WORK

Historically, the role of Kuwaiti women was confined to household and child-bearing/rearing activities. Preservation of tribal honor through female modesty and segregation of the sexes contributed important social values. Kuwaiti women maintained a passive role even when the men were absent five months each year (May–September) when they went pearl diving (Alessa, 1981; Meleis, 1982). In several cases women owned property that they inherited from their father. During the days of sea trading, the owners of some merchant ships were women, but they were inactive in trade because they always conducted their business through male representatives. Some women who needed an income for themselves and their children engaged in pursuits such as raising chicken and sheep, sewing, healing, and providing Quranic instruction. Bedouin women also engaged in selling honey and woolen cloth that they weaved (Azzam and Moujabber, 1985). Thus, the activities of most women centered around the home and children, with few exceptions. The preceding description of historical roles is similar to the one that has been reported for Arab women in general (Rassam, 1984).

As the educational profile changed, the demand for the labor of women increased concomitantly. The labor force participation rate of Kuwaiti women increased sevenfold from 2 percent in 1965 to about 14 percent in 1985. Their percentage in the Kuwaiti workforce increased from about 3 percent to 20 percent over the same time period (Table 1). Given the traditional values concerning segregation of the sexes, it was (and still is) considered desirable to employ female teachers in female schools.

Teaching has, therefore, become a primary role for Kuwaiti women, with 35 percent involved in it. In fact, female teachers have displaced several male teachers over the years. In 1961/62 there were 86 female teachers for every 100 male teachers; by 1985/86 this ratio had reversed to 124. At the same time, the percentage of Kuwaitis among female teachers has increased notably—from 32 percent in 1978/79 to almost 50 percent in 1986/87 (CSO, 1984, 1987). It should be noted here that beyond the secondary school level (i.e., 12 grades), education is usually provided in a coeducational setting. There is, however, one Faculty, the Faculty of women, which provides a facility for segregated education to those women not willing to study in a coeducational environment.

Table 1. Labor Force Participation Rates (LFPR) and Percentage of Females in the Labor Force by Nationality Among Females Aged 15 and Over (1965–1985)

	Labor Force Particip. rate			*Women in Labor Force (%)*		
Year	*Kuwaiti*	*Non-Kuwaiti*	*Total*	*Kuwaiti*	*Non-Kuwaiti*	*Total*
1965	2.0	19.0	9.2	2.5	5.4	4.8
1970	2.4	19.0	10.2	3.3	8.2	6.9
1975	6.1	24.1	14.9	8.4	13.0	11.7
1980	9.6	29.6	20.2	13.2	12.8	12.9
1985	13.8	43.7	31.1	19.6	19.7	19.7

Sources: CSO (1980, pp. 38, 39, 126; 1986, pp. 34, 128).

Social values that encouraged the employment of Kuwaiti women as teachers has led simultaneously to other forms of occupational concentration, as reflected in Tables 2 and 3. The second major occupation of women consists of clerical and related workers. Over the last two decades an interesting shift occurred in the composition of service workers. In 1965, 41 percent of Kuwaiti women were engaged in service occupations, probably as a result of economic need. In 1985 the percentage in such occupations had declined to only 7.

While the increased involvement in teaching occupations may be expected in view of the cultural values outlined above, the concentration in clerical work is relatively unorthodox. Clerical work is often placed in settings that do not permit sexual segregation, especially in government hospitals, and offices. Another point worth noting related to the fairly large involvement of women in secretarial and typing work—roles that are quite nontraditional. In terms of social status, a clerical job probably ranks lower than a school teacher, which ranks lower than a medical doctor. Yet, 38 percent of the Kuwaiti females were engaged in clerical or related jobs in 1985 (Table 2). This suggests that social values regarding appropriate female roles are undergoing an important redefinition and expansion, thus augmenting the supply of workers. Another implication of this pattern, however, is that women may become squeezed into relatively low paying, dead-end occupations that allow little chance of promotions, as has happened in several countries around the world (Standing, 1978).

The non-Kuwaiti labor force is governed by a fairly different set of demand and supply factors. The two major groups that supply the non-Kuwaiti labor force are (1) the migrant workers, and (2) those born in Kuwait, as well as other residents who accompanied a migrant worker but then entered the labor force. The former group constitutes a majority of the workers. The market structure for the labor of expatriate females is again highly segmented. The three major occupations for which non-Kuwaiti females are imported, or selected, consist of service work, professional or technical work, and clerical work (Table 2).

A further ethnic differentiation among the non-Kuwaiti women is essential for a comprehensive analysis of this group. The occupational profile of the Arab women appears to be quite different from that of Asian women (Table 3). A large majority (84 percent) of the Asians were clustered in a single occupation, domestic service, in 1985. Among the Arabs, one-third were teachers, while 13 percent were typists. Also, twice as many of the Arab women were in professional occupations, compared with Asians (12 and 6 percent, respectively). Finally, only 6 percent of the Arabs were domestic servants. The occupational concentration in low-paying, low-status jobs is hence much more extreme in the case of Asian than Arab women.

The increasing salience of service work in the occupational structure of non-Kuwaiti females is noteworthy. This category constituted 42 percent of all non-Kuwaiti jobs in 1965, but increased to 65 percent in 1985 (Table 2). Among the factors that have been significant in the expansion of domestic service, the following may be noted. First, an abundant supply of maids was available from several Asian countries, particularly Sri Lanka, at very low wages (Korale, 1986). A maid is usually paid KD.30 (U.S. $100) per month plus room and board, and an airline ticket once every two years. Second, the network of

Table 2. Occupational Structure of Kuwaiti and Non-Kuwaiti Female Labor Force (1965, 1975, and 1985)

	Kuwaiti			*Non-Kuwaiti*		
Occupation	*1965*	*1975*	*1985*	*1965*	*1975*	*1985*
Professional and technical workers	21.7	55.6	51.4	45.1	36.7	21.9
Administrative and managerial workers	3.3	0.3	0.9	2.0	0.1	0.2
Clerical and related workers	22.4	28.1	38.3	5.0	8.0	9.5
Sales workers	1.1	0.3	0.4	0.7	1.1	0.9
Service workers	40.9	15.1	7.0	41.9	53.3	65.4
Agriculture, animal husbandry, fisherwomen, and hunters	0.7	0.2	0.2	0.0**	0.0	0.0*
Production workers and laborers	2.4	0.5	0.5	4.0	0.8	0.3
Not adequately defined	7.5	0.0**	1.4	1.2	0.0	1.9
Total (%)	100.0	100.0	100.0	100.0	100.0	100.0
(*N*)	1,067	7,305	24,803	7,671	27,525	107,325

Notes: *0.01.
**0.03.

Sources: CSO (1980, p. 126; 1986, p. 128).

Table 3. Specific Occupations in Which Women are Concentrated Among Kuwaitis, Arabs, Asians and Others (1985)

		Non-Kuwaiti		
Occupation	*Kuwaiti*	*Arabs*	*Asians*	*Others*
Medical and paramedical workers	5.4	11.7	5.8	7.9
Teachers	34.9	32.8	1.1	27.7
Other professional and technical workers	6.1	2.3	0.1	1.6
Typists, stenotypists and keypunch operators	6.2	12.8	2.9	9.3
Clerks	22.4	4.7	0.4	3.1
Domestic servants	0.1	6.1	83.9	22.0
Janitors	3.2	8.6	2.9	7.3
Others	21..7	16.0	2.4	19.8
Unemployed	0.0	5.0	0.5	1.3
Total (%)	100.0	100.0	100.0	100.0
(*N*)	24,457	32,989	72,505	1,811

Source: Population Census (1985, Vol. 3, Tables 120, 127).

recruitment agencies that facilitated the supply of maids grew quickly and is responsible for the importation of the majority of maids currently in Kuwait. Third, the demand for domestic servants probably increased, partly in response to the changing roles of the Kuwaiti women. As more Kuwaiti nationals entered the labor force, they required help with childrearing and housework. Finally, it seems that the demand for maids may have increased as a result of certain status considerations. For a household that can afford the services of a maid, hiring one is almost considered a necessity. A maid is 'consumed' in somewhat the same way as other durable goods that provide a high status.

Domestic service is a low-prestige job that will continue to be 'manned' by expatriate females as long as the demand for them persists. Kuwaiti nationals are unlikely to fill such jobs in the foreseeable future. The occupations in which Kuwaiti women may displace non-Kuwaitis in the future consists of teachers, clerical workers, and medical and paramedical workers.

In terms of their contribution to the Kuwaiti labor force, women comprised almost half of all professional and technical workers, and about 28 percent of clerical workers in 1985 (Table 4). Their presence in most other occupational groups was negligible. The expansion of female roles in the future will of course depend on the interaction of the various supply and demand factors, as well as the formative and demographic constraints as the society moves from an illiterate, traditional one to a literate, modern one.

Among the non-Kuwaitis, the percentage of females increased almost seven times among the total clerical and related workers, and by four-and-a-half times among the total service workers during the 1965–1985 period. The female proportion in professional and technical occupations has remained almost constant over this time (Table 4). Thus, the concentration of non-Kuwaiti females in low-paying, nonprestigious occupations has increased over time (Shah & Al-Qudsi, 1987). The marked increase in the number of maids is, of course, an obvious reason for this trend. From 11,921 in 1975, the number of maids increased to 19,552 in 1980, and 63,250 in 1985. In the absence of the observed increase in the number of domestic servants, the rise in the labor force participation among non-Kuwaiti females may have been more modest than it actually was.

It was mentioned earlier that 97 percent of the Kuwaiti and 26 percent of the non-Kuwaiti females are employed in the public sector. Table 5 presents the distribution of private versus public sector employment in various occupations. Among the Kuwaitis, the two occupations in which most of the women were employed in the private sector consisted of sales work, and agricultural work carried out largely by illiterate (poorer) women. These two occupations contained only 139 women, or 0.5 percent of the female labor force. Consistent with the high concentration of employment in the public sector, the percentage of women who were self-employed was negligible in 1985—only 0.6 percent

Table 4. Women's Share in Various Occupations (1965, 1975, and 1985)

	Women in occupation (%)					
	Kuwaiti			*Non-Kuwaiti*		
Occupation	*1965*	*1975*	*1985*	*1965*	*1975*	*1985*
Professional and technical workers	15.2	41.7	49.1	28.6	31.5	28.4
Administrative and managerial workers	2.4	2.0	5.6	6.2	1.2	2.6
Clerical and related workers	3.1	11.5	27.9	3.1	10.9	20.9
Sales workers	0.3	0.4	1.6	0.5	1.6	2.9
Service workers	3.1	3.4	4.3	10.5	32.3	47.3
Agriculture, animal husbandry, fisherwomen and hunters	0.9	0.3	1.7	0.1	0.0	0.1
Production workers and laborers	0.3	0.2	1.1	0.5	0.3	0.2

Sources: CSO (1980, p. 126; 1986, p. 128).

Table 5. Employment of Women by Major Occupational Groups, Employment Sector and Nationality (1985)

Major Occupational Group	Kuwaiti					Non-Kuwaiti				
	Public Sector	Private Sector	Joint Sector	Total %	Total N	Public Sector	Private Sector	Joint Sector	Total %	Total N
Prof. and Tech. Workers	97.9	1.8	0.4	100.0	12,750	78.4	21.0	0.7	100.0	23,554
Adm. and Manag. Workers	49.8	38.1	12.1	100.0	223	9.5	80.5	10.1	100.0	169
Clerical and Related Workers	97.0	2.0	1.0	100.0	9,497	41.0	51.0	8.0	100.0	10,154
Sales Workers	10.8	89.3	0.0	100.0	93	0.3	98.3	1.4	100.0	919
Service Workers	97.9	2.0	0.2	100.0	1,730	6.2	93.8	0.1	100.0	70,149
Agr., Animal Husb., Fisherwomen and Hunters	0.0	100.0	0.0	100.0	46	0.0	100.0	0.0	100.0	8
Production Workers and Laborers	98.3	1.7	0.0	100.0	118	20.4	79.1	0.5	100.0	373
Total	96.6	2.7	0.7	100.0	24,457	25.7	73.3	1.0	100.0	105,326

Source: Population Census (1985, Vol. 3, Tables 126–128).

among the Kuwaitis. Similar to this pattern, only 0.6 percent of the Arab and 0.04 percent of the Asians were self-employed.

Among the non-Kuwaitis, the only occupation in which the majority of women were employed in the public sector consisted of professional and technical workers, composed mainly of teachers and medical/paramedical personnel. About four-tenths of the clerical workers were also employed by the government. Public sector employment of females may be more amenable to changes in the future, as the non-Kuwaitis are replaced by Kuwaiti nationals, while the private sector may be more resistant to such changes.

Unemployment

Kuwait has managed to keep its unemployment rate at its historically low levels—less than 2 percent—for Kuwaitis and non-Kuwaitis combined. These historically low levels have been manipulated by an amalgam of fiscal, employment and immigration policies. On the fiscal side, the continued expansion of government current and development expenditures and their multiplier effects have constantly raised the level of demand for, and actual employment of, both Kuwaitis and non-Kuwaitis. Fiscal expansions were relatively easy to engineer and implement in the presence of sizeable and rising government revenues. On the other hand, the role that the public sector assumed as a last-resort employer of Kuwaitis established a de facto floor on acceptable or tolerable Kuwaiti-specific unemployment rates. Meanwhile, and congruent with its policy of employing Kuwaitis, is the pursuit of a selective immigration policy by the executive administration. New immigrants are allowed in only if they have work permits, while existing workers can continue to reside only if they are productively employed.

Occupational Segregation

Thus far, the structure of female employment has been described in terms of concentration in specific occupations. Another important dimension according to which female occupations may be analyzed consists of the relative representation of women versus men in the occupational structure. Indices of occupational segregation enable us to measure the relative representation of each sex. Such indices point out the amount of imbalance in the distribution of persons between occupations according to any given characteristic, for example, sex. In certain cases, the indices may be indicative of discrimination against either sex. In order to measure the sexual segregation or imbalance in the structure of occupations, we have used the coefficient of female representation (CFR) in specified occupations.

The CFR measures the degree of segregation in any occupation by the relationship between the proportion of women in the occupation and the proportion of women in the labor force. Defining the coefficient of female representation

(CFR) as the ratio between these two proportions, women are said to be overrepresented in a given occupation if the CFR for that occupation is greater than unity and underrepresented if it is less than unity (OECD, 1985).

Table 6 contains the results of the calculations carried out on data gleaned from the 1985 census. The table is restricted to results based on broad occupations and a few selected detailed occupations. We found that Kuwaiti women were overrepresented in professional/technical occupations and clerical occupations, since the CFR coefficients in these occupations were 2.46 and 1.39, respectively. Apart from these two occupations, Kuwaiti women were heavily underrepresented in all the other occupations, with the CFR ranging between 0.06 and 0.28.

The degree of representation varied widely according to specific jobs within broad occupations. Among the professionals, Kuwaiti women were very well represented in teaching, physical scientist jobs, and medical jobs, with CFRs well above 2. However, they were grossly underrepresented in certain other jobs,

Table 6. Coefficient of Female Representation (CFR) in Broad Occupations and Selected Female Detailed Occupations (1985)

Occupation	*Kuwaiti*	*Non-Kuwaiti*
Professional and technical	2.46*	1.42*
Teachers	3.45	2.51
Physical scientists	2.54	1.16
Doctors, other medical workers	2.36	2.90
Jurists	0.95	0.33
Engineers	0.24	0.08
Administrators and managers	0.28*	0.13*
Clerical and related	1.39*	7.69*
Typists/machine operators	3.56	4.90
Telephone/telegram operators	1.95	0.15
Government executives	0.63	0.06
Clerical supervisors	0.22	0.05
Sales workers	0.08*	0.15*
Service workers	0.21*	2.36*
Cooks and waiters	3.28	0.31
Housekeepers, maids	2.35	3.88
Managers	0.71	0.17
Building contractors	0.54	0.65
Agriculture workers	0.09*	0.00*
Production workers	0.06*	0.01*
Tailors	3.30	0.17
Broadcasting	0.28	0.18
Food and beverage processors	—	0.12

Note: *No women in the category.
Source: Computed from the Population Census (1985).

such as jurist jobs and engineering. Among clerical workers, women were overrepresented in typing/machine operating, and telephone/telegram operator jobs, but were underrepresented in supervisory jobs. Among the service workers, females were overrepresented in cooking and housekeeping jobs.

The pattern of occupational segregation was somewhat different among the non-Kuwaitis. Females were heavily overrepresented among the clerical workers, with a CFR of 7.7. They were also overrepresented among the professionals and the service workers. In contrast to their Kuwaiti counterparts, the non-Kuwaiti women were underrepresented among the telephone/telegram operators and tailors. Thus, it may be concluded that there are distinct imbalances in the occupational structure of the Kuwaitis as well as non-Kuwaitis that relate both to the demand and supply factors discussed already.

Who Works and Why

Several sociocultural and demographic factors may exert a significant influence on the supply of the female labor force. In the Kuwaiti situation, employment of native females seems to be a direct result of their rising educational levels, because nine-tenths of the employed women had attained an education up to the intermediate or higher level, compared with only one-fourth of their nonworking counterparts (Table 7). As women have gained education, the opportunity cost of their time probably increased. At the same time, the demand for their work in occupations that are culturally acceptable and valued went up. As more and more women entered the labor force, the work role (albeit in specified areas) has probably become a legitimate sphere of female activity. Moreover, the easy availability of domestic help is likely to have further facilitated labor force entry.

In terms of their demographic characteristics, a large majority (82 percent) of the Kuwaiti working women were aged less than 35, and almost two-thirds of them were married, in 1985 (Table 7). The young ages of the workers probably reflect the recency of the education-work transition. The large percentage of married women suggests that marriage does not discourage work participation. Instead, a comparison of the participation rates of single women with that of their married counterparts in selected age groups suggests that singlehood has a strong positive association with work participation (Table 8). Although the causal direction of the above association is difficult to disentangle, the extremely high participation rate of single women aged 25–39 is worth underlining—60 percent of those aged 25–29 and 63 percent of those aged 30–39 were in the labor force.

With rising female education, the age at marriage has undergone a significant increase—of 3.5 years among Kuwaiti and 4.5 years among non-Kuwaiti females. The percentage of single women is considerably higher among working than nonworking women. Among women aged 25–29, for example, 30 percent of those in labor force were single compared with only 10 percent among the nonworking (data not shown). Thus, women may enter the labor force because

Table 7. General Characteristics of Working and Nonworking Women by Nationality (1985)

Characteristics	*Kuwaiti* Working	*Kuwaiti* Non-Working	*Non-Kuwaiti* Working	*Non-Kuwaiti* Non-Working
Age Structure				
15–24	24.2	41.2	23.3	35.6
25–34	58.0	21.2	44.9	28.7
35–44	15.1	16.2	22.9	20.9
45+	2.7	21.3	8.9	14.8
	—	—	—	—
Average	29.2	32.3	31.5	31.3
Marital Status				
Single	28.5	28.6	31.9	25.1
Married	65.2	59.1	63.4	70.8
Divorced	4.8	2.3	1.5	0.4
Widowed	1.5	10.0	3.2	3.7
	—	—	—	—
	100.0	100.0	100.0	100.0
Educational Level				
Illiterate	2.5	41.1	24.9	15.8
Read and write	1.9	11.7	33.7	12.5
Primary	4.5	22.4	2.6	24.8
Intermediate	21.4	17.0	4.2	25.4
Secondary and below university level	45.0	7.1	20.9	17.3
Graduates and postgraduates	24.7	0.8	13.7	4.3
	—	—	—	—
	100.0	100.0	100.0	100.0

Source: Population Census (1985, Vol. 3), Tables 114–116, 117–119, 122–124; CSO (1986, pp. 46, 49).

they are not yet married. As they get older, they may be pushed out of the marriage market altogether but continue to remain in the labor force. Thus, a small group of women end up fulfilling only the work role. As women gain higher levels of education, the size of this group is likely to grow.

A second group among which the participation rate is decidedly higher is that of divorced women. The working women contained about twice as many divorcees as the nonworking women among Kuwaitis (4.8 and 2.3 percent, respectively—Table 7). Similarly, Table 8 indicates that the participation rate among the divorced Kuwaiti women (25 percent) was almost twice as high as the single women (14 percent), and about 10 times higher than the widowed women (2.4 percent). A high participation rate among divorced women was documented by Youssef (1974) for several Middle Eastern countries. It seems that cultural norms

Table 9. Female Labor Force Participation Rates by Age, Marital Status and Education

	No Qualification				Elem./Intermediate[a]				Second./College[b]				University and above			
	S	*M*	*D*	*W*	*S*	*M*	*D*	*W*	*S*	*M*	*D*	*W*	*S*	*M*	*D*	*W*
Kuwaitis																
15–19	0.6	0.0	0.0	0.0	0.4	2.9	0.0	0.0	2.1	11.2	50.0	0.0	0.0	0.0	0.0	0.0
20–24	1.0	0.2	2.3	0.0	14.4	16.9	39.4	22.0	20.6	32.8	42.8	50.0*	69.3	67.2	0.0	0.0
25–34	2.2	0.8	2.2	1.0	45.5	24.8	50.6	42.9	74.3	70.4	87.0	88.9	90.3	81.7	100.0	66.7
35–44	6.9	1.8	10.2	3.5	55.8	19.7	46.9	25.0	96.7	60.8	73.7	41.7	87.5	76.6	109.0	83.3
45–54	5.6	1.2	4.8	2.3	71.4	10.0	28.6	7.4	100.0	33.3	66.7	0.0	100.0*	56.3	0.0	75.0
55–64	0.0	0.5	2.9	1.0	0.0	10.0	0.0	33.3*	50.0*	0.0	0.0	0.0	0.0	0.0	0.0	0.0
Total	1.3	1.0	5.2	1.8	5.3	18.5	41.9	24.6	28.6	54.7	74.4	58.3	83.9	78.5	100.0	76.9
N	2081	16183	636	2358	7383	5826	363	126	2699	3338	129	24	647	1207	23	13
Arabs																
15–19	24.2	1.6	50.0*	0.0	0.3	0.3	0.0	0.0	8.2	3.9	0.0	0.0	0.0	0.0	0.0	0.0
20–24	42.5	5.2	33.3	44.4	9.3	3.2	18.7	0.0	35.0	19.1	57.1	0.0	61.1	44.9	0.0	0.0
25–34	52.4	9.6	60.0	38.2	36.4	4.4	45.2	26.3	81.3	36.9	78.3	58.3	87.5	63.2	100.0	100.0*
35–44	61.3	8.8	68.6	31.9	30.4	5.1	68.8	36.1	93.8	43.3	75.0	70.4	96.7	79.3	95.5	100.0
45–54	65.5	10.2	71.4	33.1	55.6	6.7	25.0	34.3	91.4	41.6	100.0	81.8	92.9	78.2	100.0*	78.6
55–64	25.0	9.1	78.9	18.0	0.0	0.0	0.0	20.0	83.3*	21.4	0.0	30.0*	100.0*	54.6	100.0*	66.7*
Total	39.6	8.9	66.2	26.4	2.1	4.3	40.9	28.7	36.8	35.0	76.4	66.2	80.0	68.3	94.7	87.9
N	665	7770	130	754	5941	6942	71	129	2659	6270	55	71	668	3282	38	33
Asians																
15–19	91.4	73.4	100.0*	0.0	6.4	24.5	0.0	0.0	11.8	33.3	0.0	0.0	0.0	0.0	0.0	0.0
20–24	98.5	83.2	100.0*	100.0	72.0	42.5	0.0	0.0	59.1	29.4	0.0	0.0	0.0	18.4	0.0	100.0*
25–34	99.2	85.5	98.8	96.6	94.1	46.2	71.4*	100.0*	93.4	54.5	80.0*	80.0*	60.0	43.2	100.0*	100.0*
35–44	98.8	80.0	95.2	94.5	100.0	50.8	100.0*	94.1	100.0	56.1	100.0*	100.0*	94.4	48.7	100.0*	100.0*
45–54	98.4	71.9	87.5	75.3	100.0*	35.3	100.0*	70.0	100.0	54.5	100.0	50.0*	94.4*	55.4*	100.0*	0.0
55–64	93.3	68.0	100.0	46.4	0.0	25.0	0.0	33.3*	100.0*	50.0	0.0	75.0*	100.0*	40.0*	0.0	0.0
Total	97.8	80.6	97.6	81.1	38.1	45.1	76.9	79.5	69.5	52.4	75.0	97.8	86.5	44.2	100.0	83.3
N	4735	10993	164	571	1047	1629	13	39	902	2566	12	27	237	946	5	6

Notes: * Ten or fewer cases in the cell. [a]includes education up to 8 grades; [b]Includes 12 years of school and 2 years of college. *S* = Single; *M* = Married; *D* = Divorced; *W* = Widowed.

Source: Based on a 25 percent sample of 1985 Population Census.

(12 years) or two years of college, and 90 percent among those who had university level or higher education. The pattern among married Kuwaiti women aged 25–34 was similar, although they had relatively lower rates than the single women. The divorced women aged 25–34, on the other hand, had higher rates than their single, as well as married, counterparts. The strong positive association between education and labor force participation is illustrated further for married women in Figure 2.

Unlike the single Kuwaiti women, over half of the single Arab women, and more than 90 percent of the Asian women aged 25–54 who had no formal education were in the labor force. The rates for divorced women were similar. Consistent with the Kuwaiti pattern, however, education up to the secondary or higher levels also appeared to be a very important factor in encouraging the economic activity of Arab, as well as the Asian, women.

The important points that emerge from Table 9 are as follows:

1. Education up to the secondary or higher level had a strong positive association with work participation among Kuwaiti, as well as non-Kuwaiti women.
2. Almost 90 percent of the single Kuwaiti women aged 25–44 who had completed university or higher level of education were in the labor force in 1985, which is indeed noteworthy.
3. Among those who had secondary or higher levels of education, participation rates were higher among the single and divorced women compared with their married counterparts.
4. Within each educational and marital status subgroup, an inverted U shaped pattern of activity generally existed by age of respondents. That is, participation rates were usually higher in the middle of the age distribution (ages 25–54) than at the tails, as illustrated in Figure 2.
5. Participation rates were very high for women who had no formal education among the non-Kuwaitis. These women were primarily maids, who constitute an important facilitator of the work participation of indigenous women by providing household help and childcare.

The positive effect of education on the decision to work may operate through an amalgam of factors: (a) by increasing a woman's desire to work for social recognition or economic reasons; (b) by increasing her productivity in the labor market relative to home, meaning, education raises the opportunity cost of not working; and (c) increasing the probability of finding employment, especially in the public sector. The participation rate of educated Kuwaiti females has risen over the 1980–1985 period (data not shown). This implies that educated working women continue to supply work effort once in the labor market. The peak of

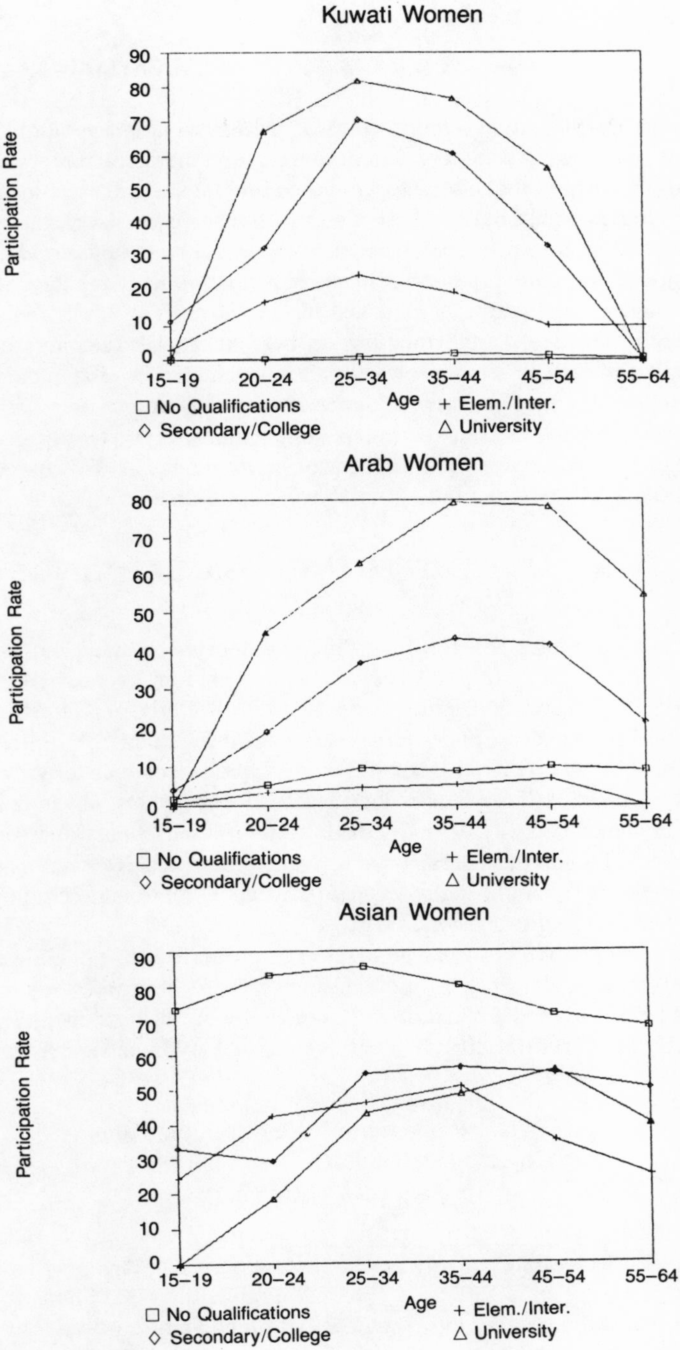

Source: Shah and Smith (1984).

Figure 2. Labor force participation rates of married women (1985)

female labor participation which occurs at relatively early ages (25–34) is attributable to the entry of recent school leavers into the labor force.

Among the factors that motivate women to join the labor force, financial need continues to be an important one even in the affluent Kuwaiti society. Despite the high and fabulous rise in real income level of Kuwaiti households, a larger percentage of the relatively poorer households allow/encourage their females to take up wage employment, as indicated in the Table 10 (below).

Although evidence on the relationship between family income and female participation in Kuwait's labor market is not conclusive, available data indicate that participation rates are much higher among the women in relatively less affluent households. Women's earnings supplement overall family income and contribute to the achievement of higher consumption levels. This pattern is true for all three ethnic groups, but is most pronounced in the case of Asians.

II. SEXUAL DIFFERENCES IN EARNINGS

This section examines the earnings differential between men and women in Kuwait's labor market. In 1983 Kuwaiti men earned an average KD. 390 per month (US $1370). Women earned under two-thirds of this, at KD. 248. In order to examine the sources of male–female earnings differential, we utilize the rich data set of the 1983 national labor survey, which was conducted by the Central Statistical Office of the Ministry of Planning. The survey covered all wage workers and included 12,076 individuals, representing about 3 percent of the labor force. The sample contained information on variables such as monthly earnings, sex, age, marital status, education, years of job-tenure, employment in public or private sector and type of occupation.

As our earlier discussion revealed, a large proportion of non-Kuwaiti (predominately Asian) women work as domestic servants. To avoid statistical biases that might arise from the clustering of Asian women in these menial jobs, the analysis below excludes all individuals who work as domestic servants. Non-

Table 10. Proportion of Women in the Labor Force by the Distribution of Household Income (private households only) (In Percent)

Households	*Kuwaitis*	*Arabs*	*Asians*
Bottom 40%	24.5	26.1	78.6
Middle 40%	16.3	19.2	39.2
Upper 20%	5.2	4.8	10.8
Average	19.3	19.1	49.3

Source: Computed from CSO (1983).

Kuwaiti men are excluded from the analysis, while the Kuwaiti men are used as the reference group against which Kuwaiti, Arab, and non-Arab women are compared. Therefore, our subsample contains information on 3,374 individuals.

The analysis of male–female earnings differentials is conducted utilizing the human-capital approach. The Oaxaca (1973), Blinder (1973), and Malkiel and Malkiel (1973) techniques for decomposing the gross earnings differentials between the two sexes according to their ethnic origin is used. The objective is to decompose observed earning differentials into components attributed to variations in human capital attributes and unexplained variations that generally measure the extent of sex discrimination in earnings. The link between measurable human capital characteristics and earnings is analyzed for men and women and according to ethnic background—Kuwaitis, Arabs, and non-Arabs. Following Mincer's (1974) formulation, separate wage equations are estimated for each sex and ethnic background as follows:[1]

$$LnY^m = \alpha^m + \sum_{j=1}^{n} \beta_j^m X^m + U^m \quad (1)$$

$$LnY^w = \alpha^w + \sum_{j=1}^{n} \beta_j^w X^w + U^w \quad (2)$$

where: LnY is the natural logarithm of monthly earnings in Kuwaiti dinars;
X is a vector of personal characteristic; and
U is the error term.
The superscripts m and w connote men and women, respectively. This specification is referred to as the basic human capital model.

Evaluating Equations (1) and (2) at the mean values for the characteristics and then subtracting (2) from (1) yields:

$$\overline{LnY^m} - \overline{LnY^w} = (\alpha^m - \alpha^w) + (\Sigma\, \beta^m\, \overline{X}^m - \Sigma\, \beta^w\, \overline{X}^w) \quad (3)$$

The first term on the right-hand side of Equation (3) represents the amount of the gross differential in earnings between men and women that has not been explained by the regressions. The second term of the differential may be broken down into two components, one attributable to differences in endowments of the productive characteristics held by the two sexes, and a second that comes from differences in the way these characteristics are evaluated in the wage equations. This enables (3) to be rewritten as:

$$\overline{LnY^m}\ \overline{LnY^w} = (\alpha^m - \alpha^w) + \Sigma\, \beta^m\, (\overline{X}^m - \overline{X}^w) + \Sigma\, \overline{X}^w\, (\beta^m - \beta^w) \quad (4)$$

The second term on the right-hand side represents the advantage (or disadvantage) in endowments of the male group. The first and third terms represent the difference between how the high-wage (male) equation would evaluate the average characteristics of the low-wage (women) group and how the low-wage equation actually evaluates them. It has become acceptable to refer to the first and third terms of Equation (4) as a measure of sex discrimination in earnings.

The basic human capital equation can be expanded to include a range of personal and institutional variables, such as marital status, sector of employment (public vs. private) and occupation. An expanded function of this sort controls for a wide range of sources of potential labor market discrimination against women. With occupation held constant, an expanded function tests the hypothesis of "equal pay for equal work." Any residual yielded by this procedure can be ascribed to wage discrimination.

The analysis below uses the coefficients of two sets of equations. The first uses the coefficients derived from the basic human capital model, which includes years of schooling, years of previous experience, measured with the help of the Mincer algorithm (Mincer, 1974), and years of job tenure, defined as the length of time workers have been employed in their current occupations.[2] The use of these coefficients will measure "total" potential discrimination against women by pushing both wage and job discrimination into the unexplained residual. The cost is that this procedure does not measure wage discrimination per se. The second set of estimates adds various dummy variables for marital status, sector of employment (private vs. public) and occupation. The inclusion of these variables may still understate the effects of job discrimination, but the residual now measures wage discrimination with some precision.

Empirical Results

Variable means for both sexes are shown in Table 11. The results of the basic and expanded human capital models appear in Tables 12 and 13. The regression results of the basic model indicate that human capital traits are rewarded differently according to sex. The Chow tests performed pair-wise on the individual

Table 11. Variable Means by Nationality

Variables	*Kuwaiti Men*	*Kuwaiti Women*	*Arab Women*	*Non-Arab Women*
Education	7.03	12.02	12.22	10.66
Previous Experience	9.37	5.42	6.85	9.36
Years of Job-Tenure	8.71	4.91	7.55	6.68
Percent Married	77.00	56.80	72.70	85.60
Percent in Public Sector	97.00	98.00	75.60	44.40

Source: Computed from CSO (1983).

Table 12. Regression Results of the Basic Human Capital Model

Variables	*Kuwaiti Men*	*Kuwaiti Women*	*Arab Women*	*Non-Arab Women*
Years of Schooling	.04542*	.07592*	.05535*	.08405*
	(24.197)	(15.700)	(16.758)	(9.183)
Previous Experience	.02017*	.00478	.00480	.02231
	(5.782)	(0.761)	(0.498)	(1.382)
Previous Experience Squared	−.00033*	−.00027	−.00018	−.00084
	(−3.184)	(−1.146)	(−0.163)	(−1.442)
Years of Job Tenure	.06805*	.02911*	.05280*	.07881*
	(21.589)	(2.769)	(7.771)	(4.334)
Years of Job Tenure Squared	−.00148*	.00052	−.00144*	−.00170*
	(−12.539)	(−0.754)	(−3.801)	(−2.101)
Constant	5.0992*	4.7035*	4.37992*	3.7462*
	(152.520)	(55.989)	(69.199)	(21.789)
R^2	0.3810	0.4620	0.4641	0.6188
F	250.065	93.055	113.756	52.629
Sample Size	2024	537	652	160

Notes: *T*-Values in parentheses; *Significant at 5 percent level.
Source: Computed from CSO (1983).

earnings equations (e.g., Kuwaiti male vs. Kuwaiti female; Kuwaiti male vs. Arab female) result in the rejection of the equivalence of regression coefficients according to sex and nationality.[3]

The explanatory power of the human capital model is higher for non-Arab women than for Kuwaiti and Arab women, which suggests that competitive forces are stronger for the former group. Of interest also is the apparently higher rate of return to education in the case of women relative to men. Years of job-tenure have a stronger impact on enhancing individuals' earnings than years of previous experience for each group considered (Table 12). The sign of the marital status dummy variable is significantly positive in the case of men (Table 13). For men, marriage provides a rationalization for the payment of higher wages because of greater financial requirements. In Kuwait, earnings are positively associated with public sector employment, which provides various allowances and fringe benefits, as was found by Quisi (1984). Participation in administrative occupations seems to be positively associated with the earnings of Kuwaiti men, as well as Arab and non-Arab women. The sign of professional/scientific occupations is positive for all groups, but its statistical significance can be ascertained for Arab and non-Arab women only. The earnings profile of Kuwaiti men is steeper relative to the earnings profiles of the three groups of women.

Table 14 is developed from the coefficients of the basic model and reports the results of the decomposition analysis of Equations (1) to (4) set out above. We

Table 13. Regression Results of the Expanded Human Capital Model

Variables	*Kuwaiti Men*	*Kuwaiti Women*	*Arab Women*	*Non-Arab Women*
Years of Schooling	.04370*	.06869*	.05593*	.07263*
	(19.580)	(11.900)	(13.277)	(7.086)
Previous Experience	.01524*	.00987	.00551	.01154
	(4.628)	(1.554)	(0.990)	(0.802)
Previous Experience Squared	−.00028*	−.00020	−.00007	−.00030
	(−2.978)	(−0.092)	(−0.309)	(−0.560)
Years of Job Tenure	.04910*	.02564*	.06077*	.07692*
	(15.371)	(2.432)	(8.699)	(4.325)
Years of Job Tenure Squared	−.00099*	−.00060*	−.00131*	−.00174
	(−8.634)	(−0.870)	(−4.422)	(−2.312)
Marital Status (Married = 1)	.26274*	−.00384*	−.0882*	.03331
	(13.574)	(−0.145)	(−2.799)	(0.332)
Sector of Employment (Public = 1)	.05277*	.03100	.00040	.33795*
	(2.215)	(0.373)	(0.013)	(3.686)
Administrators	.03023*	−.18497	.69379*	.97258*
	(6.180)	(−0.625)	(5.099)	(3.152)
Clerks	−.13032*	−.11560*	.07898	.50737*
	(−7.585)	(−2.360)	(1.804)	(4.775)
Teachers	−.08531*	.03819	−.04085	−.15958
	(−2.246)	(0.661)	(−0.903)	(−1.167)
Other Professionals	.01976	.03960	.15413*	.23485*
	(0.692)	(0.623)	(2.825)	(2.092)
Constant	5.04080*	4.7736*	4.34406*	3.59442*
	(93.052)	(40.171)	(65.089)	(23.038)
R^2	.4702	.4825	.5119	.7258
F	164.225	46.433	63.069	39.262
Sample Size	2024	537	652	160

Notes: *T*-Values in parentheses; *significant at the 5 percent level.
Source: Computed from CSO (1983).

find that out of total earnings differentials between Kuwaiti men and women, 0.220, in the logarithm term or KD. 77 per month, nearly 20 percent is diminished by the higher productive endowments that Kuwaiti women have relative to Kuwaiti men, and 120 percent is due to unexplained variables including discrimination. The earnings differentials portion due to endowments reflects the higher educational attainment of Kuwaiti women. The remaining larger differentials, 120 percent of the two groups of workers measures "total" discrimination against women; that is, the combined effect of wage and job discrimination against Kuwaiti women.

Table 14. Decomposition of Earnings Differentials

Description	Equation	Kuwaiti Women		Arab Women		Non-Arab Women	
		Logarithm	*KD*	*Logarithm*	*KD*	*Logarithm*	*KD*
Kuwaiti Men Average Salary	$\Sigma\beta^m X^m$	5.9661	390	5.9661	390	5.9661	390
Women Average Salary	$\Sigma\beta^w X^w$	5.7468	313	5.3699	214	5.1240	168
Women Salary, if paid according to men's pay structure	$\Sigma\beta^m \bar{X}^w$	6.0111	408	6.1400	465	6.0633	430
Overall Salary difference	$Ln\ \bar{Y}^m - Ln\ \bar{Y}^w$	0.2193	77	0.5962	176	0.8421	222
Endowment difference	$\Sigma\beta^m (\bar{X}^m - \bar{X}^w)$	−0.0439	−18	−0.1739	−74	−0.0972	−40
Residual (discrimination)	$\Sigma\ \bar{X}^w (\beta^m - \beta^w)$	0.2632	95	0.7701	250	0.9393	262

Source: Derived from the Basic Equation in Table 12.

The decomposition analysis also shows that Arab women have superior endowments relative to Kuwaiti men. As Table 11 indicates, the average years of schooling for Kuwaiti men is 7.03, which is much lower than the corresponding average among Arab women, 12.22.

Higher productive endowments mitigate the earnings edge that Kuwaiti male workers have over Arab women. About 29 percent of the total earnings differentials between Kuwaiti men and Arab women is offset by the superior productive endowments possessed by the latter group. The residual difference, 129 percent, is due to discrimination in favor of Kuwaiti men. By the same token, nearly 112 percent of the total earnings differentials between Kuwaiti males and non-Arab female workers is accounted for by discrimination. The better productive endowments possessed by non-Arab female workers reduce the total earnings differentials by 12 percent.

What is of particular interest for Kuwait is the result that we obtain from the residual in row 6 of Table 15, that is, the earnimgs differentials that remain even after we correct for other personal characteristics and occupational affiliation. As expected, this residual fraction is generally higher in the basic model than in the expanded model because the expanded model explains more of the endowment differences. This result therefore corroborates the hypothesis that earnings discrimination against Kuwaiti, Arab and non-Arab women persists even when the model controls with some precision for the type of occupation.

Table 16 shows the sources of earnings discrimination attributable to explanatory variables (calculated for the expanded model only). The table entries show the percentage of the differential in earnings that arises from the coefficients and the endowments. A positive entry indicates an advantage in favor of males. The most significant factors that contribute toward the endowment differential portion of earnings are education and job tenure. The percentage contribution of these factors to endowment differentials between male and female groups is in the order of 5 percent to 23 percent. Discrimination takes place through previous experience, sector of employment, occupational affiliation and marital status. Dominating the table is the contribution to discrimination of the constant term.

The above findings indicate that male Kuwaitis receive a constant premium over the earnings of females. However, the premium appears to vary according to the "ethnicity" of the female. That is, there appears to be more discrimination against non-Arab than Arab women, who in turn suffer more discrimination relative to Kuwaiti women. These findings, therefore, corroborate earlier empirical work on discrimination according to ethnic background (Al-Qudsi, 1985; Al-Qudsi & Shah, 1988; Hosni & Al-Qudsi, 1986). Thus, it is clear that Kuwait's labor market is segmented along sexual and ethnic lines. These results also indicate that even when women have higher educational attainment, their earnings are still less than men. Despite apparent equality in the educational opportunity for both sexes, women's position in Kuwait's labor market is not equal to

Table 15. Decomposition of Earnings Differentials

Description	Equation	*Kuwaiti Men vs. Kuwaiti Women*		*Kuwaiti Men vs. Arab Women*		*Kuwaiti Men vs. Non-Arab Women*	
		Logarithm	*KD*	*Logarithm*	*KD*	*Logarithm*	*KD*
Kuwaiti Men Average Salary	$\Sigma\beta^m X^m$	5.9661	390	5.9661	390	5.9661	390
Women Average Salary	$\Sigma\beta^w X^w$	5.7468	313	5.3699	214	5.1240	168
Women Salary, if paid according to men's pay structure	$\Sigma\beta^m \bar{X}^w$	5.9558	386	6.1022	447	6.0699	433
Overall Salary difference	$Ln\, \bar{Y}^m - Ln\, \bar{Y}^w$	0.2193	77	0.5962	176	0.8421	222
Endowment difference	$\Sigma\beta^m (\bar{X}^m - \bar{X}^w)$	0.0106	4	−0.1361	−57	−0.1038	−43
Residual (discrimination)	$\Sigma\, \bar{X}^w (\beta^m - \beta^w)$	0.2087	73	0.7323	233	0.9459	265

Source: Derived from the Expanded Equation in Table 13.

Table 16. Discrimination Component $\{\overline{X}_w(\beta_m - \beta_w)\}$ in the Case of Kuwaiti, Arab and Non-Arab Women (In Percent)

Variable	*Kuwaiti Women*	*(%)*	*Arab Women*	*(%)*	*Non-Arab Women*	*(%)*
Constant	0.2670		0.6967		1.4464	
Education	−0.3004		−0.1491		−0.3081	
Previous Exp.	0.0226		0.0487		0.0346	
Job Tenure	0.0997		−0.0609		−0.1305	
Marriage	0.1514		0.2551		0.1964	
Sector	0.0213		0.0396		−0.1265	
Occupation	−0.0529		−0.0927		−0.1623	
Discrim. Component	0.2086	95.2	0.7374	122.6	0.9500	112.3
Endowments Component	0.0106	4.8	−0.1361	−22.6	−0.1038	−12.3
Overall Differential	0.2192	100.0	0.6013	100.0	0.8462	100.0

Source: Derived from Table 13.

men's. Equality of education may be a necessary condition, but it does not appear to be a sufficient condition for equality of pay.

The preceding decomposition analysis is subject to two important caveats. First, the evidence presented here does not enable us to reach any conclusions about the quality of education and innate abilities of the four groups.[4] The second caveat stems from the necessity to remember that the component identified as discrimination contains unexplained differences in constant terms. It is prudent to be somewhat reluctant to call all differences "discrimination" until we are sure that they contain no remaining unidentified differences in productive characteristics.

IV. CONSEQUENCES OF INCREASING WORK PARTICIPATION

The trend toward greater labor force activity among women has somewhat different implications for the nationals and the expatriates. Two major types of consequences may be identified, namely the economic and the sociodemographic. Among the Kuwaitis, the major economic consequence of increased female work participation consists of the reduction of dependency on foreign workers, albeit in selected occupations.

The stability of the labor force in occupations where a large percentage of nationals are employed is likely to increase as part of this process. A related consequence of this trend, however, may be the concomitant increase in the importation of domestic help needed for home and childcare while the woman is at work. In the future, as an increased proportion of the professional/technical and clerical jobs are filled by nationals, a shortage of vacancies may eventually occur, resulting in the unemployment of qualified, educated women. Furthermore, Kuwaiti women may begin to seek jobs in occupations other than the present ones, thus competing with men. The latter change, however, presumes that cultural values will be modified sufficiently to encourage/enable the participation of women in nontraditional spheres of activity.

A discernible sociodemographic consequence of work participation is the increase in age at marriage of working females. In fact, the percentage who were single among women aged 30+ was much higher among the working than the nonworking women in 1985 (18 and 2 percent, respectively). A lower marriage rate among working women will obviously exert a negative impact on fertility, as will their higher age at marriage. The employed women may also serve as important agents in transforming desired fertility to lower levels. It has been shown in Kuwait that the number of children ever born among women with a secondary or higher education is substantially lower than that among illiterate women (Al Omaim & Kohli, 1984; Shah, 1988). As the educated women enter the labor force and develop serious career orientations, their fertility may be reduced further. They may adopt Western orientations concerning the number of children (Caldwell, 1982). It may be noted here, however, that the government policies in Kuwait are highly pronatalist, which may continue to encourage higher fertility than expected.

Whether the majority of the female workers will develop serious career orientations is also open to question. Most of the jobs that the nationals enter are supply rather than demand constrained. Therefore, they involve almost no competition. A Kuwaiti national seeking a job is literally guaranteed one. Consequently, labor force participation does not require a high work commitment. Furthermore, several of the jobs (e.g., clerical) may provide only horizontal rather than vertical mobility in the occupational hierarchy, thus perpetuating the low work commitment.

Despite the above factors, the increasing numbers in the work force may serve an important role in legitimizing the work role further. Economic activity may come to be seen as a significant role in its own right, and may even be considered as an appropriate alternative role (to the mother/wife role) in some cases. The Kuwaiti society is nevertheless a traditional, Muslim society, in which the values concerning female chastity and integrity of the family hold a very high salience. The wife/mother role is considered as the most important one by a majority of the society. Any redefinitions in this role will come about slowly and will occur as accommodations, rather than alternatives, to it.

The consequences of the increased demand for expatriate female workers may be viewed from the perspective of both the sending countries and Kuwait. Needless to say, female migration has in most cases helped the economy of the sending countries, because the labor of several of them (e.g., maids) would have been surplus in the home country. The social consequences of female migration, especially of domestic servants, are perhaps more noteworthy. A concern has long been expressed in Kuwait about the undesirable influence of foreign maids, who have a different cultural background, religion and language, on the upbringing of Kuwaiti children (Ministry of Social Affairs and Labor, 1983). An opposing view seems to suggest that the negative influence is not as serious as some newspaper stories make it look. Despite the debate, no reduction in the importation of maids is visible to date.

The treatment of maids in Kuwait is another topic that deserves mention. While no empirical data are available, informal observation and press reports suggest fairly serious abuse in some cases. The extent of the problem has not been quantified, however. It was in reaction to reports about the sexual harassment of maids that President Aquino recently banned the export of Filipino maids to the Middle East from February 15, 1988 (*Arab Times,* 1988). Other exporting countries, such as Sri Lanka, have hinted at the problem but have not taken any tangible action like the Philippines (Korale & Karunawathie, 1981).

Thus, several economic as well as sociodemographic consequences of work participation may be identified for the Kuwaiti and non-Kuwaiti women. The most important consequences probably are the possible expansion of roles, increased social acceptability of new roles, and greater visibility of women, particularly in jobs that are nonsex segregated. In the case of jobs based on Western models, value orientation concerning age at marriage, fertility control, family size and interspouse role relationships may undergo significant modifications. Government policies are likely to be an important factor in shaping the pace and structure of such changes, as discussed below.

V. GOVERNMENT POLICY AND THE FUTURE OUTLOOK

The central focus of population policies in Kuwait consists of devising ways and means to increase the percentage of nationals in the labor force. One important strategy aimed at accomplishing this goal is to increase the participation of females. The latest five year plan (1985/86–1989/90) identifies teaching and supervisory administrative jobs as areas that are appropriate for an increased participation of Kuwaiti females, at least in the short run. The plan also mentions the need to augment female participation in the service sector (Ministerial Council, 1985).

Two policies that appear to be contradictory to the Government's plan to expand female work participation are that of reducing the age at marriage and encouraging large families. Earlier research has shown that the fertility of women with intermediate education is about 20 percent less, while that of the women with above secondary education is about 50 percent less than the illiterate women

(Shah, 1988). Because almost 70 percent of the Kuwaiti employed women have a secondary or higher level of education, their contribution to the fertility level of the population is bound to be low. Furthermore, the percentage of single women who cannot contribute to fertility (in Kuwait) is much higher among the working than the nonworking, as discussed earlier. In the presence of the profertility cultural values and government incentives, including cash subsidies for procreation, the fertility of working women may be maintained at a higher level than could have been expected otherwise.

Although the increased female participation in clerical occupations suggests a change in attitudes toward the appropriate roles that working women may fulfill, certain constraints continue to exist. In a 1973 study quoted by Alessa (1981), it was found that 69 percent of the survey respondents agreed that women should work, while the rest did not. Among those who supported female work, 90 percent said that government jobs, preferably in education, were appropriate, because such jobs were segregated by sex. A continued preference in favor of teaching jobs is evident from the concentration in such jobs in the 1985 census. Another reason that Alessa (1981) gives for the relatively low work participation of women concerns the social definition of females as dependent. Because the husbands/fathers are expected to provide for the wife/daughter/sister, the women's incentive to work is reduced.

In an interesting study of women in the banking sector, it was reported that in January 1985, one-fourth of the total manpower in the banking sector was female (Bank Employee's Union, n.d.). Unfortunately, the nationality breakdown of employees was not provided. In order to establish the attitudes of the management toward female workers, a survey was conducted. It was found that 62 percent of the managers preferred to select men, rather than women, to work with them. Forty-nine percent of the managers stated that the work performance of both sexes was equal, while 41 percent suggested that the performance of women was below that of men. Some of the constraints in female productivity were identified to be maternity leave, frequent casual leave, and eagerness to leave work early. Finally, almost half of the managers said that women are not given an equal opportunity to occupy senior positions. These findings suggest that despite the role expansion of women in Kuwait, several additional factors which may lead to discrimination against employment of women still exist.

The government has successfully mobilized the labor of an increasing percentage of females over the 1965–1985 period. The extent to which it can continue to augment the supply will depend on the appropriateness of education and vocational training, as well as the changes in societal attitudes toward female roles. According to some researchers, the level of female activity will change, but its pattern will remain somewhat static in view of traditional values and stereotypes in Gulf countries (Azzam & Moujabber, 1985).

In view of the government policy to expand female participation among Kuwaitis, several suggestions for innovative programs are possible. First, incentives to join the labor force may be enhanced, and service benefits for men and women may be equalized. Working Kuwaiti women are provided the same social security benefits as men. Also, their basic entry salary is identical to men if their qualifications are identical. However, the fringe benefits granted to women are lower—they receive only half the social allowance of men, and are not entitled to child allowance if their husbands work for the public sector. Increasing fringe benefits may attract more women to employment. Second, the private sector may be encouraged (or even instructed) to hire more Kuwaiti women than it does at the present time. Finally, importation of maids may be allowed only for those families in which the woman is employed outside the house. Although the preceding strategies may encourage participation, social attitudes concerning appropriate female roles will continue to play a significant role in determining the supply, as well as demand, for female work.

NOTES

1. A difficulty with the specification of Equation (1) is that some control for the amount of labor supplied should be included. The dependent variable—earnings—is the product of hours worked and hourly wage rate. Economic theory suggests that hours worked depend on, among other things, the wage rate, which in turn, depends on the human capital traits. Hence, as Blinder (1973) points out, the use of earnings as the dependent variable can result in biased estimates of the parameters of the earnings function. The direction and magnitude of the bias will depend on the supply responses to wage rates. Accordingly, Blinder suggests that the appropriate specification of the dependent variable should be wage rates rather than earnings. Mincer (1974), while recognizing the problems of controlling for labor supply, introduces the log of labor supply units (weeks) on the right hand side of the earnings functions as the dependent variable. If this coefficient turns out to be unity, then this is equivalent to the specification suggested by Blinder. However, if this coefficient differs significantly from unity, the interpretation of the coefficient estimate becomes difficult. This problem is mitigated in our sample because it is restricted to a group of persons 15 years of age and over, who worked at least 35 hours per week and who were wage and salary earners having positive monthly earnings.

2. Following Mincer (1974), total experience is defined as age − years of education − 6. Previous experience is defined as total experience minus years of job-tenure.

3. The computed F-values of the Chow-tests are 37.5, 207 and 105 for Kuwaiti men versus Kuwaiti, Arab and non-Arab women, respectively. These values are greater than the theoretical values.

4. This is referred to as the self-selection problem (Willis, 1986). In the case of migrant workers, variations in earnings might also be due to variations in years of residence in the labor market of the host country (Chiswick, 1979). In our sample, the average years of residence is 14 and 10 for Arab and non-Arab women, respectively. That is, the sample contains long-term Arab and non-Arab residents.

REFERENCES

Alessa, S. Y. (1981). *The Manpower problem in kuwait.* London: Kegan Paul.

Arab Times Daily. (1988, February 11). *Arab Times Daily newspaper.* Kuwait.

Al-Omaim, M., & Kohli, K. L. (1984). The demographic situation in Kuwait. Paper presented at the U.N. Third Regional Population Conference, Amman.

Al-Qudsi, S. S. (1985). Earnings differences in the labor market of the Arab Gulf States: The case of Kuwait. *Journal of Development Economics 18,* 119–132.

Al-Qudsi, S., & Shah, N. (1988). *The relative economic progress of migrant workers in Kuwait.* Draft manuscript.

Al-Qudsi, I. (1984). *Earnings determination and differential in the Kuwait labor market.* Unpublished Ph.D. dissertation, University of Washington.

Azzam, W., & Moujabber, C. (1985). Women and development in the Gulf states. In J. A. Nasr, N. F. Khoury, & H. T. Azzam (Eds.), *Women, employment and development in the Arab world.* Berlin: Mouton.

Bank Employees Union. (n.d.) *Women's role in the Kuwaiti Banking Sector.* Kuwait: The Kuwaiti Bank Committee, Union of Bank's Employees.

Blinder, A. (1973). Wage discrimination: Reduced form and structural estimates. *Journal of Human Resources 8*(4), 436–455.

Caldwell, J. C. (1982). *Theory of fertility decline.* London: Academic Press.

Central Statistical Office (CSO). (1980, 1984, 1986, 1987) *Annual statistical abstract.* Kuwait: Ministry of Planning.

Chiswick, B. (1979). The economic progress of immigrants: some apparent universal patterns. In W. Fellner (Ed.), *Contemporary economic problems* (pp. 357–399). Washington, DC: American Enterprise Institute.

Hosni, D., & Al-Qudsi, S. (1986). *Sex discrimination in the labor market of Kuwait.* Kuwait Institute for Scientific Research.

Gunatilake, G. (1986). Sri Lanka. In G. Guntilake, (Ed.), *Migration of Asian workers to the Arab world.* Tokyo: The United Nations University.

Korale, R. B. M. (1986). Migration for employment in the Middle East: Its demographic and socio-economic effects on Sri Lanka. In F. Arnold, & N. M. Shah (Eds.), *Asian labor migration: Pipeline to the Middle East.* Colorado: Westview Press.

Korale, R. B. M., & Karunawathie, I. M. (1981). *Migration of Sri Lankans for employment abroad.* Colombo: Employment of Manpower Planning Division, Ministry of Plan Implementation (mimeographed report).

Malkiel, B., & Malkiel, J. (1973, September). Male-Female pay differentials in professional employment. *American Economic Review 63,* pp. 693–705.

Meleis, A. I. (1982). Effect of modernization on Kuwaiti women. *Social Science Medicine 16,* 965–970.

Mincer, J. (1974). *Schooling, experience and earnings.* New York: National Bureau of Economic Research.

Ministerial Council. (1985). *Development plan for 1985/86–1989/90: population and labor force* (Vol. 2). Kuwait: Author. (Published in Arabic)

Ministry of Social Affairs and Labor. (1983). *Athr al-Murabiyat al-Ajnabiat ala al-Usr al-Kuwaitiya* [Trans.]. Kuwait: Ministry report.

Oaxaca, R. (1973). Male-female wage differentials in urban labor markets. *International Economic Review 14,* 693–709.

OECD (Organization for Economic Cooperation and Development). (1985). *The integration of women into the economy.* Paris: Author.

Rassam, A. (1984). Introduction: Arab women: The status of research in the social sciences and the status of women. In UNESCO *Women in the Arab world.* Oxford: Joshua Associates.

Shah, N. M. (1988). *The population dynamics of the state of Kuwait* (Draft report). Tunis: U.N. League of Arab Nations, Population Research Unit.

Shah, N. M., & Al-Qudsi, S. (1987, April–May). *Changing characteristics of migrant workers in*

Kuwait. Paper presented at the Annual Meeting of the Population Association of America, Chicago.

Shah, N. M., & Smith, P. C. (1984). Migrant women at work in Asia. In J. T. Fawcett, S.-E. Khoo, & P. C. Smith (Eds.), *Women in the cities of Asia: Migration and urban adaptation*. Colorado: Westview Press.

Standing, G. (1978). *Labor force participation and development*. Geneva: International Labour Office.

Youssef, N. (1974). *Women and work in developing societies*. Berkeley, CA: Institute of International Studies, University of Southern California.

Willis, R. J. (1986). Wage determinants: A survey and reinterpretation of human capital earnings functions. In O. C. Ashenfelter, & R. Layard (Eds.) *Handbook of labor economics*. North-Holland: Elsevier.

Zurayk, H. (1985). Women's economic participation. In F. C. Shorter, & H. Zurayk (Eds.), *Population factors in development planning in the Middle East*. New York: The Population Council.

THE MODE OF AGRICULTURAL PRODUCTION AND FEMALE LABOR FORCE PARTICIPATION:

THE CASE OF THE GEZIRA SCHEME, SUDAN

Eltigani Eltahir Eltigani

INTRODUCTION

It has been consistently observed that the countries of the Middle East and North Africa experience low levels of female participation in agricultural production compared to levels in other countries at the same stage of development (Dixon-Mueller & Anker, 1988; Sheehan, 1978; N. Youssef, 1977).

The observed low rates of female labor force participation can be attributed to errors associated with the way economic activity is defined and measured, the special cultural/religious characteristics of these countries, or a result of the mode of agricultural production (a combination of the relations of production and type of technology used in the production process) that exist in the particular setting.

Research in Human Capital and Development, Vol. 6, pages 247–267.

ISBN: 1-55938-032-2

Women workers in the agricultural sector are disproportionately undercounted in most population censuses and surveys. The main source of this problem lies in the definition of economic activity as applied to women. For example, because of changes in the definition of economic activity and the way questions were asked, the census of India counted 49 million women in agricultural occupations in 1961 but only 26 million in 1971. By 1981 the figure had risen to 36 million (Dixon-Mueller & Anker, 1988).

Women are counted as 'economically active' if they spend a certain portion of the working week in 'productive activities.' Productive activities were defined as: "any activity which is devoted to the production of goods or services which is measurable in economic terms and in which people are gainfully employed." (United Nations, 1974, 1977). Such a definition of economic activity as applied to women results not only in excluding such important activities as food preparation, water and fuel portage, and livestock raising, but also excludes some productive activities performed by women as part of the unpaid family labor. The latest definition of economic activity includes 'all persons of either sex who furnish the supply of labor for the production of economic goods and services as defined by the UN system of national accounts and balances' (ILO, 1983). The new definition allows for the measurement of both current activity, measured in terms of a short reference period such as a week, and the usual activity, as measured in terms of a reference period of a year or a season.

Underenumeration of female participation in agricultural activities may also result from a number of other factors such as: the wording of questions regarding female 'work'; season and time reference period used; the order in which questions about economic activity are asked; the amount of probing; and the perception of enumerators and respondents regarding appropriate roles for women and men, as when farm wives are simply assumed not to be economically active and thus reported as such (Anker, 1980; Dixon, 1982; Zurayk, 1985). With respect to the reference period, a short reference period is likely to exclude many women. For example, in Peru, the 1941 census counted women as only 14 percent of the agricultural labor force when the question was based on present occupation in a specific week, but 31 percent when the question was based on usual occupation (Durand, 1975).

The low rates of female participation in farm work may not, however, be entirely due to statistical artifacts. It may result from the existence of a cultural/religious setting not conducive to, or condoning of, the active involvement of women in any activity outside the confines of their homes. In Muslim societies, for example, the low levels of female involvement in the labor force is attributed to the combined effects of the tradition of female seclusion and exclusion patterns (Anker & Knowles, 1978; N. Youssef, 1971). Another important cultural factor has to do with the way people perceive manual labor for both men and women.

The level of female agricultural labor force is also determined by the mode of agricultural production in the particular setting. Under conditions of subsistence agriculture, female labor accounts for more than half of the agricultural work force. In a survey of rural Blue Nile Province in southeastern Sudan, an area that is dominated by subsistence economic activities, it was found that women assume a much more important role in the production process compared to men and seem to participate in almost all activities. They participate in most of the agricultural activities and in all types of labor force (i.e., family, wage, and communal labor). They also almost dominate nonagricultural activities (Economic and Social Research Council, 1979). In contrast, under conditions of modern agricultural production, where the use of hired labor and modern agricultural technology is widespread, female labor accounts for a much smaller part of the agricultural labor force. As hired laborers are called in, women of the cultivators' families are released from farm work (Boserup, 1970, 1975).

The impact of technology on women's work activity can be illustrated by an example from Bangladesh. Rapid growth of mechanized rice milling has led to the displacement of an estimated 3.5 to 5 million days of female labor per year. Women from landless households had been responsible for 86 percent of all employment in rice processing, specializing in husking by traditional methods. In contrast, the newly created jobs in the new automated or semiautomated mills were almost exclusively male (Ahmed, 1987).

In this paper we focus on measuring the level and pattern of female participation in economic activities in rural Gezira. First, we measure the level of female labor force participation using an alternative definition of economic activity, adapted from the Sudan Fertility Survey (1979). Second, we examine the differentials in female labor force participation that exist among the population and the underlying socioeconomic setting in Gezira. Gezira provides a suitable setting for elucidating some of the issues mentioned above. It represents the largest modern irrigated agricultural project, not only in Sudan, but in all sub-Saharan Africa. The system of production in Gezira is considered a model for agricultural development—a model that is emulated, on a smaller scale, in other parts of the country. Thus, the implications of the Gezira type of agricultural development on female labor force participation is far reaching and can be extended to cover areas where the model of Gezira is replicated.

II. BACKGROUND OF THE GEZIRA SCHEME

The Gezira Scheme is situated in the triangle of land south of Khartoum. Two sides of the triangle are formed by two rivers: to the east the Blue Nile, and to the West the White Nile (see map). The Gezira Scheme occupies around 2.1 million feddans[1] and represents the largest irrigated agricultural undertaking in the country. Out of a total irrigated area of approximately 4 million feddans in all of Sudan, the Gezira Scheme constitutes slightly more than half.

The Gezira Scheme was established in 1925 to provide long-staple cotton for

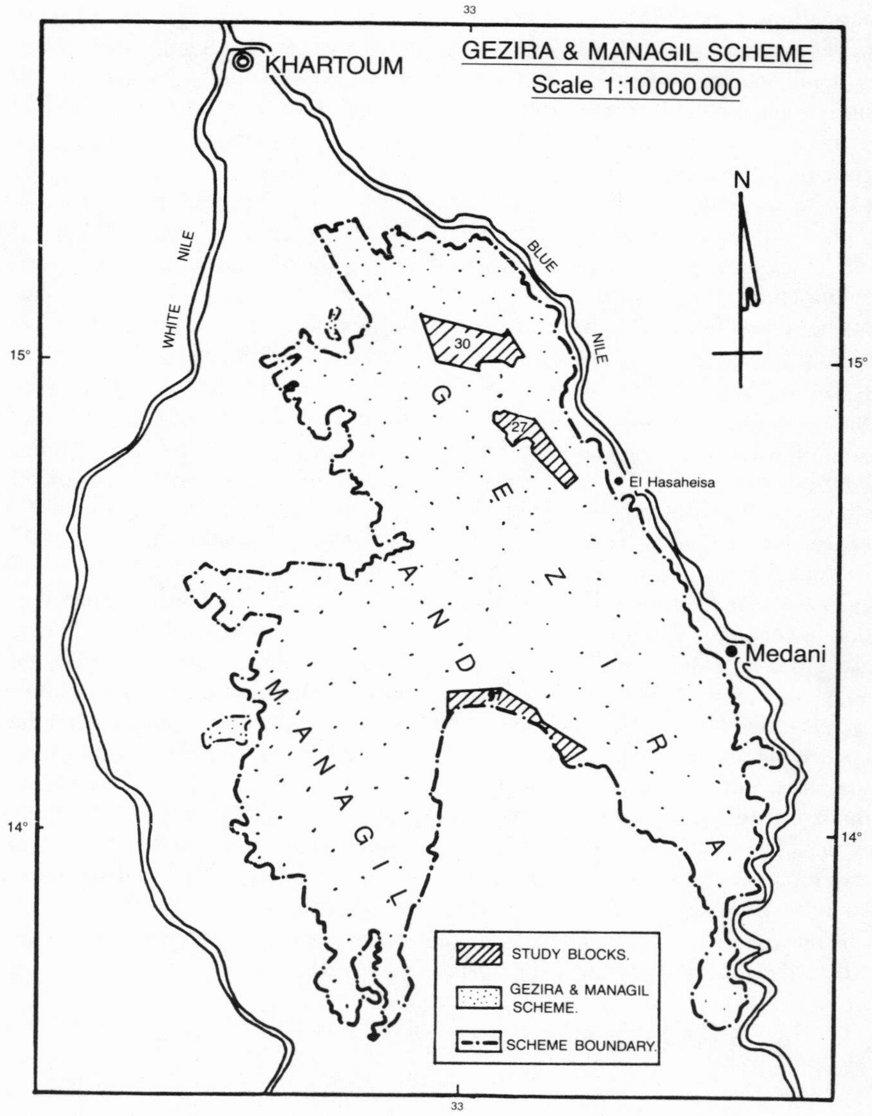

the textile factories of Lancashire, Britain. Other crops such as wheat, groundnut, and rice were introduced during various stages of the Scheme development as a part of the policy of crop diversification. However, the main function of the Scheme still remains the same—to provide long-staple cotton for export.

The Scheme contributes directly to the livelihood of hundreds of thousands of people who are involved in its operation. The Sudan Gezira Board (SGB), which manages the Scheme, employs about 10,000 staff of all grades. There are also 96,000 tenants who till the land assisted by 400,000–500,000 casual laborers.

The impact of the establishment of the Gezira Scheme on the socioeconomic structure of the region can be evaluated by considering the relations of production between the different parties involved in the Scheme operation.

III. RELATIONS OF PRODUCTION IN THE SCHEME

The organization of the Gezira Scheme has often been described as a partnership between the government, which supplied the main part of the infrastructure; the Sudan Plantation Syndicate (known as Sudan Gezira Board after the Scheme was nationalized), which manages the Scheme; and the many thousands of tenant farmers who carry out the main part of the agricultural operations within their respective tenancies. The Scheme was divided into tenancies with the size of 40 feddans in the Gezira Main and 30 feddans in Managil Extension.

The division of the gains between the three partners were distributed such that the proceeds from every bale of cotton sold were credited to a joint account. Against this account were debited the costs of seeds, fertilizers, spraying, sacks and baling materials, transport, insurance, ginning costs, and freight. The net proceeds after the deduction of all the costs cited above were distributed as follows:

- Thirty-six percent to the government.
- Fifty percent to the tenants. This includes two percent used to finance the Tenants Reserve Fund.
- Two percent to the Local Government Councils within the irrigated area. This contributes to the health and education facilities in the region.
- Two percent to the Social Development Department of the SGB. The department was concerned with the provision of water supplies and adult education.
- Ten percent to the SGB to cover administration costs.
- Profits from crops other than cotton are the exclusive property of the tenant.

Following the continuous decline in productivity in the Scheme, the above system was amended. A new system based on "Individual Accounts" was introduced in the early 1980s. Under this system, water charges were not limited to cotton only but covered all other crops. In addition, the charges were assessed against the output of every individual tenant, not from the output of all tenants taken as a collective.

The system of relations of production introduced by the Scheme was new to the area. Prior to the establishment of the Scheme, the majority of the inhabitants of the area away from rivers led a seminomadic life. During the dry season they wandered from one place to another in search of water and sparse grazing for their cattle. During the rainy season they lived in their villages and cultivated sorghum on the land around them. Economic production was organized in terms of the lineage and the tribe. Within this system of economic organization land was not a commodity because it was communally owned. It was, however, frequently vested in one man or in one family. The use of land was held in trust for the entire group (Barnett, 1975).

As a result of the change in social organization within the irrigated area, clear formation of social classes in the area started to develop. These classes did not develop spontaneously, of course. Their development was a result of a combination of preexisting social forces and social configurations within the particular structural opportunities produced by the Scheme itself.

The process by which the land was taken over and tenancies distributed was one that preserved some of the social and economic inequalities that had existed in the area before the establishment of the Scheme. Large landowners (mostly tribal and religious leaders) were able to obtain significantly larger shares in the Scheme than small landowners or those without land (Niblock, 1987). When land was registered prior to the Scheme's inception, tribal and village leaders often sought to register the communally owned lands as their own private property. In this way tribal leaders were often able to establish ownership rights over large areas that had not been their property. Further, allowing existing leaders to maintain some economic preeminence in the Gezira was seen by the colonial government as a political necessity. The government feared that these leaders might mobilize their people against the Scheme. Only by giving them some stake in the new Scheme could their support be ensured. An individual who was able to present a documented claim of ownership of 40 feddans or more was entitled to at least one tenancy of 40 feddans. If the claim was for 80 feddans or more, he was entitled to two tenancies. Such individuals were known as "Right Tenants." If a Right Tenant owned 120 feddans or more, he was entitled to name an heir, and the heir would be given a tenancy. Tenants who obtained tenancies in the latter way were known as "Nominees." Only after the needs of the Right Tenants had been satisfied could the needs of others be considered. "Preferential Tenants" were those who owned less than 40 feddans. Provided there was sufficient land available in the relevant locality, they could be granted a tenancy or half-tenancy (20 feddans). If there were still tenancies not yet taken up after the Preferential Tenants had been satisfied, the remaining plots (usually in half-tenancies) were given to landless cultivators or else to outsiders (Niblock, 1987).

The organization of the Scheme was also important in another respect. The technical conditions for successful cotton production demanded the creation of an autonomous body (Sudan Plantation Syndicate), which later became the SGB, to ensure that the right inputs were applied at the right time and in the right sequence. A high degree of regimentation and control seemed inevitable. In return for the benefits expected, the tenants had to accept a high degree of subordination. What to grow, how, when, and so forth, became decisions beyond their control (A. Salam, 1982). Thus, the role of the tenant was in many ways closer to that of a worker in a factory than to that of a small holding tenant.

Further, the watering program and the provision of services (e.g., machine operations) made it necessary to group the cultivated crops in 90 feddans units called Numbers. The whole Number is put under one crop. In the 8-course rotation, every tenant was given four separate feddans units, out of which at any one season 10 feddans are put under cotton and five feddans under sorghum. The rest is left fallow. The plots allotted to tenants did not form a compact, continuous holding but were scattered in four different Numbers. According to the rotation adopted, cotton was grown in one of the four plots. Sorghum is alternated between one's own land and his neighbor's land. Thus the producer is detached from the land; not only does his holding not form a single unit, but the rotation takes him to other people's land. He is not really a farmer but a producer of agricultural commodities, as on a 'conveyer belt' of land supplied to him by the management, and it is the management and not the farmer who cares for the land and its fertility (Gulwick, 1955). This system was modified after the 1975–1976 season.

Under the system of production emphasized in the Scheme organization, the tenant is responsible for the provision of labor in his tenancy. Thus, the work in the tenancy was supposed to be carried out by the tenant and his family. The only recognized exception to this assumption was the labor requirement during the peak seasons (sowing and cotton picking).

However, the tenants tended to employ and heavily depend on hired labor to perform tasks that were supposed to be performed by the tenant and his family. This behavioral pattern by the tenants regarding their involvement in the production process was perceived by the Scheme administration as tenant laziness and avoidance of manual agricultural work. However, the heavy dependence on hired labor can actually be attributed to demographic and economic factors.

Considering the demographic factor, as a result of the Scheme, the family structure of the Gezira tenant has become nuclearized. Thus when we talk about family labor, we are really talking about the labor potential of the nuclear family (Barnett, 1977). The nuclearization of the families was due to the fact that

> Under the new mode of production, the tenant now had control of his own specific area each year. The tenant also receives cash payment for his effort. From this income he organized his consumption. Thus the size of the production and consumption unit was effectively circumscribed . . . There is no pressing aspect of his life situation as tenant which requires that he should any longer be deeply involved in his corporate kinship group. This no longer has any crucial role to play in his role as a consumer, producer or distributor. These changes . . .

meant that the productive unit and consumption has been limited in order to fit the social unit to the carrying capacity of the tenancy. (Barnett, 1977, pp. 95–96)

It is then clear that there are demographic constraints on the amount of labor any one tenant can derive from his family. Only at certain points in his family life cycle can a tenant reckon to have enough labor from his family to reduce his requirement for hiring outside labor.

Another demographic element closely associated with the institutional structure of the Scheme encouraged the continuous dependence on hired labor. The institutional arrangement of the Scheme prohibited the subdivision of the tenancy below a minimum level of 5 feddans planted under cotton. Hence, not all of a tenant's heirs could be tenants. At the same time the relative abundance of educational facilities in the area enabled the children of tenants to be educated. Educated children leave the farms in search of other opportunities in other urban areas (mainly Khartoum and Wad Medani). Thus, the older men and women were left behind in control of tenancies. In a survey conducted by A. Salam (1976), the tenant average age was 52.1 in Gezira Main and 40.9 in Managil. About 17.6 percent of the sampled tenants were found to be over 60 years old. Thus, in such situations it is imperative for tenants to resort to hired labor with the employment arrangement either in the form of wage labor or sharecropping.

Emigration of men to urban areas may have a positive impact on female labor force participation in agriculture. Data from Zimbabwe show that sex–selective emigration of young adults intensified the demand for female labor, especially in agriculture (Dixon-Mueller & Anker, 1988). In Gezira, however, male emigration was compensated for by more dependence on cheap immigrant labor.

The dependence on hired labor was also necessitated by the fact that incomes from the tenancies are relatively low and unstable compared to income derived from off-farm activities. In a study by A. Salam (1976) it was found that during the season of 1975–1976, net income from off-farm sources amounted to 59.8 percent of total net income of the tenants. Thus the counter-attractions of sources of income off the tenancy have made it worthwhile for some tenants and their children to rely on other incomes while at the same time hiring labor (A. Salam, 1982).

The supply of hired labor to the Gezira is composed of village(s) resident landless labor, settled migrants from West and Central Africa, and Western Sudan. In addition, there are seasonal migrants drawn largely from eastern Gezira, White Nile Province, and western Sudan.

During the initial stages of the Scheme, the main source of hired labor was West and Central Africa. This was part of the immigration to the Sudan by these elements, which first started during the turn of the present century. Pilgrims from West Africa used to cross the area on their way to Mecca. During their trip they would pick up work along the way to support themselves and save enough money for the rest of their journey. However, the number of transient workers started to swell after the establishment of the Scheme. The opening of the Gezira Scheme, which happens to lie in the belt of immigration, or close to it, has led tens of thousands to flow to the area either as settlers or as itinerant laborers earning their living working in one area during part of the year and in a different area the rest of the year (Hassoun, 1952).

The influx of West and Central Africans was in fact encouraged by the colonial government. This was due mainly to the belief that they are more efficient and productive compared to the native population, but more important, the migrants were able to provide cheap labor. The availability of cheap labor in the Scheme was beneficial to the Scheme administration and ultimately to the government, because it facilitated the production of cotton at prices that can compete in world markets (Barnett, 1975).

After the nationalization of the Scheme and the political independence of the country, the policy of encouragement and recruitment of migrant labor continued. However, more emphasis was placed on attracting migrants from western Sudan and discouraging the migration of foreign labor. The SGB and the tenants, particularly the rich tenants, still conduct recruiting campaigns, mainly during the cotton–picking season, of migrant workers (Galal Eldin, 1979).

Thus from all of the discussion above, we can argue that the low and unstable incomes that can be derived from tenancies led to the outflow of the more talented, energetic, and educated elements of the area's population to seek employment opportunities elsewhere, mainly in urban centers in the country or abroad, and to the influx of cheap agricultural labor, mainly from the other economically depressed parts of the country. The implications of this on female labor force participation in Gezira will be studied in the rest of the paper.

IV. THE DATA

The data on which this paper is based were collected as part of the "Socioeconomic Aspects of Child Health in Gezira" survey conducted by the author between November 1986 and February 1987. A sample of 1241 households from 31 villages in three blocks[2] from Gezira Main and Managil Extension were covered (see map). The studied households were selected through multistage probability sampling. The data on women's economic activity were collected from ever married women who were 15–55 years old at the time of the Survey. Thus the data does not include economic activities of single women. However, because marriage is almost universal, the level and pattern of economic activity of the sampled ever-married women could safely be generalized to cover the entire adult female population of the study area.

V. DEFINING ECONOMIC ACTIVITY

Economic activity is defined here as "any type of work (apart from regular household) that is performed by women whether it was paid for in cash or in kind, whether own-account, for family or for somebody else, whether it is performed at home or outside, whether it is seasonal or all year round." This definition is adapted from the definition used by the Sudan Fertility Survey (1979). It incorporates unpaid female labor and recognizes the seasonal nature of some of the agricultural activities performed by women. To further account for seasonality, the reference period was taken as the year prior to the survey date.

VI. THE LEVEL OF FEMALE WORK PARTICIPATION

Adapting the definition above to women in Gezira, it was found that almost one-fifth of the ever-married women in the sample population are economically active. The rate of women's participation in economic activities declines to 13 percent if women who work as unpaid family labor are excluded from the definition. The rate declines further, to 8 percent, if the women who work only on a seasonal basis, in addition to women who work as unpaid family labor, are excluded from the calculations.

The observed rate of economic activity of women from this population is almost twice the rate produced by the 1973 population census of the Blue Nile Province[3] (10.4 percent). This does not mean that the rate of female economic activity has increased during the 13-year interval between the census time and our study. It reflects the extent of underreporting of the rate of female economic activity when a rigid definition of economic activity is applied.

Even after using a flexible definition of economic activity, the rate of women's involvement in work activity in Gezira is still relatively low. The 1973 census showed that the rate of women's participation, using a narrower definition of economic activity, is much higher in the western parts of the country (i.e., Darfur and Kordofan regions). The observed female labor force participation rates were 56.3 percent and 41.4 percent for the two regions, respectively (Galal Eldin, n.d.). This is due to the fact that the type of agricultural technology used in Gezira excluded women from the production process. A large portion of the agricultural activities in Gezira are carried out through the use of machines (e.g., land preparation, cultivation, wheat harvest). Thus the wide use of modern agricultural technology resulted in minimizing the role that could be played by women and children in the production process, because all of the agricultural machinery is operated by men. This was a result of the fact that when machines were introduced for the cultivation of cash crops, emphasis was made to train men on how to use the new techniques of production. No effort was made to introduce women to the new technology. Thus women were relegated to the production of subsistence crops using traditional methods of production (Galal Eldin, n.d.). However, it is important to note that there is nothing natural about sex-typing of particular occupations. Variation in what is considered men's or women's work is a product primarily of the social beliefs about appropriate male and female roles that are perpetuated in differential socialization, training, hiring and promotion practices (Dixon-Mueller &Anker, 1988).

Apart from the technology factor, the presence of the migrant labor force provided a cheap substitute for the labor of the original inhabitants of the area, both male and female, and may also have contributed to the enforcement of the cultural bias among the local population towards female active participation in economic activities.

There are, however, other important socioeconomic factors that explain the observed low rate of female economic activity. These factors are discussed below.

VII. FACTORS DETERMINING WOMEN'S ECONOMIC ACTIVITY

Whether a woman decides to participate in economic activities is largely determined by the socioeconomic status of her household, the attitudes of the woman, her household, and the community at large regarding women's work, wage level, the demographic characteristics of the woman, and availability of job opportunities. An important underlying variable in connection with the above is the education level, particularly female education. The level of education influences attitudes toward women's work and the skill level the woman brings to the labor market. However, more important, education level of the woman not only determines whether the woman wants to work, but the type of work she is willing to perform. The variables outlined above are discussed in detail below.

The woman's socioeconomic status can be approximated by the type of the household head's primary occupation. An important feature of the Gezira is the existence of socioeconomic stratification among the population of the area. First, there is the group of nonfarm wage labor (white and blue collar). Members of this group may or may not be directly involved in the Scheme's activities (e.g., field inspectors, teachers, cotton ginning factory workers and other skilled workers). Among this group, white collar workers constitute the elite group of the population. They are the most educated segment of the population; they also enjoy relatively higher standards of living. Second, there is the group of tenants who organize and supply the labor power to their respective tenancies and share the revenues from the sale of cotton with the government and the SGB. In addition, tenants also receive the entire wheat, sorghum and groundnut crops. The group of tenants is by no means homogeneous. Some tenants are rich and run their tenancies on an entrepreneurial basis, most probably as one enterprise among many. But the majority of tenants are those for whom their tenancies represent the only source of livelihood (Barnett, 1977). Third, there is the group of merchant/own account. Some of the members of this group, particularly the merchants, are involved in agricultural production, through the ownership of tenancies. Finally, there is the group of farm workers who represent the poorest segment of the population. This group is composed of the local, landless farm workers and the migrant farm workers.

Among the economically active females in Gezira, more than half of them belong to households directly involved in agricultural production (Table 1). More than a quarter belong to households headed by nonfarm workers. Only about 17 percent are from households headed by white-collar workers and merchant and own-account.

However, among the households that are directly involved in agriculture, there is a marked difference in the level of female economic activity between women who belong to tenant households and those from farm workers households. Only one-fifth of the females in tenant households are economically active compared to more than half for females from farm worker households. The low rate of economic activity among females from tenant households is at odds with the assumption, made at the inception of the Scheme, that tenant families (including women) were supposed to provide the bulk of the labor power to their tenancies. This can be explained that the detachment of the tenant from his land, alluded to earlier, has negative implications on the amount of time and effort the tenant and his family devote to investment in their land. Further, the existence of cheap landless wage labor made it easier for tenant households to substitute their own labor inputs, or at least the major part of it, with that of hired labor. This observation is supported by the fact that 40 percent of the economically active women are migrants (Table 2), despite the fact that migrant households constitute only 16 percent of the sample population. The level of economic activity among females from migrant households is three-and-a-half times the level among females from the local population of the area.

Table 1. Level of Economic Activity of Ever-Married Women by Household Head Primary Occupation (1986–1987)

Head of Household Primary Occupation	*Level of Female Economic Activity*	
	Percent Working	*Percentage of Active Women*
Tenant	21	27
Farm worker	52	28
Non-farm worker	16	28
White collar	14	9
Merchant/Own account	10	8

Table 2. Level of Economic Activity of Ever-Married Women by Area of Origin (1986–1987)

Women Place of Origin	*Percent Working*	*Percentage of Working Women*
Nonmigrants	15	60
Migrants	53	40

The high rate of involvement in economic activity of migrant women can be attributed to the fact that they are mainly drawn from areas where subsistence agricultural activity is prevalent. The strong tradition of female involvement in farm work under the subsistence mode of production is carried over by these migrants to their new area of residence in Gezira. The migrants are also, on the average, poorer than the rest of the population. This can be illustrated by the fact that almost half of migrant household heads work exclusively as farm workers, with the rest mainly engaged in casual work. Only 13 percent of the migrants have tenancies of their own. Thus women's work and contribution to the households' total income is essential for the survival of these households. Another contributing factor may be due to the type of the system of social relations between the local population and the migrants, which is largely based on tribal affiliation. Under such conditions, even if the level of poverty of tenants and workers is the same, the women of the tenants may be encouraged, either by choice or due to prohibition by their men, to retire to seclusion and to avoid all manual work outside the household, to distinguish herself from the despised and hardworking migrant female laborers.

The woman's reproductive behavior (measured in terms of average number of children ever born) may have a negative impact on the woman's work participation (H. Youssef, 1985). This hypothesis is based on the fact that the number and age of children affects the woman's child care role and hence her ability to participate in the labor force. The hypothesized negative relationship between the woman's reproductive behavior and her involvement in economic activities may not be valid if the type of work performed by the woman does not necessitate her leaving her young children for extended periods of time, or when other household members are available to provide child care during the mother's absence (Anker & Knowles, 1978; Standing, 1983).

In Gezira the average number of children ever born for working women is slightly higher compared to the nonworking women (5.72 and 5.50 live births, respectively). Among other things, this can be explained by the fact that the working women, on the average, tend to be older than their nonworking counterparts (34 and 31 years, respectively). Further, the rate of women's labor force participation increases consistently with age. The rate increases from as low as 2 percent for women in the age group 15–19 years to 33 percent for women in the age group 40–44 years. The high rate among women 40–44 years old is undoubtedly due to the fact that by this age women generally have completed their child care responsibilities and are more able to enter the labor force.

The impact of child care responsibilities on women's work participation can be assessed by looking at the rate of women's work by the age of their youngest child. Table 3 shows that the rate of women's work rises with the age of the youngest living child. Almost one-third of the women whose youngest child is at least five years old are economically active, compared to 18 percent among those whose youngest child is less than one year old.

The way the woman's child care role affects her work participation depends, however, on the socioeconomic status of her household. Women from tenant households display the lowest rate of economic activity at younger child ages (ages younger than one year old) compared to other women. More hired labor may be brought in as a substitute for the wife's labor under these circumstances. Women from farm worker households show significantly higher rates of economic activity at all levels of youngest child ages compared to the rest of the population. The difference is highest at young child ages (younger than one year). This clearly reflects the importance of the work of these women to the economies of their households.

The educational background of the woman also influences her work participation (see Table 4). It is important to note that Gezira enjoys the highest concentration of formal education services in the country (ILO, 1977). Among our female sample, 43 percent of the interviewed women have received some formal education, and almost one-fifth have completed at least primary school. These are relatively high rates of education compared to the rest of rural Sudan (Eltigani, 1989). Among the women who have some primary education, only 9 percent are economically active, whereas the rate is 13 percent for those who have completed

Table 3. Level of Economic Activity of Ever-Married Women by Age of Youngest Living Child (1986–1987)

Household Head Primary Occupation	*Age of Youngest Child* < 1 year	*1–4 years*	*at least 5 years*
Tenant	8	20	36
Farm worker	55	49	62
Nonfarm worker	19	14	21
White collar	14	14	15
Merchant/Own account	11	8	19
All women	18	19	31

Table 4. Level of Economic Activity of Ever-Married Women by Level of Education (1986)

Education Level	*Percent Working*	*Percentage of Working Women*
Illiterate	28	78
Incomplete primary	9	11
Primary and over	13	11

at least primary school. This is compared to 28 percent of the women who did not receive any formal education. This shows that women who have some formal education are less inclined to work compared to their illiterate counterparts. Educated women, particularly those who finished primary school or above, shun farm work. This attitude is hardly confined to women. This can be attributed to the fact that emphasis on the type of academic education that characterizes the education in Gezira and the rest of the country helped drain Gezira of its most educated elements, who are attracted by employment opportunities in the urban sector and away from agriculture. However, emigration among the educated elements of the population is largely confined to educated males, because it is socially unacceptable for women to engage in emigration unless they are married and move out of the village with their husbands. Because agriculture is the dominant economic activity in the area, there are limited job opportunities available for educated women to pursue and for which they have to compete with educated men. Thus, educated women may elect to stay home rather than to engage in farm work, particularly if the earnings that can be derived from farm work are relatively low and unattractive and there is no economic pressure on their households that necessitates their work.

VIII. ACTIVITIES OF THE WORKING WOMEN

Information on types of work pursued by women is useful for planning purposes. It reveals the extent to which women have access to income earning opportunities as opposed to laboring without pay. In Gezira, almost half the working women work as paid farm workers. One-quarter work as unpaid family workers. The rest of the working women in Gezira are distributed between own–handicrafts (12 percent), white collar workers (10 percent), and nonfarm workers (12 percent). The level of female unpaid family labor in Gezira conforms with empirical evidence from other countries. For example, in Sri Lanka, according to the census of 1981, 27 percent of female workers in agriculture were unpaid family labor (Dixon-Mueller & Anker, 1988).

The type of economic activity the woman pursues, however, is again determined by the socioeconomic background of the woman and her household. Table 5 shows that more than half of the working women from tenant households work as unpaid farm workers, and 38 percent work as paid farm workers. Working women from farm worker households reflect the opposite pattern. More than 60 percent of them work as paid family workers, and only slightly more than a quarter work as unpaid family workers. The relatively high proportion of women workers who work as unpaid family workers among the group of farm worker households is mainly due to the existence of the practice of sharecropping in the Scheme. Sharecropping is not recognized by the Scheme administration. It exists as an unofficial agreement between the tenant and the wage workers. The tenant agrees to give up temporarily the right to use the land. The right is offered to the farm worker who then becomes a subtenant and agrees to share the produce with the tenant at the end of the season. The crop that is widely sharecropped is sorghum, the main staple food in the area. In a small survey of 26 subtenant households in 1982–1983, it was found that each household, on the average, has about four members engaged in farming activities. This makes it possible for the subtenant to depend mainly on their household's labor and thus provide the bulk of the labor requirement in their sharecropped holdings (Abdel, 1985).

Paid farm work is also the dominant type of work performed by working women from nonfarm worker, merchant and own account households. As for working women from white collar households, they are mainly concentrated in white collar jobs (the majority work as primary school teachers).

The type of work the woman pursues is also determined by the woman's level of education. Table 6 shows that almost 60 percent of the noneducated working women work as paid farm workers, and 29 percent work as unpaid family workers. As the level of education of women increases, fewer women work

Table 5. Distribution of Working Ever-Married Women by Type of Activity and Household Occupation (1986–1987)

Head's Occupation	*Type of Activity*				
	Unpaid worker	*Handicrafts*	*Paid farm worker*	*White collar*	*Nonfarm worker*
Tenant	55	6*	38	1*	0
Farm worker	27	8	62	1*	1*
Nonfarm worker	6*	20	65	3*	6*
White collar	0	14*	0	86	0
Merchant/ Own-account	16*	16*	58	10*	10*
All women	25	12	51	10	2

Note: *Based on < 5 cases.

Table 6. Distribution of Working Ever-Married Women by Type of Activity and Education Level (1986–1987)

	Type of Activity				
Education Level	*Unpaid worker*	*Handicrafts*	*Paid farm worker*	*White collar*	*Nonfarm worker*
Illiterate	29	10	59	0	2
Incomplete Primary	26	26	48	0	0
Primary and over	3*	10*	3*	81	3*
All women	25	12	51	10	2

Note: *Based on < cases.

either as paid or unpaid farm workers. For the working women who have at least completed primary school, 81 percent of them work as white collar workers.

From the above, it is apparent that there is a correlation between the socioeconomic status of women, the rate of female economic activity, and the type of work they pursue. Uneducated women from poor households that are mainly involved in farm work get involved in farm work themselves either as paid or unpaid farm workers. On the other hand, educated women from well-off households that are not directly involved in farm work tend not to work, and when they do, they favor white collar work, which is more prestigious and pays considerably more than farm work.

IX. PATTERN OF WOMEN'S ECONOMIC ACTIVITY

Besides identifying the extent and type of women's involvement in economic activity in Gezira, it is also important to determine the pattern of this involvement. From Table 7, it appears that less than half of the working women work all year. This means that the involvement of Gezira women in economic activities is mainly of a seasonal nature. This is largely due to the fact that the production technology used in Gezira limited the role of women in the production process to only the most labor intensive aspect of the process—that of picking cotton. In fact, almost a third of all the working women work only during the cotton picking season. Slightly more than a fifth of the working women spend some time performing other agricultural activities for one period or another during the year.

Among the working women who only work seasonally, 80 percent work only during the cotton picking season. About 47 percent of the women paid farm workers work only during the cotton-picking season, and less than 30 percent

Table 7. Pattern of Work of the Working Ever-Married (1986–1987)

	Season of Work		
Type of Work	*All Year*	*Cotton Picking Only*	*Other Farming Activities*
Unpaid worker	35	31	34
Handicrafts	100	0	0
Paid farm worker	28	47	25
White collar	100	0	0
Nonfarm worker	100	0	0
All women	47	32	21

work all year. As for unpaid family workers, almost two-thirds of them work on a seasonal basis, and almost half of the seasonal unpaid family workers work only during the cotton picking season. The group of women who seem to work more regularly are drawn from among those who pursue white collar, nonfarm, and handicraft work.

X. THE CONTRIBUTION OF WOMEN TO THE HOUSEHOLD BUDGET

As was shown earlier in Table 5, 75 percent of the working women work for remuneration. To assess the importance of women's earnings to their households, we will look at how women's earnings are spent. Sixty percent of the women who work for wages spend their income to meet the daily expenses of their households, mainly on food purchase, and 11 percent spend their incomes on buying clothes for themselves and their children, purchase of furniture, and household appliances. More than a quarter save their wages to meet future emergencies. The disbursement of the women's earnings show the importance of these earnings to the livelihood of their households. However, the way the earned incomes are spent is influenced by the woman's economic background. This can be illustrated by the fact that 90 percent of the working women from farm worker households stated that their incomes are spent to buy food for the family. At the same time, only one-fifth of the working women from white collar households spend their income on food purchase. The rest of the women fall in between these two extremes.

It is important to note that excluding women's unpaid family labor from our calculations of income disbursement was mainly because of lack of empirical data. The value of such activities can contribute significantly to the net real income of the household by helping to boost the aggregate output and, accordingly, consumption of the household.

XI. CONCLUSION

The relatively low rates of women's economic participation in the rural sector in the countries of the Middle East and North Africa is usually attributed to these factors: (a) statistical artifacts associated with the way economic activity (as applied to women) is defined and measured; (b) the existence of cultural/religious attitudes not conducive to women's work; and (c) to the mode of agricultural production process that led to the minimization of the role that can be played by women in the production process.

The above arguments were discussed in the context of the Gezira Scheme, the largest modern agricultural establishment in the Sudan. It was found that, even after using a flexible definition of economic activity that recognizes the seasonal and unpaid family-labor nature of women's work, the rate of women's involvement in economic activity is still relatively low compared to rates from other parts of the country (e.g., western Sudan) where the prevalent mode of production is subsistence agriculture. This shows that the explanation of the observed low rates of women's involvement in economic activities lies elsewhere, mainly in the socioeconomic and mode of production structures of the area.

As far as the mode of production in Gezira is concerned, the relation of production in the Scheme and the detachment of the tenant from his land led to that tenant and his family refraining from putting too much time and effort in investing in their land. Further, the existence of cheap migrant farm labor became a substitute for the tenants' family labor, both male and female. The existence of cheap farm labor also led to the enforcement of an already unfavorable cultural bias among the local population against women's active economic participation. The observed differentials in rates of women's work between the migrants and the local population of the area validates this hypothesis.

Another important factor associated with the mode of production hypothesis is the impact of the type of technology used in the production process on the rates and patterns of female labor force participation. In Gezira, most of the agricultural operations are mechanized. Because the machinery is operated by men, the role of women in the production process is minimized and limited only to participation in the most labor intensive activities, particularly cotton picking. Evidence of this argument is the observed seasonal pattern of women's work.

The observed seasonal pattern of the women's economic activity shows that the level of economic activity of women in Gezira will decline below the current observed level if plans to mechanize the cotton-picking process are carried out.

Such plans are contemplated during recent years to mitigate the shortages in seasonal migrant labor who flow to Gezira for cotton picking.

ACKNOWLEDGMENT

The data on which this paper is based were collected through a grant from the Ford Foundation.

NOTES

1. Feddan = 4,200 square meters.
2. Block is an administrative unit of the Gezira Scheme. There is an average of 10 villages per block.
3. In the mid-1970s the Blue Nile Province was renamed the Central Region and was subdivided into Gezira, White Nile, and Blue Nile Provinces.

REFERENCES

Abdel, K. A. (1985). The development of sharecropping arrangement in Gezira: Who is benefitting. *Peasant Studies, 13*(1), 25–37.

Abdel, S. M. (1982, December). *Some institutional aspects and future of the Sudan Gezira Scheme* (Discussion Paper 26). Khartoum: DSRC Seminar Series.

Ahmed, Z. (1984, January–February). Rural women and their work: Dependence and alternatives for change. *International Labour Review, 123*(1), 71–86.

———. (1987, January, February). Technology, production linkages and women's employment in South Asia. *International Labour review.*

Anker, R., & Knowles, J. (1978). A micro analysis of female labor force participation in Africa. In G. Standing & G. Sheehan, (Eds.), *Labor force participation in low income countries.* Geneva: ILO.

Anker, R. (1980). *Research on women's role and demographic change: Survey questionnaires for households, women, men and communities, with background explanation.* Geneva: ILO.

Barnett, T. (1975). *Beyond the sociology of development: Economy and society in Latin America and Africa.* London: Routledge & Keegan Paul.

———. (1977). *The Gezira scheme: An illusion of development.* London: Frank Cass.

Boserup, E. (1970). *Women's role in economic development.* New York: St. Martin Press.

———. (1975). Employment of women in developing countries. in L. Tabah (Ed.), *Population growth and economic development* (Vol. 1). IUSSP, Dolhain, Belgium: Ordina.

Dixon, R. (1982). Women in agriculture: Counting the labor force in developing countries. *Population and Development Review, 8*(3), 539–566.

Dixon-Mueller, R., & Anker, R. (1988). *Assessing women's economic contributions to development.* Geneva: ILO.

Durand, J. (1975). *The labour force in economic development: A comparison of international census data.* Princeton, NJ: Princeton University Press.

Economic and Social Research Council. (1979). Socioeconomic survey of the Blue Nile Agricultural Development Project. (Research Report No. 7). Khartoum.

Gulwick, G. (1955). Social change in the Gezira Scheme. *Civilization,5*.
Galal Eldin, M. (n.d.) *The interaction between population and development* (in Arabic). Khartoum: Khartoum University Press.
Hassoun, I. (1952). Western migration and settlement in the Gezira. *Sudan Notes and Records* (Vol. 33). Khartoum.
ILO. (1976). *Growth, employment and equity: A comprehensive strategy for the Sudan*. Geneva: International Labour Office.
Sheehan, G. (1978). Labor force participation rates in Khartoum. In G. Standing & G. Sheehan (Eds.), *Labor force participation in low income countries*. Geneva: ILO.
Shorter, F., & Zurayk, H. (1985). *Population factors in development planning in the Middle East*. New York: The Population Council.
Standing G. (1983). Women work activity and fertility. In R. Bulatao & R. Lee (Eds.), *Determinants of fertility in developing countries* (Vol. 1). New York: Academic Press.
Sudan Fertility Survey. (1979). *Principal Report* (Vol. 1). Khartoum: Department of Statistics.
United Nations. (1974). Towards a system of social and demographic statistics. *Studies in Methods* (Series F, No. 18). New York: Author.
———. (1977). The feasibility of welfare oriented measures to supplement the national accounts and balances: A technical report. *Studies in Methods* (Series F, No. 22). New York: Author.
Yousef, H. (1985). *An integrated economic-demographic framework for the analysis of the factors related to the rural labor force in Gezira Scheme*. Unpublished Ph.D. thesis, University of Pennsylvania.
Youssef, N. (1971). "Social structure and the female labor force," *Demography, 8*(4), 427–439.
———. (1977). Women and agricultural production in Muslim societies. *Comparative International Development, 12*(1), 41–57.

SUMMARY AND DISCUSSION

Alan Sorkin

Each of the papers in this section of the volume deals with a society or people in transition. Female labor force participation rates are increasing quite rapidly in all three circumstances, with highly educated women responding the most to the changing economic and social environment.

The Snipp-Aytac paper is the first major study of the American Indian female labor force. Their findings and analyses, which are based on the 1980 Census "Five Percent Public Use Microdata Sample," set a high standard for future research in this areas.

The American Indian labor force is comprised of two nearly equal but very different components. The first consists of those Indian women who live on or near reservations. Most reservation economies offer limited private sector opportunities and are among the poorest rural communities in the United States (see Snipp, 1989). As a result, the majority of Indian women who are employed on or near reservations work for the Bureau of Indian Affairs, the Indian Health Service or tribal governments. In short, they hold public sector jobs. Urban Indian women, who are far less likely to reside in depressed areas than rural dwellers (Sorkin, 1978), have a higher probability of being employed in the private sector than the latter, such as in, for example, retail trade.

For Indian women (as with women in other societies) child care respon-

Research in Human Capital and Development, Vol. 6, pages 269–273.

ISBN: 1-55938-032-2

sibilities are a major barrier to labor force participation. Apparently the extensive kin networks or extended families common in many American Indian communities do not have a positive impact on female labor force participation. Moreover, in urban Indian communities the importance of the nuclear family is stronger than on most reservations.

Snipp and Aytac, in discussing the impact of husbands on the labor force behavior of Indian wives, compare two competing hypotheses. The *economic utility* perspective implies that there is an inverse relationship between the economic activity of wives and the characteristics that influence the labor force participation of their husbands. An alternative perspective, known as the *status homogamy* hypothesis, implies that people tend to marry someone of equal class or status. For most of the labor market comparisons made in their paper, the status homogamy approach seems the more appropriate explanation of observed behavior. For example, with regard to schooling, educational homogamy appears to have a major effect on the labor force participation rate of Indian women. This implies that highly educated husbands are likely to be married to highly educated wives. However, because highly educated Indian women tend to have relatively few children, both education and fertility have an effect on female labor force participation. Finally, the conventional wisdom dictates that better educated husbands are relatively progressive in outlook and are less likely to oppose their wives working than an Indian husband who is more traditional.

The group of Indian women with the most restricted economic opportunities are those individuals over age 55. Not only does this group have limited education and work skills, they also are subject to a three dimensional pattern of discrimination: that is, based on age, sex, and race.

Most of the relationships discussed in this paper are "two-way" comparisons. These give a general picture of the important relationships and interactions under consideration. However, as Snipp and Aytac indicate, in-depth multivariate modeling of the Indian female labor force behavior is the next analytical step in providing a fuller understanding of the relationships between the independent and dependent variables.

The Eltigani paper focuses on female labor force activity in rural Sudan. More specifically, the study considers the economic activity of women who live and work in proximity to the Gezira Scheme. This project, with its vast irrigation program, was begun in 1925 and emphasizes the growth of long-staple cotton.

Eltigani points out that most developing country studies of female labor force participation in agriculture underestimate the actual level of female economic activity, because workers engaged in unpaid family labor are generally excluded. Moreover, seasonal employment of female labor is often underreported in labor force surveys (see, e.g., Dixon, 1982). For example, in Gezira, 20 percent of the female labor force is economically active. However, if unpaid family workers are excluded, only 13 percent of women workers are in the labor market. Furthermore, only 8 percent of women work for wages on a full-year basis. Among seasonal workers, about four-fifths are employed only during the cotton picking season.

Although in theory, the Gezira scheme emphasized the development of family-based farm tenancies (with contributions from both male and female family members), in practice this has not proven to be the case. Tenants are increasingly dependent on hired labor to perform tasks that were supposed to be performed by the nuclear tenant family. In Gezira the emigration of men has caused an increased dependence on cheap immigrant labor instead of female tenant labor. Moreover, the introduction of labor saving machinery has reduced the role of women and children in the production process. This trend is intensified by the fact that the operators of this machinery are almost exclusively male.

In Gezira, the highest rate of labor force participation for women is among those who are least educated. On a cross-section basis, as the educational level of women rises, fewer are employed, particularly as paid or unpaid farm workers. Moreover, working women from white-collar families tend to engage in white-collar work. These women are mainly employed as primary school teachers.

Most women in Gezira are spending the bulk of their income on food. Thus 90 percent of working women from farm worker households spend their income in this manner. However, only a fifth of working women from white collar households spend income on food purchases. This indicates the importance of women's economic activity in provisions of a basic necessity in all but relatively high-income families.

The bulk of the female work force in Gezira is in a vulnerable economic position. There are plans to introduce more machinery into the cotton harvesting process. This would tend to displace the large number of women who have been seasonally employed in that activity.

Although women with young children are less inclined to be economically active than women with older children (as is the case in most parts of the world), women who are migrant workers are about as likely to work with a child less than one year of age as they are if the child is at least five years of age. This indicates the necessity for working among the relatively poor migrant workers. At least in rural Gezira, the economic utility perspective, discussed earlier, seems to have some empirical verification.

The Shah and Al-Qudsi paper considers female labor force participation in a society that is undergoing rapid economic change. In Kuwait, development is largely based on the export income generated by the relatively high price of oil. Kuwait is unusual in that only 40 percent of the population are Kuwaiti. The remaining 60 percent are from other Arab countries or Asia.

Much of the labor force information in this paper focuses on the 1965–1985 period—an era of incredible economic development in Kuwait. The labor force participation rate of Kuwaiti women rose from only 2 percent in 1965 to almost

14 percent in 1985. At the same time the participation rate for non-Kuwaiti women rose form 19 percent in 1965 to 43 percent in 1985. About 35 percent of all employed Kuwaiti women were teachers in 1985.

The second largest occupational grouping of Kuwaiti women was in clerical or related jobs. Some of these workers may spend their careers in positions with little or no advancement—certainly a situation that has occurred in many highly industrialized countries. An increasing number of these women are employed in circumstances that do not permit segregation of the sexes—a situation that would have been unthinkable a generation ago.

Unemployment in Kuwait is less than 2 percent. In comparison with Kuwaiti men, Kuwaiti women are proportionally overrepresented in professional and clerical occupations and proportionally underrepresented in all other occupations. A similar situation exists for non-Kuwaiti women.

Among non-Kuwaitis the group with the highest labor force participation rate are the Asians, most of whom work as domestics. These women have played an important role in the rapid increase in the labor force participation of indigenous women by providing household help and child care to the families of the latter. There is increasing concern expressed in the Kuwaiti press about the effect these "outsiders" may be having on the cultural heritage of the children and families for whom they are employed. In addition, concerns have been raised that these domestics are being exploited.

Among all racial and ethnic groups of women in Kuwait, participation rates are higher among women in less affluent households. This implies that many women work because of economic necessity. This finding is similar to that observed by Eltigani in rural Sudan.

Using a human capital approach to measure the impact of discrimination, Shah and Al-Qudsi find that Kuwaiti men receive a constant premium over the earnings of women (see Mincer [1974] for a formulation of the relevant wage equations). However, the economic advantage of the Kuwaiti men varies with the ethnic origin of women. The intensity of discrimination is greatest against Asian women. Arab women are subject to less discrimination than Asian women but receive more discrimination than Kuwaiti women. This finding substantiates earlier research that also showed that Kuwaiti's labor market is segmented based on sex and ethnic origin (Al-Qudsi, 1985).

Regarding Kuwaiti women, the major economic consequence of increased female work participation is a reduction of the dependency on foreign workers. One consequence of this trend may be an increase in the importation of domestic help to assist in child care activities. Moreover, Kuwaiti women may begin to seek jobs in occupations in which they have traditionally been underrepresented, thus increasing their competition with men. This is more likely to occur if economic growth slows down and, as a consequence, there are fewer vacancies in traditional female occupations.

REFERENCES

Al-Qudsi, S. (1985). Earnings differences in the labor market of the Arab Gulf States: The case of Kuwait. *Journal of Development Economics, 18,* 119–132.

Dixon, R. (1982). Women in agriculture: Counting the labor force in developing countries. *Population and Development Review, 8*(3), 539–566.

Mincer, J. (1974). *Schooling, experience, and earnings.* New York: National Bureau of Economic Research.

Sorkin, A. (1978). *The urban American Indian.* Lexington, MA: D.C. Health.

Snipp, M. (1989). *American Indians: The first of this land.* New York: Russel Sage.

of High Level Manpower Requirements in Iraq, *George T. Abed and Atif Kubursi, IMF, McMaster University.* **Sectoral Employment Projections with Minimum Data Base: The Case of Saudi Arabia,** *Naiem A. Sherbiny, The World Bank.* **PART III: POLICY ISSUES. Labor Adaption in the Oil Exporting Countries,** *M. Ismail Sirageldin, The World Bank.* **Labor and Capital Flows in the Arab World: A Policy Perspective,** *Naiem A. Sherbiny, The World Bank.* **Index.**

Volume 3, Health and Development
1983, 364 pp. $63.50
ISBN 0-89232-166-0

Edited by **Ismail Sirageldin** and **David Salkever,** *The Johns Hopkins University* and **Alan Sorkin,** *University of Maryland.*

CONTENTS: PART I: CONCEPTS AND MEASURES. A Conceptual Model of Health, *Hector Correa, University of Pittsburgh.* **A Conceptual Framework for the Planning of Medicine in Developing Countries,** *Peter Newman, The Johns Hopkins University.* **Health and Development: A Discussion of Some Issues,** *Oscar Gish, University of Michigan.* **PART II: HEALTH IN HUMAN CAPITAL FORMATION. Adolescent Health, Family Background, and Preventive Medical Care,** *Linda Edwards and Michael Grossman, National Bureau of Economic Research.* **An Economic Analysis of the Diet, Growth and Health of Young Children in the United States,** *Dov Chernichovsky, Ben-Gurion University and NBER and Douglas Coate, Rutgers University.* **The Demand for Prenatal Care and the Production of Healthy Infants,** *Eugene M. Lewit, New Jersey Medical School.* **Life Environments and Adult Health: A Policy Perspective,** *Anthony E. Boardman, University of British Columbia and Robert Inman, University of Pennsylvania.* **Summary and Discussion, Part II,** *David Salkever, The Johns Hopkins University.* **PART III: HEALTH IN DEVELOPMENT. Correlates of Life Expectancy in Less Developed Countries,** *Robert N. Grosse and Barbara H. Perry, University of Michigan.* **The Power of Health,** *Wilfred Malenbaum, University of Pennsylvania.* **Health Planning in the Sudan,** *Ronald J. Vogel, University of Arizona and Nancy T. Greenspan, Health Care Financing Administration.* **Health Expenditure in a Racially Segregated Society—A Case Study in South Africa,** *M.D. McGrath, University of Natal, Durban.* **Analytical Review of the World Health Organization's Health Manpower Development Program 1948-1978,** *W.A. Reinke, The Johns Hopkins University and T. Fulop, WHO.* **Summary and Discussion, Part III,** *Alan Sorkin, University of Maryland.*

Volume 4, Migration, Human Capital and Development
1986, 185 pp. $63.50
ISBN 0-89232-416-3

Edited by **Oded Stark,** *Havard University and Bar-Ilan University*

JAI PRESS